Cyril Birch, who edited the volume, is Associate Professor of Chinese at the University of California. Formerly Lecturer in Chinese at the London School of Oriental and African Studies, he is the author of *Stories from a Ming Collection and Chinese Myths and Fantasies*. He has also written numerous articles on twentieth-century fiction and poetry.

CONTENTS

CHINESE COMMUNIST LITERATURE

CHINESE COMMUNIST LITERATURE

Edited by CYRIL BIRCH

FREDERICK A. PRAEGER, *Publisher*

New York · London

FREDERICK A. PRAEGER, PUBLISHER
64 UNIVERSITY PLACE, NEW YORK 3, N.Y., U.S.A.
49 GREAT ORMOND STREET, LONDON W. C. 1, ENGLAND

Published in the United States of America in 1963
by Frederick A. Praeger, Inc., Publisher

Published in the United Kingdom in 1963
by Frederick A. Praeger, Inc., Publisher

First published in Great Britain in 1963
as a special issue of *The China Quarterly*

Library of Congress Catalog Card Number: 63-18538

This book is Number 131 in the series of
Praeger Publications in Russian History and World Communism

Printed in the United States of America

Contents

Publisher's Note

In August 1962, The China Quarterly *embarked on what was for it a completely new project: the sponsoring of a full-scale academic conference. The subject chosen was Chinese Communist literature and the articles printed in this book represent the fruits of the considerable amount of work put into the conference by its distinguished participants.*

The conference was held from August 13–17 at the new Anglo-American conference centre run by the Ditchley Foundation at Ditchley Park near Oxford and much of the enjoyment of the proceedings sprang from the co-operativeness of the Ditchley Park staff and the charm of the Manor itself and its impressive grounds.

Ten papers were presented and thoroughly discussed. All the participants seemed conscious of the importance of establishing a sound basis for a critical approach to Chinese Communist literature at this first conference to be held on the topic in the West. Our only regret was that a few other scholars specialising in Chinese literature were unable to accept the invitation because of previous commitments. At some of the sessions, the participants were joined in their discussions by leading British specialists on contemporary China.

Two of the papers were not presented at the conference. Professor Hsia's "Twenty Years After the Yenan Forum" was commissioned to provide a rounded conclusion to this book. Mr. Ng's "The Poetry of Mao Tse-tung" was offered separately and in view of the intrinsic interest in the topic, we decided that it ought also to be included.

When all contributed so thoughtfully to the discussions, one would not want to single out the work of any particular participant. But we would like to stress that whatever the conference had was in large measure due to the ideas and efforts of Professor Cyril Birch. He also contributed considerable editorial advice for the preparation of this book.

CHINESE COMMUNIST LITERATURE

The Particle of Art *

By CYRIL BIRCH

"WHERE ideology restricts, art frees . . .": the opening section of T. A. Hsia's paper provides an eloquent statement of a fundamental distinction, a distinction which is at the centre of a dilemma. How is a group of men whose inclinations and commitments are to literature as art to approach a literature which is ideological in inspiration and intent? For this, we agreed, is a fair statement of the nature of Chinese Communist literature. It is more than a matter of guidance, or direction or control. It is not at all to be taken for granted that control is disastrous for literature. Great works of literature emerged in the past from under the control of despotic monarchs and authoritarian religions. Dante did not necessarily understand the authority of the Church to impose some kind of fetter on his work; it was a measure of restricted freedom that Chinese writers of the past knew and felt at home in. Great literature endures, as Mao Tun maintains, "not because literature is independent of politics but because it serves in a way much more profound than can be assessed at the moment."

The ideological nature of Chinese Communist literature is determined rather by the nature of that truth at whose service the writer places himself. It may well be a truth nourished by personal conviction. There is indeed a kind of "truth of myth": the myth or archetypal truth, for instance, of landlord villainy, which enables Ho Ching-chih from his deep conviction of this myth to create a drama, *White-Haired Girl*, with full power to compel sympathy. But there is also for the ideologist (in contrast with the artist) a truth which has nothing to do with conviction, which is objective, which exists independent of and outside of the human personality. Howard Boorman gives the game away when, discussing the Soviet critical theory of Socialist realism, he speaks of "truthfulness, or 'party-mindedness' (*partiinost*)."

* In these prefatory remarks I attempt to underline some of the leading arguments advanced in individual articles, and also to record some of the ideas expressed during the discussions of the Ditchley study group. "Conclusions" would imply that discussion led to compromise and agreement, which was seldom the case. Nor am I either qualified or authorised to act as spokesman for the fifteen or so scholars who engaged in the discussions. This introduction, then, should be regarded as a reflection of one man's understanding of what was said, rather than as a collective statement or as a personal statement of my own. I cannot over-emphasise the value of the contribution made to the study group in general and to the preparation of this introduction in particular by Mark Lavery, who brought both great patience and a sensitive understanding of the issues involved to the task of rapporteur.

Literatures of the past have known control. The innovation is the intrusion, in addition to "don'ts," of "shoulds" and "musts" as well. Miss Li Chi offers a nice instance of an artistic conception driven to defeat by the force of ideology in her discussion of Chou Erh-fu's story *Yen-su Crag*. Here art has certainly tried, but failed, to make headway. Yet sometimes the victory may go the other way, as is apparent at several points in T. A. Hsia's analysis of Yang Mo's *Song of Youth*. We may take encouragement in our search from a statement confided by Zhivago to his diary in Varykino. The passage bears repetition here in that, cited during the opening session of the Ditchley discussions, it proved prophetic of the approach most characteristic of those present: the search for the particle of art:

> "I have always thought that art is not a category, not a realm covering innumerable concepts and derivative phenomena, but that, on the contrary, it is something concentrated, strictly limited. It is a principle that is present in every work of art, a force applied to it and a truth worked out in it. And I have never seen art as form but rather as a hidden, secret part of content. . . .
>
> Primitive art, the art of Egypt, Greece, our own—it is all, I think, one and the same art through thousands of years. You can call it an idea, a statement about life, so all-embracing that it can't be split up into separate words: and if there is so much as a particle of it in any work that includes other things as well, it outweighs all the other ingredients in significance and turns out to be the essence, the heart and soul of the work."

Whether or not much art is to be found, we must in any case acknowledge the energy and scope of the literary effort of the Chinese Communists. In sharp contrast with preceding decades, when the régime showed a large indifference to such writing as was not actively seeking its overthrow, writers in China in the forties and fifties were recalled to national service. "Recalled": for there is indeed a precedent for the role of the new writer in that of the historian of imperial times, conscious of his task to give guidance to the administration. Writers under Communism, funnelling guidance through to the people in their work towards the construction of Socialism, have produced already a corpus of staggering size.

The huge quantity of material, and the imminence to our own lives of its social and political implications, increase the difficulty of the search for quality. But that is where our task lies. If we study problems of literature at all, we must concentrate on works of art as the essence or basis. After we have done enough close observation of this essence, we may expatiate on the social significance and political connotations of the work. In the study of poetry, the examination of poetic quality comes first; as S. H. Chen put it, "certain poems just sing and touch the heart; even though afterwards we might feel repulsed, yet that force is there, just by a certain combination of words, diction, imagery."

The twin dangers, the Scylla and Charybdis of the search for quality would be the risk of impatient rejection of great masses of material as turgid non-literature, mere propaganda, over against excessive tolerance of bad writing, the suspension or lowering of standards of excellence in the hope of finding something worthwhile. But the particle must be sought to satisfy "our" point of view, before we go on to consider "their" point of view. The latter embraces such things as *partiinost*, educational function, establishment of patterns of conduct. And, of course, we are in no way prevented from examining these things from a non-Communist standpoint, as C. T. Hsia does when in his paper he finds the story *Warmth of Spring* to illustrate the principle that "in a Communist society a woman is closer to her husband when sharing his kind of drudgery than when merely content to perform her traditional wifely functions."

True enough, we must remember that we are hardly the readers the Communist author has in mind. He is writing for a mass public, and there is plenty of evidence that he is reaching a mass public. First printings of eighty or one hundred thousand for a new novel, commune libraries, the space occupied by literary men in daily newspapers, these things and more are evidence of the régime's commitment to what may prove a huge fallacy: that the masses, made literate, may by the same token be made literary. Against this possibility are the distressing facts that literary tastes can certainly not be ascribed to the broader literate publics of the western world, and that literary taste must necessarily involve some degree of freedom of choice. Of this the Chinese reader, it seems certain, enjoys much less even than his Soviet Russian counterpart: directed reading, in fact, is likely to account for a considerable proportion of his literary experience. For his reading is politically important. It provides, not an education in the sense of a heightening of his sensitivities, a deepening of his understanding of life, but a practical training in the attitudes which are necessary to him in the new society. This particular type of educational function is performed most conspicuously by the stories about life in the co-operative or commune and in the factory, as Miss Chung-Wen Shih and Richard Yang respectively show very clearly. Ho Shih-chieh, in Prof. Yang's extended quotation from Lei Chia's novel *Spring Comes to the Yalu River*, establishes an interesting pattern of model cadre behaviour. Faced with a critical lack of trained managers in industry, the régime made shift with inexperienced but politically dependable cadres. If chaos was to be avoided it was essential that old concepts of "face" be rooted out, that the new leaders be prepared to admit their ignorance and to learn of technical matters from their inferiors if necessary. Which is exactly what we find Ho Shih-chieh doing. An important behaviour pattern is here defined; many further patterns, for peasants and especially for women, are described in the papers by Miss Shih and by C. T. Hsia.

This extremely specific educative function is a significant part of the burden the writer under Communism must be prepared to bear. With large areas of the field of writing closed to him—the literature of personal experience, the exploration of subjectivity, really incisive social protest—he must be constantly aware, under what Prof. Chen calls "the vigilant Communist high noon," of the propaganda requirements for his work. Although his predecessor in imperial times would indeed often be conscious of the need to conform to a sacrosanct official ideology, he could still "walk out of the examination hall and do something very different by himself." That is no longer possible—or, at least, no longer publishable. The mere reporting of reality is, of course, no more acceptable from a Chinese writer than it would be from an English or American writer: but the *interpretation* of reality, there's the rub, must be made in accordance with—what? Not, definitely not, his own understanding of life and the world, his personal vision of God or his fellow men; rather, "reality as it develops"—the Party's vision of the future. Some of the perplexities to which this demand gives rise are expressed in T. A. Hsia's enigmatic quotation from Wu Ch'iang in "The Conditions Under Which I Wrote *Red Sun*."

There will naturally be periodic changes in the apparent weight of the burden on the writer's shoulders. It will feel heavier, no doubt, when the guidance of the Chinese Writers' Union is undertaken by men who are, like Chou Yang, more interested in politics than in creative work; it will lighten when the "interpretation" of reality does not have to show a fantastic remove from actual conditions. A novelist depicting the renewal of activity in a power-station which has been stripped by the retreating Japanese and ignored by the harassed Kuomintang, will have an easier time of it than a man who must dream up, in the face of widespread hunger and the failure of farm plans, a picture of joyful collective abundance. There is some evidence, indeed, that the power-station novel will prove more satisfactory than the farming piece simply because the straining of facts need be less pronounced (Ai Wu's *Steeled and Tempered* compares very favourably with any novel about an agricultural co-operative).

Reference was made in discussion to an article published by Pa Chin in May of 1962 (in *Shanghai Wen-hsueh*). The article reveals more than the limited extent of Pa Chin's enthusiasm for the régime. It indicates both the pressures writers feel themselves to be under, and the encouraging possibility that these pressures, allowed recognition in this way, may be reduced. Yet it seems clear that the principal effort in censorship comes, and long will continue to come, from the writer himself as he sits at his desk. Unlike T. S. Eliot, whose best lines, as he claims, were written " at moments of inattention "—from the deepest and least conscious part of his being, that is to say—the writer under Communism must be all attention, all cognisance of what is going on around him.

The third section of Hellmut Wilhelm's paper underlines some of the wide dissimilarities between the literary situation of China after 1949 and that of post-revolutionary Russia. Nothing comparable to the New Culture Movement or " Chinese Renaissance " had taken place in Russia; there was no move towards the wholesale rejection of a literary tradition. Indeed, some of the very *leit-motifs* of the Russian literary tradition, as Boorman pointed out, were precisely what appealed to the revolutionary Chinese intellectuals of the " renaissance " period: themes of social idealism, patriotism, the possibility of salvation through burying oneself, even losing oneself in a great cause. This literary life of Russia, itself more firmly established, more safely anchored than the Chinese experience of the 1930s could possibly be, was in turn subjected in the early revolutionary period to a political direction very much less stringent. Controls were applied in China even before 1949 which in Russia, their country of origin, had taken years to develop. And during those at least relatively " free " years Soviet literature, drawing strength from the Russian past, was able to prepare the ground for work of a quality not yet seen in Communist China. No Chinese story of industrial life, for example, has reached the standard of Gladkov's *Cement*. These considerations must be borne in mind by those who hopefully await some kind of " Chinese *Zhivago* ": not only is the specific religious dimension absent, but the underlying literary tradition also has received too profound a shock to leave much likelihood of such an achievement. A shock, in fact, compounded: for the imposition of the ready-to-hand Soviet-type controls of 1949 was a new blow to the maturing modern literature of China. The work of the novelist Pa Chin, treated in Vincent Shih's paper, reaching its highest level at the end of the war against Japan in such a book as *Winter Night,* relapsed appallingly into the absurdities of his Korean War stories. Miss Li's study of war stories generalises this falling-off of quality under the suffocating effect of political interference after 1949, when, as she says, there is " no longer room " even to make a creative mistake.

" If control were total," Prof. Wilhelm commented early in the discussions, " I would say there would be no hope whatsoever. But even in China the degree of control can never be total: there is always a margin for life to escape into, which could be the region out of which future creativity will come."

T. A. Hsia indicates a local habitation for this "margin" when he speaks of the significance of detail in a novel, detail which may well be exempt, as it were, from conformity to the propagandistic framework of the story; or when he writes "if there is still some sign of bewilderment left, some sign of ambiguity or mental reservation, it becomes apparent that the surrender is not total." And no doubt the writings branded as revisionist are often to be placed in our margin. This is not to pretend, of course, that whatever we find in the margin will automatically represent high quality. Feng Ts'un's story *Beautiful* has sincerity and much interest, yet C. T. Hsia finds it none the less "a rather poor story."

The tendency, marked in very recent times, to go back to the 1930s for material may well represent a means of escape into a "margin of creativity." Yang Mo can take the latitude she does in her novel *Song of Youth* because her story is of the early history of the Party: behaviour similar to that of her heroine would not be tolerated in a figure of the present time. The Communists in the novel are depicted in heroic terms, but in shadow, as figures mysterious and brooding, almost one would say as Byronic heroes. Although the rediscovery of a lost *élan* and the need to create myths for a new generation must be two powerful forces behind this noticeable historicism, we may see in it also one region in which a writer may enjoy a greater scope for creativity than the present offers.

As to the recall of styles and attitudes from very much earlier times, there is here a paradox I point to in my own paper. However thoroughly Westernised may be the external appearance of writing of the 1920s and 1930s, the values we find there are consonant with the great tradition of the past, private, questioning or contemplative; whereas the Communist writers, public, acquiescent, optimistic, in essence and underlying modes break with the past, yet assume familiar guise by tricking themselves out with forms from past tradition. Such borrowings from old popular genres as I describe in my paper would, of course, be most helpful towards the popularisation of new works: and these new works, it must be remembered, had the task of replacing the immediately pre-Communist "new writing" which, although never known to a really broad public, had attained a degree of excellence and a popularity of its own. The past popular tradition was therefore conscripted into the service of a new "official" literature. The heroic temper in particular, now so frequently invoked, was a constant of the old novel and drama: the esoteric classical tradition had little place for this, unless it was for the tragic hero (as Ssu-ma Ch'ien's Hsiang Yü) whose presence is no longer required.

Communist treatment of the Chinese literary heritage has been highly selective. What we might characterise as the literature of protest—from Ch'ü Yüan and Tu Fu's poems against war all the way to the satirical novel of the *Ju-lin Wai-shih* type—is to be prized in its historical context but hardly to be imitated, since protest is out of place in Utopia. On the contrary, it is the despised and discarded relic of feudal subservience, the eulogy (dynastic or merely personal, as in the exquisitely-worded application for patronage) which is now revived: the eulogy, and the entertainment. The works discussed in my paper, the *Heroes of Lü-liang* or Chao Shu-li's *Magic Spring Caves*, are, after all, mere entertainments of an unsophisticated order. With the increased complexity of national life, with, for instance, the need to treat of the factory worker rather than the guerrilla hero, these borrowings from the " step-child of the literary tradition," the old novel or play, are seen to offer inadequate help and to diminish in significance.

At the same time nationalistic pride has stimulated revivals from the esoteric classical tradition itself. Classical writers are annotated and reprinted on a considerable scale; scholars seek and find refuge in classical researches. And writers follow classical models, at times with surprising scrupulousness. Individual papers of this symposium offer evidence: for example, the formal severity of Ko Pi-chou's fourth poem in Professor Chen's paper. Other instances emerged in discussion: the publication of Mao Tse-tung's wholly traditional *tz'u* poems in a wholly traditional " thread-bound " format; the revaluation (in the *People's Daily* in March of 1962) of Yuan Mei's *Sui-yuan shih-hua*, a study of classical criticism made by Kuo Mo-jo in a style wholly consistent with his subject.

Over against these echoes from a more distant past C. T. Hsia in discussion drew attention to a revival of a different kind: the re-emergence of the modes of leftist writing of the early thirties, becoming more marked, even predominant, after the mid-fifties. At the 1960 Congress of the All-China Federation of Literary and Art Circles, as usual a listing was made of approved works of the preceding years; and it was noticeable that the lion's share of these works came not from the popular entertainers of the type of Chao Shu-li, but from writers schooled in the earlier leftist tradition. When these men cling too close to their models they may well be carried over into " revisionism," as C. T. Hsia makes clear in his concluding pages. To avoid this fate they must perform some strenuous gymnastics. The defiance and negation characteristic of young people in the novels of the early thirties (Pa Chin's *Family* is the classic model) must give place to a new image of affirmation and enthusiasm. The disharmony between youth and age must be replaced, not indeed by the classic harmony which resulted from recognition of interdependence, but by a new harmony brought about by the harnessing of young and old shoulder to shoulder in the service of Socialist construction. Yet images survive from the early days: witness the image of the Communist Party which T. A. Hsia finds in *Song of Youth*, as " a political party composed of a number of dedicated but otherwise mysterious human beings deeply engaged in a conspiracy to overthrow a government."

An obvious manifestation of these recalls of earlier modes is the existence of distinctive styles of language. Of personal style there is not much to observe, but, on the contrary, a general anonymity in keeping with the " public " character of thematic material. But we can distinguish at least three general types of written styles. The first, the " traditional " style, strongly influenced by the old *pai-hua,* is the style I attribute in my paper to Chao Shu-li as a leading practitioner. The remaining two we could label respectively " National Language " (*Kuo-yü*) and " common speech " (*p'u-t'ung hua*). The former was developed from the old " plain speech " (*pai-hua*) after the " Literary Revolution " of 1917. Its syntax and vocabulary were influenced by contacts with English, French and Japanese, and it was the language of education in school and college prior to 1949. The writers of the Literary Revolution used such a style, be it noted, *not* primarily to reach a mass public but to provide a more effective means of expression than the classical written language offered to a modern literary man. It is this " National Language " style that we find recalled so strongly in the stories that go back for their material to the thirties, in *Song of Youth*, in the revisionist fiction C. T. Hsia discusses.

" Common speech " is a newer development, and not easy to characterise. It is the result of a process of broadening out of the *Kuo-yü* of previous decades; while retaining a certain degree of " Europeanisation," it finds room also for dialect expressions, for more colour than before. It is a welcome development, a more natural standard for a modern Chinese that can be used by peasant as well as intellectual; and it is seen at its best in a writer like Chou Li-po. Chou, " a propagandist at war with the artist within him," as T. A. Hsia describes him, has made conscientious and successful efforts to incorporate good material from local dialects into his written style; and he is not alone in this.

Apart from such linguistic innovations, what else is new in the new literature? Obviously, a good deal of interest in the stories on industrial themes. New locales, shipyards, steel plants, are often vividly evoked, and technological processes described with admirable clarity (Richard

Yang has an excellent instance from the veteran novelist, Ai Wu). War stories also are new to China, as Miss Li points out—war stories, that is, which concern current or recent conflicts rather than battles long ago. Models from Soviet literature were inevitably drawn upon when the scale of warfare was expanded from the guerrilla operations against Japan to the complex campaigns, with planes and armour and divisions on the move, of the Civil War and the Korean War which followed.

Whether or not, as C. T. Hsia maintains, women in the new literature appear as creatures devoid of human dignity is open to question. At least they do appear, far more significantly than in the literature of the past. They are, it is true, shown to have little choice: all achievement is owed to the help and guidance of the Party. Yet they may well be held to have achieved dignity, in their literary identities at least, through self-fulfilment. This sense of fulfilment may very well inspire the woman who, discontented with the chore of cooking for her husband, finds herself under the new order cooking for thousands in a commune mess-hall.

One of the conspicuous failures, a problem that has shaken the heads of many critics, has been the attempt to create heroes. The war stories are subject to interpretation as a move towards the establishment of a professional military caste, but they are matched in mood by stories of model workers and labour heroes on the farm, in the factory and in the huge construction projects. These men and women display the same virtues of zeal and self-sacrifice, even use the same vocabulary as their armed counterparts: "shock troops," "declare war against Heaven," a "front-line worker" carries out a "night attack." Here Socialist realism is at its most visionary in depicting reality in the course of revolutionary development: the future at hand today. The heroes whose exploits so raise our eyebrows are here at least in the making, and must certainly come, men who will shoulder impossible burdens gladly for the sake of the building of Socialism. They will appear in every trade, and so every trade must be glamourised, with stories about load-carriers and poems about collectors of manure. To just what lengths of absurdity the process has been carried by writers of fiction may be seen from Vincent Shih's description of Pa Chin's Korean War stories. T. A. Hsia's is probably the most apt comment: "There is no surer way of debasing heroism than by multiplying heroes."

A process of debasement is evident again in the sphere of poetry, "a huge spoiled metaphor." Of the fourth poem from Ko Pi-chou quoted in his paper, Prof. Chen said in discussion: "It is very touching, and we respond easily—until we come to the very end. 'But we do not complain that we parted too soon': this is the important line, the turning away from the traditional ending which would be in sadness and pathos. And now, what is it the poet offers that is new? 'All rivers will concourse in the great sea.' The poet and his old friend will never be parted, but submerged in the great sea of humanity. Individuality disappears, human beings are identified with natural imagery, after so much literary emotion has been built up in the poem, finally it is obliterated. Ko's poem is a good poem, effective within its limits, but it finally has to hit on a public theme: and once the theme becomes public, all that has led up to it is shown as false." It is indeed possible that we come too early to judge, that Ko Pi-chou, having met as Goethe said a poet must "*die Forderung des Tages*," has here created something which will grow with time, a work of art. His metaphor may indeed be not fully conscious, have a broader eventual significance than the poet himself could conceive, be capable of relation to basic Chinese philosophical concepts of the organic unity of the whole of humanity. But we who live in the time of the poet and know something of the background of his society cannot but find his metaphor public and transparent. "A slogan here becomes most powerful poetry": Feng Chih's line clearly indicates his awareness of the character and immensity of the contemporary poetic task. The poems Prof. Chen quotes from Feng Chih bear witness to a major shift in the poet's relation to nature. Gone is the ancient harmony man sought to establish with nature, that harmony whose image is the glory of great poetry of the past. In place of harmony now comes confusion: is nature a willing partner in the building of Socialism, only too anxious to have her rivers tamed, her mountains mined? Or is she a stubborn enemy to be warred against? Or both at once? Or which, when?

To gauge sincerity is the most difficult of the tasks facing the student of Communist literature. Established writers by and large chose to remain on the mainland in 1949; though some perhaps lacked only the means to escape, there was no such exodus as from Russia in 1917. The case of a man like Shen Ts'ung-wen is full of ironies. The modern master of the rural idyll, he has remained unproductive at a time when idylls are most vociferously demanded. Then why, after early bewilderment and later years of silence, should he now print poems whose references are all to a tradition of criticism of the régime in power—unless it is that he has found here, as Vincent Shih suggests, a means of outwitting the censor? And if this is so, are Pa Chin's fantastic heroes of the Korean War to be interpreted in terms of satire, as objects of ridicule whose "heroism" no censor nevertheless could disclaim? We are on more certain ground with Chou Li-po. Here is a favourite, a Stalin Prize winner, who has achieved a kind of Hegelian freedom. From this he profits to depict scenes almost as critical as we can find of the régime's difficulties: witness the scale and intensity in his novel, *Great Changes in a Mountain Village*, of local resistance to collectivisation. Yet there is no reason to doubt his sincerity in so constructing his tale that all problems are resolved with the help of Party guidance: Socialist realism, with its new corollary of revolutionary romanticism, demands only that life be shown *as it is going to be* on the *basis* of what is.

The possibility of such a sense of security is a hopeful sign. Mao Tun appears to have carved himself a similar niche in his work as a critic, a place from which he now can express personal and not merely official interpretations. The virulence of personal attacks has abated, as has the hallucinatory frenzy of the time of the Great Leap Forward. It is possible to find, as S. H. Chen finds in one instance from Feng Chih, a good poem, with nothing hollow or forced about it. Whatever ideological problems may rage, writers in China continue to strive after goals of technical proficiency. All these facts encourage the belief that a real literature may, however haltingly, at length emerge.

For the moment, no doubt a leading attraction of Communist writings will be their interest as social documents. This aspect is discussed at some length by Miss Shih in her paper, and indeed, her whole treatment of the " stories of co-operatives and communes " shows a more immediate relation between government policy and the work of the writer than is observable elsewhere. We do not, of course, have to accept that there is any correspondence between vignettes of life in the Socialist paradise and conditions as they actually are in mainland China But there is a particular interest in the " before taking " sections, the unsatisfactory states of affairs before the people have properly understood or accepted Party guidance. There is a true enough ring to Lei Chia's dramatisation, quoted by Richard Yang, of problems of the early stages of industrialisation. In the same paper reference is made to the situation, in Ai Wu's novel, *Steeled and Tempered*, of conflict between plant manager and Party branch secretary. The manager concerned with technicalities, the secretary with ideological correctness; the manager impatient to secure an immediate production increase, the secretary committed to the long-term political objective of making thorough-going Communists out of the workers: the conflict here engendered represents a real and major source of friction in the new society, which the standardised mode of solution in Ai Wu's novel cannot obscure.

From C. T. Hsia's paper on " residual femininity " we may trace, in this one sector of the position of women in works of fiction, certain most interesting effects which shifts in the political line exert on approved or permissible behaviour patterns. It is this kind of chronological development in the relation between politics and literature in Communist China which in the present state of our studies is most difficult to establish. All the papers which follow could be said to represent pioneer work: their authors are happy if they have laid down some tasks and some guide-lines for further study.

The Literary World of Mao Tse-tung *

By HOWARD L. BOORMAN

"Who says we have not had any creative workers? Here's one right here!" (Laughter).

Mao Tse-tung, *Oppose Party Formalism* (February 8, 1942).

POETRY and politics are rare companions in the competitive world of practical affairs today. In Moscow, Nikita Khrushchev, with peasant shrewdness, is addicted to Russian proverbs to enliven his rhetoric; but there are few indications that he is sympathetic with the creative writer and none that he himself will rank with Pushkin in the annals of his nation's literature. In Washington, the appearance of Robert Frost at John F. Kennedy's inauguration in January 1961 was an event at once exceptional and gratifying to admirers of Frost's artistic integrity; the elderly poet's advice to the young president of the United States to stress the Irish and underplay the Harvard in his background may yet have enduring significance. Only in Peking, however, do we find a world leader who combines distinctive political abilities and literary talents. Indeed the juxtaposition of strategic and artistic instincts in Mao Tse-tung is so unusual in the post-Churchillian world that the case merits more than passing note.

The outsider surveying the literary world of Mao Tse-tung confronts several possible avenues of approach. Contemporary Chinese literature may be studied, first, as the subject of literary criticism; second, as the source of data regarding the society which has produced it; or, third, as the product of particular political and social conditions. The first approach is predominantly aesthetic; it views literature as a verbal art form, studies the artistic devices peculiar to creative writing, stresses appreciation of the unique qualities which inhere in a work of literature to give it distinctive beauty, emotional power, moral verity, or new awareness of the potentialities of life. The second approach attempts to delineate and describe a society through the mirror of its literature. The third approach aims—not at literary, aesthetic, or social criticism—but rather at the establishment of a sense of historical perspective.

Clearly Chinese Communist literary policies cannot be made intelligible without reference to what the Chinese authors themselves have

* I acknowledge with gratitude the assistance provided by Mr. Yong-sang Ng of the research project on Men and Politics in Modern China, Columbia University.

actually been writing or without reference to aesthetic considerations. Such appraisal, however, is outside the scope of this article. Nor do I attempt the use of contemporary Chinese literature as social documentation, if only because the existence of nation-wide controls over literature has sharply limited traffic on this avenue. Chinese writing today appears to have become a literature unlikely, except by omission or oversight, to reveal much about the real problems of real people living in the People's Republic of China.

Rather this article attempts to survey the evolving political influences which have shaped Chinese imaginative writing in the past two decades. During the 1930s and 1940s, despite the Nationalist censorship so sharply condemned by the literary left, a genuine literature of social protest—a literature which served as a sort of national conscience—did emerge and exist in China. Since the Communist victory in 1949–50, the authorities at Peking have erected a new control system designed to inhibit the production of imaginative writing as that term is conventionally used in the West. Aware of the function of literature as an instrument of social stimulus, the Communist leaders now emphasise the production of what appear to the bourgeois mind to be essentially propaganda and educational materials cast in the forms traditionally employed by literature: fiction, drama and verse. At the same time, the attitudes which Communist China displays toward its writers and artists, and the views which it holds of the proper position of art and literature in the life of the society afford important insights into China's deeper aspirations. Peking's theories regarding the social role of literature do delineate the values held by the ruling group, the leadership of the Chinese Communist Party, and the style of life which its policies are shaping. The following pages outline some basic assumptions and aims of Chinese Communist literary policies as expounded by Mao Tse-tung, and describe some salient features of the bureaucratic structure through which creative writing is now controlled in the People's Republic.

I

The political control of literature in Communist China rests ultimately upon the theoretical foundations of Marxism-Leninism. Though precise definition of the relationship between European Socialism before Lenin and Chinese Communism after Mao Tse-tung is elusive, some important strands do link the remote worlds of nineteenth-century Europe and twentieth-century China. These strands are both theoretical and practical. Of major importance is the instinct inherent in Marxism that its doctrine offers a new instrument for systematic analysis and radical reshaping of history and human society, the crusading faith based upon a set of imperatives both philosophical and political. Chinese Communism owes its theoretical faith in dialectical and historical materialism to Karl Marx. But it owes a more practical and penetrating debt to Vladimir Lenin. Lenin it was who developed a specific analysis of " imperialism," a framework for supporting the concept that non-Western nationalism would be a useful ally of the Western proletariat in the general revolutionary struggle against capitalism. At the same time, Leninist doctrine laid emphasis upon conscious action as a critical factor in stimulating social change. And Lenin laid stress, finally, upon the need for organisation as a key to action, on the vital necessity of developing a disciplined political party with absolute authority to lead the revolution and build the new society.[1]

More immediately, Chinese Communist literary policies have been affected by Russian experiments and experiences in fashioning " Socialist realism " as the main doctrinal guide in shaping literature and art in the U.S.S.R.[2] The most succinct definition of Socialist realism in its classic form was given in a statute passed by the First All-Union Congress of Soviet Writers in August 1934:

> Socialist realism is the basic method of Soviet literature and literary criticism. It demands of the artist the truthful, historically concrete representation of reality in its revolutionary development. Moreover, the truthfulness and historical concreteness of the artistic representation of reality must be linked with the task of ideological transformation and education of workers in the spirit of Socialism.

This innocent formula embraces, on the one hand, a link between Communist " Socialist realism " and the earlier critical realism of nineteenth-century Europe and, on the other, an element which the Soviets described as new and distinctive in literary theory.[3] The link lies in the

1 For concise and lucid appraisal, see Alfred G. Meyer, *Marxism: the Unity of Theory and Practice* (Cambridge: Harvard Un. Press, 1954) and *Leninism* (Cambridge: Harvard Un. Press, 1957). See also Edmund Wilson, " Marxism and Literature," in *The Triple Thinkers* (London: John Lehmann, 1952), pp. 188–202. Originally published in 1938, this remains a perceptive essay by a distinguished literary critic who has also read Marx thoughtfully.

2 Of the large literature available on the subject, see especially the recent books by Avrahm Yarmolinsky, *Literature under Communism: the Literary Policy of the Communist Party of the Soviet Union from the end of World War II to the Death of Stalin* (Bloomington: Indiana Un. Press, Russian and East European Series, Vol. 20, 1960), and Harold Swayze, *Political Control of Literature in the USSR, 1946–1959* (Cambridge: Harvard Un. Press, 1962). A classic account written from inside the movement is Leon Trotsky, *Literature and Revolution* (New York: Russell & Russell, 1957). Originally published in 1924, this volume remains a brilliant short analysis, charged with Trotsky's usual polemical gusto, of the problems confronting Russian authors during the early period after the Bolshevik revolution.

3 See the revealing examination of Soviet literary doctrine offered by an unknown writer. Abram Tertz (pseudonym), *On Socialist Realism* (New York: Pantheon Books, 1960), pp. 24–25, with an introduction by Czeslaw Milosz. Milosz himself has discussed the relationship between political responsibility and artistic creativity in *The Captive Mind* (New York: Vintage Books, 1955), a brilliant volume confirming the fact that it is simpler to write about the intellectual under Communism than to be one.

truthfulness of the representation, a quality shown by earlier writers in the stream of modern realism: Balzac, Maupassant, Tolstoy and Chekhov, for example. The distinctive element lies in the alleged ability of Socialist realism to portray the future in the present, to grasp reality " in its revolutionary development," and to instruct readers in accordance with that development " in the spirit of Socialism." Viewing literature as the artistic crystallisation of the political aspirations of the Communist Party, Socialist realism is concerned not only with portraying " life as it really is " but also with depicting " life as it ought to be." On the basis of this theory, official Soviet criticism during the Stalinist era erected three fundamental standards for estimating the merit of a work of literature: first, the truthfulness, or " Party-mindedness," of its portrayal of reality; second, the work's pedagogical potential; and, third, its intelligibility to the " broad masses " of the people.[4]

In China, the impact of Marxism-Leninism helped to create the type of intellectual and emotional environment necessary for the existence of a Chinese Communist movement and for the emergence of Mao Tse-tung as its leader. Essentially, Mao's historic role stems from the fact that he has been a man of sufficient stature and imagination to adopt Marxism-Leninism and to apply its mystique and its radical faith in a technologically primitive peasant land which no European or Russian Communist leader ever truly comprehended viscerally, however much he may have attempted intellectually. In the same fashion, Mao was able to absorb the general elements of the Soviet pattern of political control over modern Russian literature and to apply them to the specific stream of modern Chinese literature as it had developed during the 1920s and 1930s. Peking's official doctrine has conventionally stressed the point that Mao's success has lain in his integration of the " universal truth " of Marxism-Leninism with the concrete " practice of China's revolution." The same claim may be made for the evolution of Chinese Communist literary policy under Mao's direction.

The development of a unified literary line in the Chinese Communist Party first took place during the Sino-Japanese war, as Mao consolidated his control over the central Party apparatus. After the Japanese action in north China in July 1937, Mao and the Chinese Communist leadership evolved a strategic programme at once simple and comprehensive: total conquest of national power. In pursuit of this goal, the Chinese Communists fashioned a working programme which affected increasingly broad areas of the countryside of north, east and central China. This programme included, for example, mobilisation of peasant discontent wherever possible; manipulation of the latent forces of Chinese patriotism; and the projection of Mao's " New Democracy " as the most

[4] See Swayze, *op. cit.*, p. 17.

progressive political programme in China. Utilising these and other devices, Mao's commanders, commissars, and cadres gradually wove a network of " liberated areas " in the face of the Japanese invasion. Since the Chinese Communist movement was in armed opposition to the Nationalist Government, its doctrine and practice were of necessity overwhelmingly oriented toward problems of power. Yet Yenan's doctrine was often discreetly muted to encompass the political logic of the united front, and practice was consciously patriotic to embrace the logistical and intelligence requirements of guerrilla warfare in the rural areas.

One mark of the growing political shrewdness of the Chinese Communist leadership was the fact that it came to emphasise the " cultural front " as of equal importance with military operations. Mao himself argued that literature was as critical a factor as guerrilla warfare in the total revolutionary programme in China. In retrospect, this emphasis provides a notable measure of the calibre of the two major antagonists of the period. Mao consistently recognised the important social role of literature as an instrument of criticism and reform during an interlude of political disintegration. Chiang Kai-shek just as consistently viewed the war against the Communists solely in military, never in intellectual, terms.

Though Mao's view of the social role of literature was doubtless influenced by earlier Marxist or Soviet analysis, his grasp of the problem was nevertheless consciously native.[5] Mao himself was a man of the May Fourth generation, and his diagnosis inevitably began with examination of the seminal outburst which had been the May Fourth movement of 1919.[6] In his major statement, *On New Democracy* (January 1940), Mao placed the May Fourth movement as the principal line of demarcation running through China's " democratic revolutionary movement " and dividing the old from the new.

> The May Fourth movement was an anti-imperialist as well as an anti-feudal movement. Its outstanding historical significance lies in a feature which was absent in the revolution of 1911, namely, a thorough and uncompromising opposition to imperialism and a thorough and uncompromising opposition to feudalism.[7]

Bringing orthodox class analysis to the phenomenon, Mao argued that before 1919 China's new cultural movement, her " cultural revolution,"

[5] A convenient summary of Mao's views is given in *Mao Tse-tung on Art and Literature* (Peking: Foreign Languages Press, 1960), translated from the Chinese text published by the People's Literature Publishing House in December 1958. Arranged chronologically, most of the contents are taken from the *Selected Works of Mao Tse-tung*, with some additions of more recent materials.

[6] The most extended study of the movement, based on wide research in contemporary sources, is Tse-tsung Chow, *The May Fourth Movement: Intellectual Revolution in Modern China* (Cambridge: Harvard Un. Press, 1960).

[7] See Mao Tse-tung, *Selected Works* (New York: International Publishers, 1955), Vol. III (1939–41), pp. 145–146. The following quotations are taken from this translation of *On New Democracy*, p. 145 *et seq.* The Chinese text is found in *Mao Tse-tung hsuan-chi* (Peking: Jen-min Ch'u-pan-she, 1952), Vol. II, pp. 655–704.

had been led by the bourgeoisie and directed against the " old culture of the feudal class." The May Fourth movement opened the way for a distinctly new historical period, the era of the " new-democratic culture," defined as the " anti-imperialist, anti-feudal culture of the broad masses of the people under the leadership of the proletariat."

Since the dawn of Chinese history, according to Mao, " there had never been such a great and thorough-going cultural revolution." As the " ideological reflection " of the political and economic revolution, the cultural revolution from the May Fourth movement to the time of Mao's speech (January 1940) was divided into four periods: (1) 1919–21; (2) 1921–27; (3) 1927–37, and (4) 1937–40. The first period, from the May Fourth outburst to the founding of the Chinese Communist Party, was an interlude during which the cultural revolution was confined to the intelligentsia and had only limited contact with the workers and peasants. The second period, from 1921 to 1927, was the era of the temporary Communist-Kuomintang alliance and of the Northern Expedition. In class terms, this was defined as a united front of the proletariat, the peasants, the urban petty bourgeoisie, and the (national) bourgeoisie. The decade from 1927 to 1937 was a " new revolutionary period " comprising " on the one hand a period of counter-revolutionary campaigns of ' encirclement and annihilation,' and on the other a period of the deepening of the revolutionary movement." And the fourth period was, of course, the then current period of the " war of resistance " against Japan.

The core of the " new democratic culture " section of *On New Democracy* summarised what was to become the conventional Communist analysis both of the May Fourth movement and Lu Hsün, the most articulate and influential critic of the post-1919 Chinese society:

> Its influence is so great and its power so tremendous that it is practically invincible wherever it goes. The vast scope of its mobilisation is unparalleled in any other period of Chinese history. And Lu Hsün was the greatest and the most militant standard-bearer of this new cultural force. He was the supreme commander in China's cultural revolution; he was not only a great man of letters, but also a great thinker and a great revolutionary. Lu Hsün had the most unyielding backbone and was totally free from any trace of obsequiousness and sycophancy; such strength of character is the greatest treasure among the colonial and semi-colonial peoples.[8]

Writing only about three years after Lu Hsün's death in October 1936, Mao lauded an already near-legendary " Lu Hsün, the Communist," as the " giant of China's cultural revolution," conveniently ignoring the fact that the real Lu Hsün had never joined the Party. Despite increasing contact with the underground Communist apparatus in Shanghai during

[8] *Ibid.* p. 144.

the period of the repressive Kuomintang actions of the early 1930s, he remained an intransigent individualist. Though Lu Hsün became China's most prominent symbol of left-wing intellectual opposition to the Kuomintang, he never succumbed to the lure of institutionalisation in the Marxist-Leninist faith.[9]

The sweep of Mao's vision may explain, if not excuse, his imprecision. Nearly a decade before Communism gained power at Peking, he was attempting during the winter of 1939–40 at his remote Shensi base to describe the system of " New Democracy " which, even then, he planned to bring to fruition in China. " National in form, new-democratic in content ": such was Mao's prescription for the cultural sector of his general revolutionary formula. Culture should be " national, scientific, and mass." It should be national in the sense that it should oppose " imperialist oppression " and uphold the " dignity and independence of the Chinese nation "; scientific in the sense that it should oppose all " feudal and superstitious ideas " and stand for the " unity of theory and practice." And it should be " mass " in the sense that it should be " in the service of the toiling masses of workers and peasants who constitute more than 90 per cent. of the nation's population, and it should gradually become their culture."

In essence, Hu Shih's earlier " literary revolution " and the entire May Fourth movement had incorporated a bold attack upon the classical language in favour of a simpler medium which could be understood not only by trained scholars but also by all Chinese with a minimum standard of literacy. So too did Mao Tse-tung in his *On New Democracy* (January 1940) call for linguistic and literary reform as an integral part of the Communist programme of cultural reorientation. Yet Mao's proposals were more drastic than those of the explorers and experimenters of the 1917–27 decade. Mao argued not only that a written form of the everyday spoken language of China should properly be used for general communication but also that the intellectuals should consciously learn the language of the common people. The Chinese written language, he stated, " must be reformed in certain ways, and our spoken language must be brought close to that of the people; we must know that the people are the inexhaustibly rich source of our revolutionary culture."

Two years later, in May 1942, Mao framed a more specific definition of the new policies through which the Communists planned to control the course of literary development in China. This definition was offered at the Yenan Forum on art and literature, a landmark in the history

[9] See Harriet C. Mills, " Lu Hsün and the Communist Party," *The China Quarterly*, No. 4, October–December 1960, pp. 17–27.

of Chinese Communist cultural policy, where Mao made two significant speeches.[10]

The first, on May 2, was designed to raise issues for discussion. Observing that since the outbreak of the Sino-Japanese war in July 1937 more and more " revolutionary artists and writers " had come to Yenan and other Communist base areas, Mao referred to the necessity of merging the talents of these individuals with " the people." The purpose of the meeting, he stated, was " to fit art and literature properly into the whole revolutionary machine as one of its component parts, to make them a powerful weapon for uniting and educating the people and for attacking and annihilating the enemy. . . ." To achieve this objective Mao presented several problems requiring solution: the standpoint, the attitude, and the audience of the writers.

The proper standpoint (*li-ch'ang*), Mao stipulated, should be " that of the proletariat and the broad masses of the people." The correct standpoint in turn determined the appropriate attitude (*t'ai-tu*): whether to " praise " or " expose." Both were necessary, Mao stated, in accordance with whether the writer was dealing with (a) the enemy, (b) the allies in the united front, or (c) " our own people, namely, the masses and their vanguard " (*i.e.*, the Communist Party). With respect to audience (*kung-tso tui-hsiang*), he stated that literary works produced in the Shensi-Kansu-Ninghsia border region and other anti-Japanese bases should be designed for a specific audience: workers, peasants, soldiers and revolutionary cadres. If " writers from the intelligentsia " were to produce works which would be welcomed by the common people, they must first " transform and remould their thoughts and feelings." If such writers were to become Communist revolutionary writers, they must have a serious knowledge of Marxism-Leninism. True, the essential task of the writer is to create literary works. But " Marxism-Leninism is the science that all revolutionaries should study, and artists and writers cannot be exceptions."

Three weeks later, Mao summed up the forum's deliberations. In a concluding talk on May 23, 1942, he drew a firm line across the page of modern Chinese creative writing and promulgated what has since become, with some later variations, the " correct " analysis of the literary and aesthetic principles designed to guide the " progressive " writers and artists of China.

With characteristic pragmatism, Mao began: " In discussing any problem we should start from actual facts and not from definitions." After summarising the " present situation " as viewed from Yenan in the

[10] See Mao Tse-tung, *Selected Works* (New York: International Publishers, 1956), Vol. IV (1941–45), pp. 63–93. The Chinese text is found in *Mao Tse-tung Hsuan-chi* (Peking: Jen-min Ch'u-pan-she, 1953), Vol. III, pp. 849–880.

spring of 1942, Mao turned to " our problems." These, he stated, were basically two: " for whom " to work, and " how to serve." Quoting Lenin's famous 1905 statement, *Party Organisation and Party Literature*, Mao echoed this classic definition of the ideological basis of proletarian literature. Mao concurred that literature must be shaped by a clear " Party spirit " and must be designed for the masses, specifically for the workers, peasants and soldiers. As to the problem of " how," Mao stipulated that " popularisation " was a more pressing task than " elevation," that is, that literature should be brought down to the level of the common people to explain Communist programmes in simple, concrete language. Writing should be consciously native: in substance drawing upon China's rich storehouse of " revolutionary tales " and folk literature capable of being interpreted in an appropriate political light; in style drawing upon the pithy language of the common people. Writing should turn its back upon bourgeois themes or subjective inspiration, and should be based upon immersion in the everyday life of the common people of China.

Mao then turned to the broader issue of the relationship between literature and politics. In the world today, he stated, " all culture, all art and literature belong to definite classes and follow definite political lines. There is in reality no such thing as art for art's sake, art which stands above classes or art which runs parallel to or remains independent of politics." Literature, in short, exists primarily for politics (interpreted as meaning " class politics and mass politics "), not for amusement or entertainment. Thus Communist literary activity occupies a definite and assigned place in the Party's total revolutionary work and must serve the particular political purposes defined by the Party. Commenting finally on literary criticism as a principal method of " struggle," Mao distinguished two basic criteria: political and artistic. At the time Mao spoke (May 1942), the foremost problem confronting both China and the Chinese Communist Party was " resistance to Japan." According to the political criterion, therefore, all literary works were " good " which encouraged national unity and resistance to Japan. At the same time, Mao recognised that, to be politically effective, literary works also had to be artistically effective. " What we demand is unity of politics and art, of content and form, and of revolutionary political content and the highest possible degree of effectiveness in artistic form. Works of art, however politically progressive, are powerless if they lack artistic quality."

In a general way, the literary standards prescribed by the leader of the Communist Party of China in 1942 were similar to those created by the doctrinal demands of Socialist realism in the U.S.S.R. Literature must, first of all, be truthful in its depiction of real life as seen through the glass of *partiinost*, the " Party-minded spirit " which views all situations in relation to the " correct " Communist Party line at any given point in time. It must, secondly, incorporate a pedagogical element to give it maximum effectiveness in inculcating appropriate ethical and political values as required by the Communist revolution. And it must, thirdly, be intelligible to the common people. To be socially effective as a device for instruction and edification, a work of literature must be successful in creating an impact that is extensive as well as intensive.

Mao's Yenan talks on literature were neither original nor unopposed. In large part, they represented his summation of theories which had been widely discussed in leftist literary circles in China since the 1930s. His call for linguistic and literary reforms echoed programmes advocated earlier by leaders of the League of Left Wing Writers. His stress on the necessity for popularisation was as much pragmatic as political, a reflection of the fact that *pai-hua* literature, as it had developed during the 1920s and 1930s, was tending to become almost as incomprehensible to the average Chinese reader as classical *wen-yen*. Nor did Mao's ideas go unchallenged; a small but influential group of left-wing writers and literary critics continued in fact to oppose his dictates through the 1940s and even the early 1950s.

Because of his personal position as unchallenged leader of the Chinese Communist movement, Mao's 1942 statements did nevertheless have widespread practical importance, both in the Communist-controlled areas and outside. Within the " border regions " the Communists increasingly attempted to link imaginative writing with the political demands of nationalism, agrarian reform and the united front. Genuinely interesting talents, displayed by new authors working completely in the new native " revolutionary " pattern stipulated by Mao, did emerge. Chao Shu-li, for example, Shensi peasant born and bred, demonstrated an authentic command of rural idiom; a considerable virtuosity in linking humour, satire and pathos; and notable effectiveness in creating peasant literature with a political message for peasants.[11] In the Nationalist areas, the major established authors of twentieth-century China, increasingly dissatisfied with the intellectual turbidity and artistic aridity of the Kuomintang leadership, gradually moved towards the political left. Yenan's resolute anti-Japanese stand, its lack of venality, its Spartan way of life and its nascent " New Democracy " constituted potent appeals which Chungking could hardly match.

II

All was not simple and sweet. In the Communist areas, both in Shensi and elsewhere, the unavoidable frictions created in attempting to wed

[11] See Cyril Birch, " Fiction of the Yenan Period," *The China Quarterly*, No. 4, October–December 1960, pp. 1–11, followed by Birch's translation of the short story " Mai-chi " (" The Sale of a Hen "), pp. 12–16.

literary creativity and political orthodoxy were apparent during the 1940s, as similar tensions had earlier been manifest at Shanghai during the 1930s. Yet the broad fact remained that Chinese Communism, well before it won national control, had gained substantial support from many thoughtful and patriotic Chinese writers. The assassination in July 1946 at Kunming of Wen I-to, prominent poet, scholar and spokesman of the liberal Chinese intellectuals who opposed the National Government, aroused national attention and widespread criticism of the Kuomintang. By the late 1940s, almost all the serious writers of China had indicated their tacit agreement with Mao Tse-tung's political programme; after 1949, every top-ranking author remained on the mainland.[12] Such a beginning appeared auspicious. The literary front could lay claim to a substantial body of writing produced despite frustrating conditions of military conflict, political suppression and censorship, and economic insecurity during the three decades following the May Fourth movement. With optimism tinged by fatalism, the literati looked forward to reaping the benefits which Mao's consistent attention to "cultural work" appeared to promise.

The situation of the writers since has been largely a tale of ingenuous affection deceived. In practical terms, the establishment of the Central People's Government marked the close of the literary period sparked a generation earlier by Ch'en Tu-hsiu, Hu Shih, *New Youth* and the Chinese Renaissance. The post-1949 era has been marked by total emphasis upon the creation of a "people's literature" on a truly national basis. This emphasis has been accompanied by the establishment of a new control mechanism capable of applying rigorous standards to all writers on the mainland, Communist and non-Communist alike. The hypothesis that politics has a profound impact upon literature has ripened into the axiom that politics is the essence of literature. Understanding of the relation between the two may thus best be assisted by an assessment of Peking's general policy intentions.

In the political sphere, Peking's primary objectives have been, first, consolidation of total power and construction of an effective apparatus of political control and, second, forced development of maximum national power. The driving ram-jet engine behind this programme of social engineering is the distinctive organisation-cum-ideology which is the Communist Party of China. Leninist by tradition and by necessity, the Communist Party now dominates all aspects of life on the mainland, acting in part as the innovating agent in imposing change, in part as

12 Of the top-ranking literary figures, only Lao She, who was in the United States at the time, was absent when the new government was established in October 1949. He returned to China slightly later, toward the end of 1949, and has remained in Peking. See Cyril Birch, "Lao She: The Humourist in his Humour," *The China Quarterly*, No. 8, October–December 1961, pp. 45–62.

the reflector of evolving forces and aspirations in contemporary Chinese society. The new totalitarian marriage of apparatus and doctrine, coupled with a technological control system which never existed before in China, thus gives the Chinese Communist élite a degree and a type of power which is in important respects completely new.

As the nature of the society is now being shaped to correspond with the priorities of the Communist political system, so too has the position of literature in the society changed drastically. Now, as formerly in the Communist-controlled areas in the countryside, the Party seeks expository works which preach a simple, social moral attuned to its immediate purposes. But now the mobilisation of fiction as the handmaiden of politics has been carried through on a national scale. In pursuit of its ambitious goals, Peking confronts the problem of purposeful stimulation of over 650 million Chinese dwelling within the borders of the People's Republic. To that end, Peking must strive to eliminate illiteracy to make literature comprehensible to the common people [13]; while simultaneously it must use literature to reach those who can read in order to secure maximum public support for its programme of planned national modernisation. The political structure of Communist China is in important respects similar to a military organisation which operates through command, not consent. Within this command context, literature is a sort of independent regiment staffed by technicians skilled in the use of prose, poetry and drama for the mobilisation of mass support for centrally determined political objectives.

An outstanding characteristic of modern single-party dictatorship is its reliance upon bureaucratic organisation to render its controls effective on a broad scale. As in other realms of Chinese life, it has been necessary to create a large bureaucratic apparatus to translate the Communist Party's literary precepts into actual practice. The political control of literature in the People's Republic of China has been little studied to date, and the following account is confined to description of the apparatus affecting the production of literary works. It does not attempt to analyse the precise techniques of control or to assess the manner in which changes in the political climate within China have affected the style and operation of the system.

The primary instrument of political control in Communist China is the central apparatus of the Communist Party itself. Thus the Party's central organisation, specifically the department of propaganda of the Central Committee, acts as the general source of ideological orthodoxy and the central arbiter of its transmutation into "literature." Director

[13] See Father Paul L.-M. Serruys, *Survey of the Chinese Language Reform and the Anti-illiteracy Movement in Communist China* (Berkeley: University of California, Center for Chinese Studies, Studies in Chinese Communist Terminology, No. 8, February 1962).

of the propaganda department of the party is Lu Ting-yi, long a high-ranking figure in the central hierarchy, an alternate member of the Political Bureau since September 1956 and a member of the Secretariat of the Central Committee since September 1962. Of the seven deputy directors of the department, the most prominent is Chou Yang, an alternate member of the Central Committee and the key figure in articulating the Party line in the field of literature. The propaganda department of the Central Committee also includes a literature and arts division, headed by Sung Yang, of whom little is known.

The Communist Party rules mainland China through an apparatus composed of what are ostensibly governmental organisations and institutions, but it has ensured from the outset that all such organs function only under its own political supervision. In the national government structure at Peking, the principal channel of direction and control is the Ministry of Culture. Since its establishment in 1949, this ministry has been headed by the novelist Mao Tun. Creatively inactive in recent years, Mao Tun has been the ranking government official in the field of literature and the arts though he himself is not a Communist Party member. He has eight vice-ministers, of who Ch'ien Chun-jui, now an alternate member of the Central Committee, is probably the most influential Communist. The Ministry of Culture has broad administrative authority in the cultural field, including literature, and is the top level in a nation-wide pyramid of subordinate bureaus which direct cultural affairs at the provincial and local levels. Neither Mao Tun nor the Ministry of Culture, however, plays any major role in policy formulation.

The Chinese Academy of Sciences, also a part of the governmental machinery at Peking, may be mentioned because of its position as the principal centre of advanced research in the People's Republic. President of the Academy since 1949 has been Kuo Mo-jo, one of the most versatile of living Chinese intellectuals and a significant force on the cultural scene since the 1920s. Prolific as poet, playwright, novelist, short story writer, essayist and critic, Kuo formally joined the Communist Party in 1959. Under its department of philosophy and social sciences, the Academy has an Institute of Literary Studies, where senior scholars pursue advanced research on China's classical literature, as well as other organs which have more indirect connection with literature and literary history: the research institutes on linguistics and philology, minority nationality languages and archaeology.

Outside the Party and government structure, the key apparatus facilitating Party direction of literature is the All-China Federation of Literary and Art Circles. The Federation, established in the summer of 1949 slightly before the establishment of the Central People's Government, is one of the largest and most influential of the " people's organisations " which Peking has created to channel political controls throughout the country.[14] Reorganised at its second congress in 1953, the Federation held its third national congress of writers and artists at Peking in July–August 1960. That meeting elected a national committee of 224 persons, from among whom were elected the chairman and fifteen vice-chairmen of the Federation. Kuo Mo-jo was re-elected chairman, with Mao Tun and Chou Yang as the top vice-chairmen. Other vice-chairmen elected in 1960 included Pa Chin, Lao She, Hsu Kuang-p'ing (widow of Lu Hsün), T'ien Han, Ou-yang Yu-ch'ien (died 1962) and Hsia Yen, as well as Mei Lan-fang (died 1961) and other senior figures in the arts. Well-known literary figures who became members of the national committee in 1960 but were not elected to vice-chairmanships included Chang T'ien-yi, Ch'eng Fang-wu, Hsieh Ping-hsin (previously a vice-chairman), Hsiung Fo-hsi, Liu Pai-yu and Yü P'ing-po.

The All-China Federation of Literary and Art Circles is essentially a holding company responsible for co-ordinating the activities of nine national organisations representing major branches of the arts: literature, drama, painting, music, dance, folklore, vocal music, films and photography. The literary subdivision of the Federation is the Chinese Writers' Union. Like its Russian counterpart, the Union of Soviet Writers, this organisation is intended to be the principal professional body in contemporary Chinese literary life,[15] responsible to and supervised by the Central Committee of the Party. The Writers' Union is designed to provide a forum for the interchange of ideas, an organisation through which professional writers may aid and stimulate each other, and a direct channel through which the Communist Party, aided by the Party fraction in the Union, can transmit its mandates and elucidate its view of the tasks confronting contemporary Chinese literature. Mao Tun, in addition to his post as Minister of Culture in the government, has also served as chairman of the Chinese Writers' Union since 1949. The Union now has four vice-chairmen: Chou Yang, Pa Chin, Shao Ch'uan-lin and Lao She. As a national association, the Writers' Union also supervises branches in the provinces and autonomous regions, and at the sub-provincial level as well. In organisation and operations, these branches are similar to the national Union, though their apparatus is naturally simpler.

Information about the activities and interrelationships of the various parts of the bureaucracy which controls the complex range of activities involved in the production of literary works in Communist China is

[14] See *The People's New Literature* (Peking: Cultural Press, 1950), for English translations of four reports given at the first Congress of the All-China Federation of Literary and Art Circles in July 1949. Reports are by Chou En-lai, Kuo Mo-jo, Mao Tun and Chou Yang, and the pamphlet has a foreword by Emi Siao.

[15] For an appraisal of the Soviet Writers' Union, see Swayze, *op. cit.*, Chap. 6, "Bureaucratic Controls and Literary Production," pp. 224–258.

scanty.[16] As a general rule, policy decisions of the central apparatus of the Party, speeches by top Party officials, leading editorials in the major newspapers and theoretical journals published in Peking—all these have the force of military orders. In specific cases, the top Party echelons may issue instructions through the propaganda department of the Central Committee. And, not least important, Peking's ranking literary bureaucrats, both vice-chairmen of the Chinese Writers' Union, are also ranking Communists. Chou Yang has been close to Mao Tse-tung since the 1930s; Shao Ch'uan-lin, while less prominent, is now secretary of the Communist Party fraction in the Writers' Union. The Party thus exercises continuing political surveillance through the editorial offices of the leading literary journals and publishing houses.

The two leading literary magazines in China today are *Jen-min Wen-hsueh* (*People's Literature*: PL) the organ of the Chinese Writers' Union, and *Wen-yi Pao* (*Journal of Literature and the Arts*) the organ of the All-China Federation of Literary and Art Circles.[17] Both are monthlies; and it is hardly surprising to record the fact that, in both influence and circulation, they dominate the literary scene throughout the country. *People's Literature*, normally running about 80 pages, prints current short novels and some poems; *Wen-yi Pao*, with about 40–50 pages, specialises in shorter literary pieces and literary criticism. Though the precise techniques of Party control are often cloudy, it is clear that few are exempt from pressures. Feng Hsueh-feng, for example, at the time of his downfall, was both a vice-chairman of the Writers' Union and editor-in-chief of the People's Literature Publishing House. This company, one of the specialised houses established by the Communists to publish literary works for the general reader, occupies a key place in the preparation and distribution of approved books. Here, as elsewhere in the publishing realm, editors, cultural cadres, and authors are doubtless plagued continually by the tensions created by the potentially conflicting demands for ideological reliability and artistic potency.

The organisation of writing on a national basis may be viewed, at one level, as an aspect of the programme of coercive persuasion and indoctrination which has been so prominent a part of the Communist

[16] Some guidance is provided by Franklin W. Houn, *To Change a Nation: Propaganda and Indoctrination in Communist China* (New York: The Free Press of Glencoe, 1961). See especially Chap. 3, "The Printed Word and the Dogma," pp. 91–154.

[17] A useful index guide to the contents of *Jen-min Wen-hsueh* is given in Takashi Aiura, "Jimmin bungaku sodai shosetsu, sambun, ho-koku ichiranhyo," *Journal* of Osaka University of Foreign Studies, 1961, No. 9, pp. 93–145. Prepared in the Chinese literature seminar, this guide lists 947 items included in *Jen-min Wen-hsueh* during the period from October 1949 to November 1959, arranged by year and month with summary of contents.

Samples of three short novels, translated from PL (issues of October through December 1961), are given in *China News Analysis* (Hong Kong), No. 414, March 30, 1962.

control system in China.[18] This programme, played in a distinctively Chinese key and aimed at a higher degree of saturation than superficially similar programmes in other totalitarian political systems, has been a major element in Peking's mobilisation effort. At another level, the Chinese Communists have gone beyond the general thought reform programme to launch specific attacks against writers accused of being lax in political reliability or lethargic in production of the approved brands of fiction. The primary instrument employed in these campaigns has been public criticism by the Communist Party. The major purpose has been to compel the writers thus stigmatised to recognise and accept the strict guidance of the Party in literary, no less than in political, matters.

This series of campaigns aimed at reaffirming the primacy and purity of Party leadership has encompassed both non-Communist and Communist writers, including some veteran Party members. The roots of these attacks may be found in the period during the Sino-Japanese war when the Communists, confronted with expanding Party membership and with extended geographical lines of control, embarked upon a thorough-going programme of tightening intra-Party discipline along strict Leninist lines.[19] Both at Yenan during the early 1940s and in the Communist-controlled areas of the North-east after 1945, the Party authorities dealt abruptly and harshly with Communist writers who ventured overt criticism of Mao's official policies.

Since their victory on the mainland, Communist attacks on writers and literary scholars have intermittently been intensified.[20] One major campaign, launched in the autumn of 1954, focused upon Yü P'ing-po, leading non-Communist scholar of classical Chinese literature, for alleged ideological errors in assessment of the famous eighteenth-century novel, *Hung Lou Meng* (*The Dream of the Red Chamber*). The essence

18 The most informed brief introduction to this controversial subject is Harriet C. Mills, "Thought Reform: Ideological Remoulding in China," *The Atlantic*, special issue on China, December 1959, pp. 71–77. More extended first-hand accounts and academic studies include the following: Theodore H. E. Chen, *Thought Reform of the Chinese Intellectuals* (Hong Kong: Hong Kong Un. Press, 1960); Robert Ford, *Wind between the Worlds* (New York: David McKay, 1957); Robert Jay Lifton, *Thought Reform and the Psychology of Totalism: a Study of "Brainwashing" in China* (New York: Norton, 1961); Allyn and Adele Rickett, *Prisoners of Liberation* (New York: Cameron Associates, 1957); and Edgar H. Schein *et al.*, *Coercive Persuasion: A Socio-Psychological Analysis of the "Brainwashing" of American Civilian Prisoners by the Chinese Communists* (New York: Norton, 1961).

19 See Boyd Compton, *Mao's China: Party Reform Documents, 1942–44* (Seattle: University of Washington Press, 1952). Compton provides a solid introduction, followed by translation of twenty-two documents used in "study" and discussion groups in the Communist areas during the *cheng-feng* campaign. A slightly revised group of documents is given in *Cheng-feng Wen-hsien* (Peking: Hsin-hua Shu-tien, May 1950).

20 In addition to the summary provided by Franklin W. Houn, *op. cit.*, pp. 130–40, see also Shau-wing Chan, "Literature in Communist China," *Problems of Communism*, VII, No. 1 (January–February 1958), pp. 44–51, and Cyril Birch, "The Dragon and the Pen," *Soviet Survey*, special China issue, No. 14 (April–June 1958), pp. 22–26.

of Peking's criticisms of Yü, a prominent authority on the novel, was that he had failed to emphasise that the novel portrayed the class struggle and exposed, through its characters, the evils of China's feudal society. Having vilified Yü for his failure to employ Marxist categories of analysis, the Communists went on to denounce him as a " bourgeois idealist " tainted with the poisonous doctrines of Hu Shih, attacks which were as virulent as they were manifestly absurd, since Yü P'ing-po had often differed with Hu Shih's opinions concerning early Chinese fiction and drama. Feng Hsueh-feng, then a vice-chairman of the Chinese Writers' Union and editor of the influential *Wen-yi-Pao,* lost his editorship for having taken Yü's part in the controversy. Yü P'ing-po in the end emerged from the sustained attack, made the necessary concessions to Marxist interpretation, and applied himself with remarkable resilience to his *Hung Lou Meng* studies.[21]

Less fortunate was Hu Feng, himself a leading independent Marxist literary critic who had been a disciple of Lu Hsün in Shanghai in the 1930s. After the establishment of the new régime at Peking in 1949, Hu Feng became increasingly critical of the attempts of his old antagonist, Chou Yang, and of Chou's fellow bureaucrats in the central apparatus to dominate all literary activity in China. This smouldering resentment erupted in a general statement, " Views on Literary Questions" which Hu Feng boldly submitted to the Central Committee of the Party in July 1954. In reply to this overt criticism of the sterility of literature under its rigid rule Peking launched a massive counter-attack. The Communist authorities declared Hu Feng of " bourgeois reactionary " thinking and in July 1955 arrested both Hu and other members of his " clique " on charges of " counter-revolutionary " activities.

Though the charge that he disagreed with Peking's current literary policies was valid, there was no evidence proving that Hu Feng's ideas were anti-Marxist in principle or that he actually intended to subvert or sabotage political authority. Peking's manipulation of the case demonstrated that the political aspects of the controversy overshadowed the literary. Peking's programme of political mobilisation during 1955 required that heterodox views be exposed and eradicated. A revolutionary by conviction, Hu Feng found himself unable to sustain his stand in favour of freedom of expression for the creative writer during a period when the demands of political utilitarianism outweighed those of artistic integrity.

An interlude of liberalisation in ideological controls came during the " hundred flowers " campaign launched in mid-1956 with the explicit aim of giving intellectuals and " cultural workers " a greater sense of

21 I am indebted to Professor David Hawkes of Oxford University for background information on Yü P'ing-po.

participation in the tasks of "Socialist construction" and of leavening the literary scene with fresh forms of expression. The apparent relaxation in Communist policy heralded by Lu Ting-yi's speech of May 1956 [22] did in fact bring forth a short-lived spasm of literary realism. One short story, "Young Newcomer to the Organization Department," published in the September 1956 issue of *People's Literature*, provides a perceptive account of the growing disillusion experienced by an enthusiastic Communist Party worker in the face of bureaucracy, lethargy, and indifference.

Yet the attempt to win over and mobilise the intellectuals was too brief to sustain significant new literary production, and the interlude of criticism was followed in 1957 by a new rectification campaign in the Party and a general nation-wide drive against "rightist elements" antithetical to Peking's policies. The most dramatic case affecting the literary world during this period was that of Ting Ling, prominent Chinese Communist authoress and Stalin Prize winner, who was attacked for leading an "anti-Party conspiracy" within the Communist ranks. Chou Yang himself led the attack on Ting Ling and her associates.

Amidst the tangle of polemical verbiage contributed by Chou Yang and other pillars of orthodoxy,[23] many questions regarding these major cases of non-conformity remain obscure. It is clear, however, that the Communist authorities at Peking still affirm the validity of the general literary principles enunciated by Lenin in 1905 and articulated in China by Mao Tse-tung in 1942.[24] They still decree, first, that literature must be subordinate to politics; second, that the Communist Party must direct the course of contemporary Chinese literature; and third, that the essential purpose of literature is to educate workers, peasants, and soldiers in the policies determined by the Party leadership. The continued relevance of Mao's literary precepts was again stressed in May 1962, on the twentieth anniversary of the talks at the Yenan Forum on art and literature, when Peking's policy line stressed the ultimate political responsibilities of the creative writer. "China's literature and art must bring into full play its militancy and inspire the whole people to strive for the nation's prosperity and make efforts to establish a new socialist life," the official *People's Daily* stated.

22 Lu Ting-yi, *Let a Hundred Flowers Blossom, a Hundred Schools of Thought Contend* (Peking: Foreign Languages Press, 1958). The speech was given in Peking on May 26, 1956, and published originally in the *People's Daily* of June 13, 1956.

23 One sample may suffice to indicate the style of the discourse. Chou Yang, in denouncing the errant behaviour of Ting Ling and Ch'en Ch'i-hsia, summarised the official line: "Instead of remoulding themselves in the spirit of collectivism, they want to remould the Party and the revolution according to their individualist outlook." See Chou Yang, *A Great Debate on the Literary Front* (Peking: Foreign Languages Press, 1958), p. 13.

24 See Lin Mo-han, *Raise Higher the Banner of Mao Tse-tung's Thought on Art and Literature* (Peking: Foreign Languages Press, 1961).

By intent and by necessity, Chairman Mao remains the Male Muse of the Arts in Peking's current mythology. In the real world, however, it is clear that neither the Central Committee of the Party, the Chinese Writers' Union nor the Party officials in the principal editorial offices at Peking and Shanghai are omnipotent. The process of influencing and controlling literary production depends also upon author and reader.

At one level, the task begins at the desk of the individual author, where the subtle process of personal censorship inherent in the Chinese Communist political system is first activated and finally resolved. Supported by stipend and encouraged by royalties, the creative writer nevertheless occupies a precarious position, constantly measuring his margin of freedom between the wall of schematism and the brink of non-conformity. At still another level, the enormous and newly literate reading public plays an essential role as ultimate consumer. Though the choice of Chinese literary works to be approved and published, and of non-Chinese works to be translated, is determined in large part by the Party's prescriptions as to what he should read, the reader himself is still not defenceless. Reader reaction (reception or resistance) is not an integral part of the control process, but it is still influential in China as in the Soviet Union. The authorities at Peking thus temper their proletarian predilections with a measure of pragmatism in publishing policy. The major traditional works of Chinese fiction are available, as indeed is a wide range of Chinese translations of Western books. Shakespeare, Dickens, and Hardy; Mark Twain and Jack London; Zola, Maupassant, Balzac, and Victor Hugo; Goethe and Heine: all are part of the literary fare still available in Chinese translation in the People's Republic of China today.[25]

III

Available they may be, but Western works form only a minor pattern in the literary world of Mao Tse-tung's China, dedicated as that nation is to the downfall of bourgeois society. The dominant motif is still the distinctive blend of nationalism and radicalism which has come to mark Chinese Communism today. Within this larger political context, the meshing of doctrine and discipline is as notable in literature as in any other major field of activity in China. Indeed the very speed and sureness with which the authorities at Peking have moved in imposing political controls over literature (much faster than the Communists in Moscow did during a comparable period after 1917) suggest that Mao Tse-tung and his associates have been working in harmony with some

[25] See the special article on translations into Chinese from Western languages in *The Times Literary Supplement*, September 21, 1962, p. 741.

longer historical trends. On any realistic estimate, neither Marx, Lenin, Stalin, nor Mao Tse-tung may be held solely responsible for the pattern of intellectual and social revolution in contemporary China. The new formulae are supported by elements in the Chinese political tradition. They are also buttressed by the Russian impact on China during the three decades before Communism engulfed that country, and by the particular demands, frequently turbulent and usually strident, of modern Chinese nationalism and anti-imperialism.

Mao Tse-tung's brand of totalitarianism has certain roots in the massive tradition of bureaucratic government, variously labelled authoritarian or despotic, found in dynastic China. The paternalistic Confucian system, dependent as it was on status and hierarchy, on obligation and obedience, was based in part upon autocratic assumptions and administered by a sophisticated bureaucracy well attuned to the practical requirements of wielding power. For centuries prior to the metamorphosis of mainland China into a major power in the international Communist system, the Chinese political heritage consistently placed greater emphasis upon group ethics and group responsibility than on individual autonomy.

Peking's present programme of intellectual and literary reorientation has also been aided by the impact of Russian ideas among the Chinese intelligentsia after 1917.[26] While the Western powers were still dominant on the China coast during the 1920s and 1930s, the influence of Russian literature was both strong and subtle. The works of the nineteenth-century titans—Pushkin, Gogol, Turgenev, Dostoyevsky, Tolstoy, and Chekhov—were all found in China's bookshops. Gorky was also popular, and considerable attention was paid to Soviet authors of the early post-revolutionary authors despite the Kuomintang censorship during the 1930s.[27] The attraction of modern Russian fiction arose partly because it depicted problems and tensions which paralleled those with which sensitive Chinese were naturally concerned. Thus the inflow of Russian ideas, particularly the themes of social idealism, patriotism and humanitarianism, fed the mole of intellectual revolution in its burrowing under the bustling international concessions in Shanghai and the other treaty ports.

Another manifest segment of Russian influence was, of course, sharply focused and highly political. After the 1917 revolution, the

26 See Benjamin Schwartz, "The Intelligentsia in Communist China," *Daedalus* issue on "The Russian Intelligentsia," Summer 1960, pp. 604–621.

27 A list of translations of foreign works into Chinese up to March 1929 is given in Chang Ching-lu (ed.), *Chung-kuo Hsien-tai Ch'u-pan Shih-liao* (Peking: Chung-hua Shu-chu, 1954), Vol. I, pp. 271–323. Russian authors and their works are given on pp. 277–287. Another list in the same work gives the names of Soviet authors available in Chinese translation up to May 1930, *ibid*. Vol. II, p. 280 *et seq*. Almost all important writers of the Soviet period are represented.

Soviets brought to China a shrewdly conceived, partially true, and reasonably palatable diagnosis of Chinese national frustration. Foreign "imperialism" and domestic "feudalism," the Leninist argument ran, were the twin evils blocking progress toward independence and modernisation. The blending of Russian and Chinese revolutionary styles has also been aided by two particular elements inherent in the mystique of Marxism-Leninism: a probing insight into mass psychology in countries attempting the process of rapid transition from traditional to industrial society and, second, a deep passion for material improvement and modernisation.[28] All these elements helped Communism in China before 1949 to take advantage of the growing mood of protest; they have unquestionably helped Communism in power since 1949 to enforce discipline, regimentation and centralisation of decision.

Yet the intellectual component in Marxism which allegedly provides "scientific" description and analysis of reality is only the warp of the ideological pattern in contemporary China. The pattern also embraces an indigenous emotional woof, dyed in the vat of modern Chinese nationalism. The projectile force of nationalism, which Peking has now seized and directed into anti-American channels, is in part a newer version of the deep Chinese antagonism toward Western intrusion manifest during the nineteenth century. The traditional hostility of the official-gentry class toward foreigners was sharpened and broadened during the early twentieth century as a result of the impact in China of the Russian revolution and the ideas of Lenin. Both the Chinese Communist Party and the post-1924 Kuomintang were strongly, often violently, anti-imperialist. Harnessing the deep-seated Chinese distrust of the West and of its ambiguous intentions toward China, Mao Tse-tung has now organised modern Chinese nationalism for his specific political purposes. Peking's "anti-imperialist nationalism" lays primary stress upon the demands of national solidarity over competing demands for individual rights. Though giving little place to what the West would define as democratic participation, Peking's appeal to Chinese nationalistic aspirations has tapped significant sources of popular energy in that country.

Viewed against this backdrop of historical and cultural motifs, the peregrinations of the Party line toward contemporary Chinese literature gain additional significance. Peking's political emphasis today is on the sustained expansion of national power. In pursuit of his objective, the Chinese Communists have made a massive effort to instil a sense of unity into the Chinese nation and a sense of purpose into contemporary Chinese life. The long-term success of their endeavour is problematic.

28 See Adam B. Ulam, *The Unfinished Revolution: an Essay on the Sources of Influence of Marxism and Communism* (New York: Random House, 1960).

But the immediate accomplishments, as well as the obvious shortcomings, must be recognised. For some in China, the Communists have transformed uncertainty into conviction. For many others, the Communists have restored a sense of confidence in China as a vigorous nation capable of decisive action (not least, of expelling the Westerners and extirpating the Western enclaves) and have inculcated a renewed sense of self-respect for China as a distinctive cultural entity with a proud past and a manifest destiny.

Perhaps the major requirement in assessing tradition and transition in the literary world of Mao Tse-tung is, therefore, a sense of perspective.[29] In the non-Communist tradition, literature is conventionally held to be an individual expression of experience, real or imagined; and the normal relation between writer and product is assumed to comprise integrity, spontaneity and sincerity. For the writer working on a large scale, the purpose of creation is the communication of a complex vision, inherently personal and frequently moral, of man and of life. Secure in his individualist bias, the non-Communist critic is thus likely to conclude that the authorities at Peking, through their collectivist preconceptions and prejudices, have doomed the Chinese literary field to stunted growth for an indefinite period.

Actually, however, the links between literature and society are inevitably intricate.[30] Contemporary Chinese literature may be of dubious value as a guide to present social reality in China. But it still has substantial significance in clarifying the values of the society which has shaped and produced it. In earlier centuries, the traditional historian of China had a definite didactic function: he was consciously constructing a corpus of precedents to guide future generations of scholar-officials in the theory and practice of public administration as it should be conducted in accordance with Confucian ethical standards.[31] Today the writer in Communist China is, in a perverse way, similarly charged with a didactic mission: he is attempting to channel all the energies of his nation into the construction of the "New China."

29 See T'ien-yi Li, "Continuity and Change in Modern Chinese Literature," *The Annals* of the American Academy of Political and Social Science, Vol. 321, January 1959, pp. 90–99.

30 Irving Howe, *Politics and the Novel* (New York: Horizon Press, 1957) is a provocative study of some aspects of this subject. The volume has chapters on Stendhal, Dostoyevsky, Conrad, Turgenev and Henry James; a section on American novelists ("The Politics of Isolation") commenting on Hawthorne (*The Blithedale Romance*), Henry Adams (*Democracy*) and Henry James (*The Bostonians*); and an appraisal of several distinctively twentieth-century writers: Malraux, Silone, Koestler and Orwell. Leo Lowenthal, *Literature and the Image of Man: Sociological Studies of the European Drama and Novel, 1600–1900* (Boston: Beacon Press, 1957), is a thoughtful study of the changing image of man in relation to society as revealed in some of the major literary works of the Western world during the past three centuries.

31 See E. Balazs, "L'histoire comme guide de la pratique bureaucratique," in W. G. Beasley and E. G. Pulleyblank (eds.), *Historians of China and Japan* (London: Oxford Un. Press, 1961), pp. 78–94.

IV

The vision of social change, while itself a major feat in a tradition-bound civilisation, is certainly not new in modern China. But the implementation of change on a national basis under determined and dedicated direction is new. Chairman Mao has added implementation to imagination, and the political results of the addition process are certain to outlast him.

In the literary realm, however, the situation still shelters deviant conduct. While all professional writers in the People's Republic must follow the demands of the " mass line in literature " in writing for " the people," one prominent non-conformist amateur stands aloof from Peking's doctrinal demands. Contemporary China's best-selling and most-translated author is—in his poetry at least—a conspicuous exception to the rules articulated in Peking.

Snow Scene (1945)

The grandeur that is the northern country—
an expanse of the good earth ice-bound,
snow-covered for thousands of miles around.
Surveying the Great Wall, to its north and south,
nothing but whiteness meets the eye.
The torrents of the mighty Huang Ho
into insignificance pale.
Silver snakes dance atop the mountains,
waxen elephants roam the plains,
as if to wrest heaven's domain.
Let us wait for the sky to clear
when, clothed in radiant colours,
the land becomes more magnificently dear.
For such an enchanting empire, little wonder
countless heroes matched wits with one another.
Alas! The ambitious emperors of Ch'in and Han
could scarcely boast of literary lore.
E'en the founders of the great houses T'ang and Sung
became nought before the sages of yore.
As to the redoubtable Genghis Khan,
pampered child of fortune he was,
excelled only on the field of battle.
Gone are they all.
For leaders truly worthy of homage,
must yet be sought among men of our own age.[32]

[32] Mr. Yong-sang Ng has prepared this translation. Peking's official English version appears in *Mao Tse-tung: Nineteen Poems* (Peking: Foreign Languages Press, 1958), p. 22, and is also quoted on page 65 below.

Written in the *tz'u* form, the poem marks a definite return to the past in both conception and style. Its presentation is in the orthodox Chinese statesman-scholar tradition, opening with a reference to the beauties of nature and then turning to a political theme. Blending sharp imagery and vivid metaphor, manifesting a strong sense of history and of change on the part of the author, the poem stands as an unusually effective example of traditionalism, formal excellence, and romantic heroism.

The culprit?

Mao Tse-tung himself is the outstanding exception to the canons of proletarian and utilitarian literature which he has brought to his country and his people.[33]

[33] Aware of this stubborn fact, Mao has suggested that it is inadvisable to encourage young people to write verse in the classical style "because these forms would cramp their thought and are also difficult to master." See his January 1957 letter to Tsang K'o-chia, then editor of the magazine *Poetry*, included in *Mao Tse-tung on Art and Literature, op. cit.*, pp. 135–136. See also Ping-ti Ho, "Two Major Poems by Mao Tse-tung: a Commentary, with Translations," *Queen's Quarterly* (Kingston, Ontario, Canada), LXV, 2, Summer 1958, pp. 251–262. Robert Payne has a chapter on "The Poetry of Mao Tse-tung" in his revised biography, *Portrait of a Revolutionary: Mao Tse-tung* (New York: Abelard-Schuman, 1961), pp. 230–248.

Metaphor and the Conscious in Chinese Poetry under Communism

By S. H. CHEN

Poetry as I understand it flows through history and in collaboration with real life.

—Boris Pasternak.

Proletarian art and literature . . . as Lenin said are " a wheel and a screw " in the whole revolutionary machine. Therefore the position of art and literature in relation to the whole revolution under the Party is definitely set and well affixed. They are obediently to serve the revolutionary task defined by the Party at any given period of the revolution.

—Mao Tse-tung.

COMMENTING on literature as a human record, Goethe once called it " The fragment of fragments: The smallest part of what has been done and spoken has been recorded; and the smallest part of what has been recorded has survived." I find this observation a very sobering and instructive reminder for a discussion of Chinese poetry under Communist rule. Goethe was speaking of literature in general. And poetry, formally at least, being but one of its branches, is by deduction a fragment of " the fragment of fragments." Over a decade many things have been accomplished under the régime. Many deeds have been done, immense work of material reconstruction has been completed, and more is in process, on the débris of destruction of comparable quantity; and unfathomable tribulations, pains and frustrations in soul and body are felt and muttered, as well as the hue and cry of zeal and enthusiasm exclaimed among massive crowds.

A moment's reflection on the magnitude of all these in the actual life of over six hundred million people should place whatever printed word we obtain as poetry in the right perspective and proportion. Whatever has survived severe censorship and embargo, though trickling to us cumulatively in millions of words as poems and songs, would still appear precious tiny bits of refractions of a gigantic human phenomenon. The phenomenon being a contemporary, living reality imminently concerning our life, we may become too eager and seize upon these refractional bits to pass judgment on, or imagine we were seeing directly that reality as a whole. Or, contrarily, if taking poetic expressions literally for actual life is below the intelligence of most people who care for poetry, there is still another pitfall. Different traditions breed different aesthetic preferences. If we attempt to treat the Chinese poetry in question as human data, we have to submit that it is produced under unprecedented conditions, and intended for a different kind of purpose and appeal. It would be all too easy to criticise, reject, or laugh out of countenance the poetic efforts produced under changing circumstances of which we know but very little and have experienced even less. What we would so ill-treat might indeed be poor or downright bad verse, but might we not have dismissed them too rashly, for the wrong reasons, and therefore miss what we should be looking for?

I have learnt to reflect thus while writing earlier for *The China Quarterly* a short study which I called "Multiplicity in Uniformity: Poetry and the Great Leap Forward." [1] The title I hoped would somehow signify a quality, even though this was the hardest to recognise off hand, because it was the impressiveness and significance of the tremendous *quantity* of the mass products of a "multi-million poem" movement that was dealt with, a movement conducted among the vast population under intensive, uniform political direction. To discern quality before the exercise of judgment I believe is the first obligation of literary study, even though our ultimate aim may be to gain some understanding of the political and social life that has produced the works. Taste may incline us toward attraction or repulsion as an immediate reaction, but it should not be allowed to hold too long its all too often wayward sway. It should be at least suspended, so that we can contemplate and analyse the quality once it is recognised. Quality is what we with our faculties trained in literary and historical discipline want to distil from the precious "survivals" that have come to us now, and that will have to stand the test and ravages of much longer time. A historical perspective in our mind will aid us with enough detachment to deal with our materials not only in reference to past standards, but also with a view of how they may look in the future. Our immediate task of distillation, on the other hand, be it surely from "the fragment of fragments" of much greater doings and happenings, may by its very nature of concentration on the essence of a poetic work, hold a microscopic picture. It will be the sharper the more it deals with the particular, and may thus reveal at least a segment of Chinese mental state of being, that by inference may the more effectively cast some light on the whole today.

In this article I will therefore attempt to discuss Chinese poetry under Communism by drawing enough attention to those elements which since the dawn of literary criticism have been recognised as the quintessential basis for the distinction of poetic quality, especially the making of metaphor. Here metaphor is meant in its broad sense of poetic function,

[1] *The China Quarterly*, No. 3, July–September 1960.

which will often include also the simile, regardless of the merely formal syntactical distinction. Along with metaphor, image will naturally come under consideration both for its mediatory function as a vehicle to convey the idea, and more importantly for its effect of fusing the idea and the object so that some verses or whole poems attain the vividness and concretion of poetically imagised representation of life. When such vivid image is achieved, and we translate it back into terms of the actual life it represents, it is then a symbol, and we are attempting a symbolic interpretation. Furthermore, poetic form, though it is difficult to discuss by exemplifications in a foreign language, will also have to be touched on, if only because it is inescapable when we want to indicate the change and re-establishment of vogue under new social and ideological circumstances. Needless to repeat is the truism that form is inseparable from content.

The making of metaphor is the continual basic effort of any poet worthy of the name in any age. Indeed most often it is by his metaphors, together with their felicitous imagistic effect, that a poet, if he is successful, is usually remembered; and moreover the traits of his age are thereby symbolically recognised, if his works survive. We may praise or condemn a poet himself if it is to be seen that his metaphorical expression comes from private sources, is based on singular visions and represents ingeniously personal aesthetic or moral views. In such cases the poet may be regarded as entirely responsible for himself and to his sources, which are drawn from his individual consciousness, but more fundamentally from his subconscious or even unconscious. But we should be called on to take more cognisance of his age and his milieu rather than himself, when we discover all signs pointing to the fact that his sources are distinctly public, his vision and views are working in total conformity with officially sanctioned morals and aesthetics, that his self-denial must be complete in favour of the all powerful collectivism, and that his metaphors, always having to express a superimposed national purpose, make his poetry all shadowless public consciousness, without adumbrations from deeper regions of the mind. It is precisely in this milieu, unlike anywhere else in this world today or any other age, that Chinese poems and songs, of all brands and labels, new or old, are currently produced on the mainland by hundreds of millions.

If the staggering quantity of poems that has been publicised defies any attempt at complete study, and even if most of them can be disregarded as too rough and hasty synthetic manufactures, still it will be revealing to observe a limited number that possess certain quality by poets who are considered successful at least in view of that particular milieu, if not by our yardstick which is of a different world. And though political and ideological concerns pervade every piece without exception, we want to refrain from any extraneous debate, but first only reach to what is most essential to the works as poetry, noting especially their metaphorical components, imagistic effects and symbolic meaning, and their formal distinction, keeping in view their possible revelation of an important part of the present Chinese mentality shaping and shaped by the finer expression of poetry. Of real life here we may only get a refracted glimpse, but interpreted and understood with detachment, they may inform us more.

We shall take as our first examples four very recent poems by a remarkable poet, Ko Pi-chou, published on March 24, 1962, which should be very revealing of the situation up to date. In four quite different forms they make an integral whole, under the general title "New Songs (*hsing*) of Pei-Mang Mountain, Four Pieces." [2] Despite their length we present them in full so that our impression can be intact before we treat them in detail. A translation can never be a facsimile. I shall try neither to beautify nor to parody the original, but do my best to preserve and convey some of the original sense of form, rhythm and diction, good or bad, for such fair judgment as we are capable.

The first piece is clearly derivative in form and structure,[3] harking back to ancient poetry, while expressing a contemporary Chinese Communist world-view:

I

A New Song of Pei-Mang

Ancient elegies written on Pei-Mang,
All lamented the impermanence of life.
Now atop the Pei-Mang Mountain,
Where does one see the desolation?
I do not see broken stones or deserted tombs.
I only see young wheat fields green, green;
I do not see decayed cypress or old pine,
I only see new buildings one by one;
Cocks crow, dogs bark,
Villages front, hamlets behind;
Geese swim and ducks at play
In rivulets and in the ponds.
New forests grow all round the Hill of Shou-yang,
Water below the Dam of the Golden Valley is swelling, flowing.
Behold, where are the ruins of old Lo-yang City?

[2] *People's Daily* (*Jen-min Jih-pao*), March 24, 1962.
[3] One example in classical poetry to show the derivation is available in English translation, "Ruins of Lo-yang" by Ts'ao Chih (A.D. 192–232), translated by Arthur Waley in *Translations from the Chinese* (New York: Alfred A. Knopf, 1941).

I see only clouds and water, and oceans of trees densely
without limit.
The old dies, new life is born—life, life, never to end,
Today the evening glory of nimbus—tomorrow, the morning sun.

The second piece in the sequel presents a very different state of affairs, a scene dominated entirely by Chinese Communist "new world" sensibility. It is obviously proletarian consciousness, garbed in new typical jargon to serve immediate political ends. And even newer of course is the theme, for since when but the very present has any Chinese poet on Mount Pei-Mang been impelled to single out invisibly remote Albania to vow friendship in behalf of his nation, and, why if not for some very imminent reason at this particular moment?

II

What I See In The Assembly Workshop
—Tractor Factory No. 1 is
assembling trucks for Albania—

In the assembly workshop
The machines are thundering.
The workers are intently working
Yet all seems so calm.
Everyone's face is solemn,
So true to his task.
Row after row of trucks are happily roaring,
Rushing to embark on a voyage of ten thousand li.
If you ask what they are carrying,
The Chinese people's friendship in full load.
Even though from oceans away,
You see clearly in this workshop,
That our hearts,
Under the banner of Marxism,
Are so closely to each other drawn.

The third reverts to ancient formal tradition like the first, but only halfway, and then the impact of sentiment turns to rest heavily on the militant present, like the second. And the style is more rhapsodic:

III

Gazing Afar From Pei-Mang

I stand before Shang-ch'ing Temple to gaze afar at the
Gorge of Dragon Gate,
Hoping to see the walled city of Chou, and Han, and T'ang,

The capital of nine epochs was long buried below,
I only see clear streams, red-tiled roofs, and green woods
in mists and clouds.
What of the famed magnificence of the Han capital,
And what of the vaunted glory and splendour of T'ang?
In our new town of Lo-yang,
Where is the old city to be found?
Among nimbuses of many hues the Yi River dances like
a phoenix,
In the white clouds the River Lo arches like a dragon;
See the immense ocean of green trees,
And jungles of smoking chimneys row after row,
Factories stand like gunboats in battle array,
O fighting ships one by one,
A voyage of ten thousand li you have begun.

The fourth and last piece is in form nearly a perfect traditional *wu ku*, "pentasyllabic old style," of good ancient Han vintage. Even its tenor may appear traditional, dealing as it does with the meeting and parting of old friends. Yet in its final metaphorical effects we see something monolithically characteristic of today's Chinese Communist poetry:

IV

To A Comrade

On the bank of the Yen River [4] once we parted,
By the side of River Lo now we meet.
Together several days like body and shadow,
To each other our stories are too long to tell.
The wine we drink is Dragon Gate brew,
But the moon of Ch'iao Shan we both recall:
How we shared a mud cave for our lodging,
And how on mountain tops we "learned" [5] as a group.
To till the virgin land we used the same hoe,
Our happy songs we sang to the same beat.
Now I look at the land in front of your house,
I see beans and melons you planted by hand.
You eat very little, and your duties are many,
To wield the hoe for you means even a rest.
But since you've imbibed water of the Yen River,
You act like the same hero of the years past.

[4] Near the Communist war-time headquarters of Yenan.
[5] "Learned," *hsueh-hsi*, is treated as a special term, which in Communist China has come especially to mean training to be a member of the new revolutionary society.

Do not say the towering pine is growing old,
The young forests are soon to reach the sky.
Waving our hands, we go again each his own way,
But we do not complain that we parted too soon.
All rivers will concourse in the great sea,
How can clouds and mountains ever keep us apart?

These four poems by such a skilful poet as Ko cannot represent the average, particularly since the mass production of the last few years makes it necessary to even them up with perhaps hundreds of millions of verses if a true average is to be obtained. But Ko's four poems nevertheless are manifestly typical of the most recent trends in their important features. A consideration of the poems in detail will therefore sufficiently epitomise the general situation of poetic creation. at least among poets who can produce works of recognisable quality.

First, let us see briefly what is involved in the matter of form for this group of Ko's poems, in so far as this technical point discussed even in a foreign language can show its broad significances. The " multi-million poem " movement of four years ago has with its success in " meeting the projected quota " raised an immense nationwide wave to drive the poets to " learn " sedulously from folk form. The " folk form " current today among the several hundred million Chinese peasants being still predominantly either the pentasyllabic or the septasyllabic stich (scanned 2-2-1 or 2-2-2-1), the poets accordingly adopted either metre from the sacrosanct and infallible " people " with a hallowed sense of " correctness." But these metres are precisely identical with those which dominated classical Chinese poetry for at least two thousand years. So in seeking for China's great poetic future in the grass-roots of the people, the course reverts to reaching for the great poetic past and meeting with the elegant genteel tradition of classical poets.

But every " contradiction " under Communism is dialectically explained away and justified. Under these circumstances, for Chinese poetic form today, the earlier slogans of inheriting, preserving, and profitably using national cultural heritage are now supposed to have been realised with bounteous fruition. Of course for the new sanctity, there is in addition a higher influence, not just a new lease of life for the classical forms along with folk metre. It is from an even more zealously avowed sacrosanct and infallible source. In this case it is from Mao Tse-tung himself, whose masterly classical verses, though rather small in number, have been acclaimed as the supreme example.

Under the aegis of the new synthesis of folk form and classical tradition, therefore, we see that three out of four of Ko's poems as a group make a typically ingenious mixture, if not always a happy fusion, of traits of both folk and classical poetry in their formal apparatus, including diction, phrasing, tonal exactitude or laxity (which should distinguish the folkish and the classic after all) as well as metrical imitation or derivation. Poem II may be singled out as distinctively in the "modern" tradition, in form as well as content, with its colloquial speech rhythm and bi-syllabic endings throughout. But this also betokens the result of a fruitful debate during the "multi-million poem" movement, when a few very able poets and critics [6] of influence, though supporting the "correctness" of imitating folk and classical poetry, nevertheless asserted the necessity of keeping up the "modern" colloquial forms experimented with since the May Fourth Movement (1919), in order to develop a new poetic "metrical discipline" (*ko lü*), more compatible with everyday living speech to express life in the Marxian paradise. Though tempers flew high during the debate, and typically Communist strong language was exchanged as if a verbal holy war were being fought, the end result was a compliment to Chairman Mao's "hundred flowers" policy. For it was after all an innocent issue taken up by opponents who were politically all considered absolutely safe. The modern contemporary colloquial form, initiated by the May Fourth intellectuals, continues to blossom amidst immense varieties and mixtures of the rustic and antique species in a tremendously prolific plantation. Ko Pi-chou's group of four poems we have brought under consideration represents therefore really a typical cross-section of the high vogue of today in Communist China's poetic forms. And this matter of form, as we have seen, on the one hand is heavily charged with political overtones, while on the other it bears intimately upon the characteristics of the poetic products.

Now, metre affects diction, and diction is basic to the substance of metaphor. Metaphors the poet can create or recreate, in inspired moments and under felicitous circumstances; or he may borrow, readapt, or tritely repeat, for the lack either of talent, or of the new individual vision which is essential for him to make original linguistic discoveries to achieve fresh metaphors that give totally new perspectives on human life and nature. The lack of new individual vision, however, is often not caused by the deficiency of the individual poet's innate capability, but by his times and conditions. Decadence and escapism forced by circumstances may of course make the consciousness of the poet recoil and render his vision indigent. But there are also times and conditions when the poet suffers what I would call the overstrain of apparent consciousness and the loss of individual vision and creativity. It is when the poet's whole attention is summoned by an overbearing

[6] Most of their articles on the *ko lü* problem were published in several numbers of the *Wen-xue P'ing-lun* 1959–60, a bi-monthly on literary theories, perhaps the best of its kind.

outward power of which he must be always intensely conscious, to see what he is desired by that power to see, and thus to say what he is desired to say. And he must be furthermore always conscious of his form which in metre and diction should not just suit his own poetic impulse, but will be bound to have ideological or ritualistic significance attached to it and be criticised, justified, or rationalised according to state interest. We may easily be reminded of like conditions for poetic composition in earlier times at court examinations, under the Chinese dynasties, when the poet must have been all awareness as regards the prescribed form and desired content. The ritualistic homage having been correctly paid, however, he could then walk out of the examination hall and do something very different by himself. But today the Chinese poet must be constantly mindful of the wish and interest of the Party and the State, which he must will into his consciousness all the time in order to serve as an approved intellectual worker. As a consequence, this mental state, this constant strain of the consciousness, infuses into his poetry a distinct, pervading quality in all cases, be the verses competent or incompetent. This quality we may easily recognise, and call it the transparency of theme. And the poet, having "surrendered his heart" entirely to Party and State, *chiao hsin,* as innumerable slogans have cheered it, and thus lost himself in the gigantic collectivity, cannot but inflate his language into that of the grandiose collective mind and thus speak most often in hyperboles.

Transparency of theme and hyperbolism therefore may be said to characterise all the poetry produced so far under Communist rule both by able poets as well as by the masses. These two qualities are clearly exemplified in Ko Pi-chou's poems we have cited. We can immediately feel them in the general tenor of the poems, in the rhythm and diction, and they are most tell-tale in the making of the metaphors. So far as metaphors are concerned, our first impression may indeed be the paucity of them. For most of the lines are direct statements. And where metaphors in the strict sense are formally present, they are in most cases diaphanously obvious ones, or borrowed from too familiar sources: "The evening nimbus and morning sun" to stand for unending life; "the banner of Marxism"; "phoenix dancing" and "dragon arching" to depict the flowing rivers; "the young forest" succeeding "the old pine" like future generations. Though the poems are clothed mostly in old imagery, the poet's intent is to say something very new. And we should not disregard the whole work by picking out only the fragments. But the "newness" neither appears to be in the way he says things, nor strikes us as any too fresh an individual perceptive discovery. It is rather that the subject is all too consciously about newness itself. Consequently we see the poetisation of the apparent public knowledge of the new living China contrasted with the dying old, as in Poems I and III. Poems II and IV attempt to depict new types of human activity and human relationships, which, again, have been too often publicised. All four poems are eulogistic, and in one way or another moral pieces, like every other Chinese Communist poem, typically exhorting to a uniform purpose. This purpose we may sum up in the phrase collective militant optimism, and it dictates the glorification of the present and a happy outlook for the future, to be realised by the fighting forces of solid collectivity, that will not only vanquish ideological enemies, but conquer nature and transform man's individuality into a body of massive power, with the common aspiration to serve Party and State. This common purpose so fully occupies the entire consciousness of the poet wherever he writes, that it shines through every one of his poems like a piece of perfect glass. When the theme is so glaring, other details of the poem dissolve into mere foils or ornaments.

But Ko Pi-chou is no doubt a poet of real talent, as is evidenced by his facility with versification and the dexterity of his formal adaptations. And like a talented poet, he can achieve poetic devices in the face of any situation to suit the moment. In employing all the ingredients of sanctioned forms, as in his "Four Pieces," he demonstrates technical versatility, showing results in each case far superior to the average. Even when the "common purpose" is so pressing, we see him serve it dutifully, yet with a discernible poetic method. Diaphany being the criterion, both psychologically necessitated and socially demanded so that the individual voice change and merge into the collective body and be there entirely accepted, he has to use old or familiar diction and facile rhythm. Most of his metaphors are derivative and even rather hackneyed. And their connotative effects are further delimited to a very narrow range in the presence of so many denotative statements. But the "Four Pieces" read as a whole unit are saved from being completely trite. The contrast between the old and the new is made distinct. From the technical point of view, the poet is attempting to force the old idioms and images to work for him so that in the whole context they symbolise either the dying old history or the self-same old nature taking on a new aspect. New landscape and new scenes seem to emerge in a new human society.

An especially interesting feature of the four poems is that ever present among the four, despite their great differences in subject-matter, there is the image of ocean or sea, the more remarkable considering the fact that Pei-Mang Mountain near Lo-yang is far away from all oceans and seas. Here the sea or ocean becomes the dominant metaphor in the whole group. Variously it stands for the visual aspect of the vast growing forests (Poems I, III), the all-embracing collective immensity that obliterates all distance between individuals as well as submerging them all (Poem IV), and, though in a direct statement (Poem II), it is highly charged with emotion to indicate the expansiveness of the Chinese Communist nation, extending comradeship to a small country in Europe. But above all, the ubiquitous image of the sea gives the " Four Pieces " a portentous sense of dynamism and mobility. Metaphorically, even when it seems to be only for visual effect, it conveys a feeling of tremendous change of the face of nature, a kind of metamorphosis felt in Communist society, where growing trees are looked on as endless billowing waves, while factory chimneys are counted as trees in a jungle. The same sea metaphor with its mobile force indicates the vast flowing change of human relationships in quick progress. And in all this mobility and dynamism, we distinctly see the ultimately militant purpose. that the factories are not standing statically, not spoken of even as means for production and prosperity, but are riding on rolling waves as battleships for the conquest of all.

Now, to liken a whole mountain landscape to the sea, and factory buildings to battleships upon it, would strike us as rather the play of fancy than an act of imagination. Judged as metaphor making, the one appears facile but loose, and the other whimsical. Both would fit better, as the English Romantic poets discovered, light verse rather than serious poetry. But Ko's poems, as we can see, are all seriousness and solemnity. The poems may have succeeded in bringing about an emotional impact to bear upon the reader with the poet's talent to lend it vividness and colour, and even some tender touches. But in the last analysis, they show a certain incongruity and lack of cogency. And we think the reason is that the publicly dictated and dutifully obeyed " common purpose " has overwhelmed the poet's consciousness, and he has strained it to find metaphors and to superimpose on them the weight of a poetic intent they are not normally the best fit to carry.

This strain of the consciousness, this constant wide-eyed attention to Party policy and ideological dictates, as effects on their poetry, is best expressed in these two lines by Feng Chih, another experienced and very gifted poet[7]:

In front of their concentrated attention
Nature has lost all her mysteries.

With such loss of all nature's mysteries, we would add, poetry has to lose all its depth. It has to be all surface and externality, to carry out a transparent official purpose with unflaggingly vigilant consciousness. The

[7] All Feng Chih's works quoted in this paper are from his *Shih-nien Shih Ch'ao*, published in Peking in 1959.

individual would have no dreams, no streak of subconscious vision or unconscious will to be allowed to appear in his poetry. " Nature has lost all her mysteries " in the face of intensely purposive " attention," our poet says, and perhaps means it as an actual experience. But is it not truer to say that before this " attention " nature has been reduced to only some very limited manoeuvrable conceptualities, which can be wilfully directed for the manufacturing of a poetry to serve an external purpose that overwhelms the poet's consciousness? Under such conditions, easily disregarded will be the congruity and cogency of what must be concretely sensed in nature for making happy metaphors and creating the convincing poetic image.

The lines we quoted are from Feng Chih's poem " The Surveyors," where he could write like this:

How high is the mountain? and how deep the water?
How many cubic feet per second does it flow?
How much weight can the rocks carry,
How hard are they, above ground or below?

For all its plain, matter-of-fact appearance, I read this at least as a promise of competent verse considering the nature of the subject, and I am trying to convey some of its quality even in translation. But then he has to chant in the last stanza:

Our great task is just at the beginning,
The Yellow River has surrendered to us now,
Whatever the sons and daughters of New China do,
Is to the cheers of our friends, and to our enemies' woe.

Strained consciousness and over-attention, as when one keeps vigil at night, can make one see and hear things, those phantom shapes and sounds of friends and enemies! Yet since they are produced with that kind of consciousness, they sound as if meant to be perfectly real, not adumbrated into metaphors. Or on certain occasions, the overwhelming collective purposiveness to conquer nature and man invests their poetry with what we may call mass pathetic fallacy. For it is oftenest hylozoism of gigantic proportion, panpsychically perceived by the poet, not so much with his individual eye at a peculiar illusory moment (" the cruel, crawling foam "),[8] as through the collective vision of the masses on a wide-awake day. It consequently makes hyperbolical metaphors, grandiose personifications of the most obvious kind. We have just seen the Yellow River " surrender to us," like a vanquished stubborn enemy of the People. But in another poem, " Song of Liu Chia Gorge," by Feng Chih, too, the same River is an object for pity and sympathy, and to be liberated:

[8] From Kingsley's " Alton Lock," quoted and criticised by Ruskin.

The Yellow River, like a Titan,
Has been for eons here enthralled,
Groping, he could not reach the vast earth,
Gazing, nor could he see the distant sky. . . .
Now, he is to get liberated. . . .

When nature, by an act of will, is despoiled of all her mysteries, she can only in a too much manhandled way yield tired or false metaphors and images to poetry, like all specious prefabricated articles.

I do not doubt Feng Chih's personal sincerity. Under the circumstances the personal and individual elements become practically negligible anyhow. His total submission to the official will, to the public common purpose, directed by Party and State, has to be real enough for him to articulate as a poet at all. Feng Chih's unquestioned poetic talent has been proven by his pre-revolutionary works, lyrical, tranquil, tender and capable of philosophic profundity. In the present situation, where his conformity is sufficiently wholehearted, his intellect, still vigorous, does not stop to search for new technical possibilities even within rigorously delimited paths, and he still writes mostly in the modern colloquial tradition, to continue some of the experimental spirit in the development of new "metrical discipline" or *ko lü*. But in his search, since Nature has been pre-empted, so to say, in the way we have seen, something else of considerable interest seems to appear from another direction. This we may call scientism welded into his poetry. He resorts to using numerical figures of weights and measures, poetising, as it were, the Communist belief in statistics. We have already seen some of this in his "Surveyors." And in another poem, "Wang Ch'ung-lun's Workshop," he offers this stanza:

You saturate twenty-two hundred seventy-seven "bench" hours,[9]
With a capacity production of units ninety-four hundred twenty-nine,
So much noble sentiment in them is contained,
That the statistic figures do loudly sing their song.

So eager is the poet to hammer what has been hitherto considered remotest to poetry into poetic substance, and with such conscious effort, that he cannot help making everything obvious by protesting to us, though in fact to himself, too, as he says in the same poem:

Since it reflects a living reality,
A slogan here becomes most powerful poetry.

But it is always pleasant to see any success of an artist's search, especially when we realise the limitations of his arduous conditions. Here

[9] *T'ai shih*, to signify the hours actually spent at work on the *t'ai*, literally "bench" or table.

I believe we have found such a good example, rare among thousands of poems produced with the same intent. It is Feng Chih's " Coal Mining District," a short piece in two stanzas which may be rendered as follows:

> Day and night, day and night, the mountain creek purls,
> Day and night, day and night, coal trains on the rail shuttle,
> At hundred fifty metres below ground,
> Day and night dins the electric drill sound.
>
> By the creek happily the market noises flow,
> Women laugh and talk, and children sing everywhere,
> But inaudible to people are the electric drills below,
> Like the people's own heartbeats that they cannot hear.

Here we see the same resort to figures of measurements, which, in the light of the poet's consistent technical experiments, may be regarded as the same touch of scientism for the spirit of exactitude. And there is in the second stanza even also a touch of the prevalent hylozoism. But the statements are well under control. The metaphorical construction and its imagistic effects in the juxtaposition of what is above and what goes on underground are convincing enough. And even the sound pattern in rhythm and rhyme (which in a translation we can only simulate), with, for instance, " day and night, day and night " repeated for the " creek " and " coal train " rushing without stop on the surface of the earth, and the same phrase muffled into a single one for the busy electric drill far down below in the shimmering dark, show the authenticity of poet insight. Hence in the second stanza where sound seems apparently diffused on the visible earth, there is effectively driven home the feeling of oneness of the seen and unseen, the sense of unity and identification of man and nature, which is being busily conquered, however, by man in a Communist new society, all with the same heartbeats towards a great aim. This still of course fits perfectly the official common purpose. But in its own way it attains artistic quality and, ideologies aside, it reveals its own poetic truth by conveying a real experience in its organic construction of poetic properties.

But such precious examples are hard to come by, too easily lost among millions of effusive political doggerels, spasmodic fulminations of ideological jargon, and pious hallelujahs to the Party and its Chairman. Better poems like this, we may note incidentally, are mostly the shorter pieces of the Chinese lyrical tradition. It is as if the poet's over-strained consciousness cannot hold long enough without stretching itself into statements of the obvious, transparent over-all theme in so many dead tired metaphors. One would expect that such a great epoch-making movement as the Chinese Communist revolution would produce epics worthy of it, especially when conspicuous efforts have been encouraged to " learn " from the folk-song stories, such as the *hsin t'ien yu* form of Shensi Province. But after scrutinising the long narrative poems of this decade under Communist rule, we do not yet find such epics.

Li Chi, a popular young poet, among a few others who have attempted the epic genre, has followed the *hsin t'ien yu* metre, written several long works, and is perhaps best known in his role as the recognised " People's bard." His works include *Wang Kuei and Li Hsiang-hsiang, Chrysanthemum Stone,* and *Yang Kao Chuan* in several sequels, each published in a separate volume. As epic, not only their " heroes " and " villains " are too crudely typified in too garish contrast to rise above the level of slapstick comedy, their climaxes and dénouement too easily foreordained, and their narrative language as a whole too often jarred by artificial rhythm and diction, but their author's over-anxiety to praise the Party forces some otherwise innocent passages into downright bathos, absurdities even to the most sympathetic reader. Here is one such example. In *Yang Kao Chuan,* Part I, " The Fifth of the Fifth Moon," the hero Yang Kao, as a herdsboy, is running away from his employer, the rich landlord, to join the Red Army. He secretly says goodbye to his sheep. We are supposed to hear in his voice all love and solicitous care for the animals, but he is actually indoctrinating them and making a fantastic political promise to them in his farewell speech:

> You are sheep and I am a man,
> But the rich men oppress us in the same way.
> The rich men spend money to keep you,
> That he may eat your flesh or sell you.
> Sheep, sheep, do not be heartbroken,
> When the rich are overthrown, I'll herd you again,
> The Red Army will march to victory,
> All cattle and sheep will belong to us poor men.
> With enough pasture, plenty of water, you will be fat,
> Every one grows lots of flesh and long, long fur,
> Then your small folds will become large folds,
> The hills will be full of sheep, more and more.

As we follow passages like this, willingly submitting to the style of folkish *naïveté*, and without ideological considerations or discrimination by subjective taste, still a disturbing question cannot but arise by the force of simple logic. If the rich men " oppressed " the sheep by eating their flesh or selling them, what does the hero, being a " poor man " himself, think the poor men in the Communist society will do with the sheep after the victorious Red march, when they are so gleefully watched to " grow lots of flesh and long, long fur?" Even as political propaganda this defeats its own purpose.

All the time we do not forget that we are supposed to be in the presence of serious literature, by a poet of celebrated stature, who published tens of thousands of lines, with the important Writers' Publishing House (Tso-chia Ch'u-pan-she), and the People's Literature Publishing House (Jen-min Wen-hsueh Ch'u-pan-she), sponsoring him. To understand his case, we say again that Li Chi, still a young man, is not entirely without talent, and certainly with plenty of perseverance and sedulous efforts to learn and practise as a poet in the Communist milieu. His long verses occasionally demonstrate his ability to glean and order genuine folk idioms and to paint rustic scenes with bright local colours. He travels far and wide, participates in hard labour with the declared wish to enrich his poetry, more recently in the north-western regions of oil and iron mining fields. But what he draws from the "people's" sources he seems to over-spend on the political end for his poetry, and too quickly, without time to digest or ruminate. The political directive for poets, especially for those as active as Li Chi, as revealed under the new dictum of "combining romanticism with realism," is, in effect, that they should not only describe but transform, not only record but idealise.

Still over above all this, reigns the supreme categorical imperative, "be absolutely optimistic!" Consequently, no misery is described but it is transformed into happy outlook, no frustration or hardship recorded, but idealised into a heroic process of invincible conquest; and poetry is no consolation, certainly not expression, for tribulations, but always exhortation to high aspirations. No opportunity should be lost by the poet to convey this whole attitude into his verse, whether poetic logic requires it or not, as we have seen in Li Chi's passage just cited, which was published in 1959, about pre-revolution events. In recent days, especially when reality is the more miserable and hard, romantic transformation and idealisation to exhort to absolute optimism becomes the more urgent. Wholehearted conformity to the dictum and imperative insures a young poet's career.

Examining some actual poetic works so produced as evidence, our natural immediate impression would be that the romantic optimism is blown all out of proportion, into megalomaniac highfalutin' nonsense to an extraordinary degree, if the poems are measured as products of a sane individual. But we have to realise that the mentality which makes him gush out such utterances is no longer the individual's own. Circumstances have made him will his own individuality into the huge collective body, so that to the utmost of his capacity he can try to think with the collective mind, see with the mass vision, and speak with a mythicised "people's voice," directed of course by the infallible Party and its Chairman.

With this unified, purposive mass mind and vision, which, in the spirit of high romanticism, look at all nature and the human world as objects of emotion-charged conquest and transformation, panpsychism and hylozoism expressed in the " people's " language become the use and wont of the day. Furthermore, as the poet represents no individual personality but that of the collective masses, pathetic fallacy takes a strange turn. No longer is it the individual emotional state, as in usual cases, subconsciously imposing itself on outside objects, but it appears to be a mass feeling, conformed to with all too clear consciousness by the poet whose intention is to cast a collective image of the " people " on natural phenomena. In the Communist neo-romantic ideal, to employ poetry to transform actual misery into blissfulness and arduous task into happy undertaking, merely to represent Nature as a stubborn but conquerable enemy seems no longer enough. More often in recent poetry all her resources become not only animated, but converted into comradely, docile, willing and loyal citizens like the People themselves, anxious to give away all for the construction of the Communist paradise.

Li Chi's shorter poems published in a volume, *Unforgettable Spring*, furnish some of the most revealing examples. In his " Just One Day on Iron Hill " he takes us into the hills of the iron-producing district on the Ch'i-lien Mountain Range. There " the peaks stand up to sky, one after another," and " every piece of rock is iron." One hill was already developed and named Mirror-like Iron Hill. But as soon as the poet ascends that hill and looks away at the other hills,

> Not waiting to be introduced by the surveying guide,
> Each vies to speak out that it is an iron hill too.

Then in genial voices and affectionate familiar terms like a clan of good people, the hills offer themselves:

> The Mirror-like Iron Hill is the eldest brother, and we the younger,
> And we have many other brothers and sisters in big crowds. . . .
> Settled by the Ch'i-lien Mountain Range,
> What desolation and solitude we suffered.
> To see people's faces is our hearts' desire,
> But we waited and waited thousands of years.
> We are grateful to the kindly shepherds
> Who brought over the geological experts. . . .
> They are just the kind of people we love,
> Elated, we sign away to them all our hearts. . . .
> Please carry a message when you go back,
> Come to develop us with all speed. . . .
> For thousands of years we just slept,

But we have no patience to wait another day.
If you just mobilise us in good time,
In fifteen years England will drop behind far away. . . .

It is not for us in a translation to improve anything. We can only do our best to retain as many of the original elements as we can, and recapture some of the original voice. In the Chinese original Li Chi uses ostensibly the popular folk-song metre, interspersed with modern colloquial polysyllables with which he manages to preserve a suggestion of some sort of rhyme endings. To us the whole texture is loose, and the diction stilted because of the slogan words. We feel that the voice indeed sounds hollow, and the imagination seems even hollower. It is a big fantastic affair, yet without either the dark appeal of a dream or the innocence and charm of a child's fantasy. If we feel this way about it, as we naturally would, however, it is because we as free individual readers are instinctively applying our experiences and judgments developed in a world which is no longer there, where this poem and many others like it are produced. We want to understand, if we can never appreciate, the poem as the product of a peculiar human condition as of this day. We may be tempted to wonder whether a Pasternak, or even an Evtushenko, or even a few Ehrenburgs may be there. There might be some time in the future, who can tell? But there is none at present. And it is the present time that we are talking about, a time on the Chinese mainland which as a point in human history is intensely interesting to watch, from the viewpoint of its poetry as well as from any other.

Li Chi's poem just cited would exemplify the result also of a laborious search by younger Chinese poets who make themselves a success in the stringency of a given inescapable condition. In what seems to us so apparently hollow and garish, the poet may be confidently feeling that there he has best succeeded in total self-surrender, as has been constantly demanded, to the overpowering, all-conquering oneness of a humanity. Its great common purpose spelt out by endless dinning Party slogans and directives, has been made all his consciousness. This consciousness he exploits and over-exploits to make his poetry. The poem we have seen may be taken as a clear example of many others of the over-exploitation of the conscious, with the result of a huge spoiled metaphor. We realise that, despite all the faults the poem may seem to show us, it is a peculiar kind of work, produced in a peculiar mental state. We are not to treat it as sham, but see in it this extraordinary mental state working upon the poetic product, especially the making of the metaphor which is basic to all poetry, even including this type.

Now, efficacious metaphors must come as discoveries of somehow hidden relationships between apparently disparate matters or situations; hence new metaphors present new visions, and even effect new beliefs. In such metaphors felicitious images cohere, the more convincing and revealing the more far-fetched, as if in a prophetic dream, drawing themselves from darker, deeper regions of subconscious or unconscious sources. But in today's Chinese Communist world, at least as evidenced in their published works which we are able to see, the poet's mental energy seems to have drained itself entirely into ever-wakeful consciousness in the vigilant Communist high noon. All the world, natural or human, is flat visibility under its artificial light generated by supreme state power. There is supposed to be nothing hidden in the individual mind but it is exposed and aired in innumerable public vows, declarations and confessions. Just as nothing is supposed to be hidden on or in the earth, but it is to be dug up as coal or iron to serve the People's Republic, what subconscious or unconscious forces there may be in the individual are thus commanded by the power of the strained conscious will to be surfaced, to be baked in the sun, as it were, to become obviously serviceable articles.

The poem cited from Li Chi thus regarded becomes an extremely interesting illustration. We have pointed out its apparent fantasticality. It first reminds us of dreams, or childhood fantasy, but immediately we recognise that it has the qualities of neither. It is just too glaringly distinct. The whole work is no doubt intended as a large metaphor: The iron-producing hills declare themselves as loyal clans of brothers and sisters; they love the geological experts; they cannot bear the solitude any more, but must " sign away " (*chüan hsien*, a standard term in political slogans to exhort the people to make free offerings) all their hearts, they are impatient to be dug and opened up; and they are very anxious that China should surpass England. All these could have been the stuff of dreams. But here clearly no dream is by any intention conveyed. There is on the contrary only the saturating, coercing political consciousness, expanding and over-reaching itself from the human to the natural realm. Nature is supposed to have no mysteries, we have been told with the cocksureness of Communist confidence. Such is indeed the case here with the metaphor which has no more mysteries, therefore no more hidden truth either, to reveal. It has no more any dimension for them, because no matter to what enormous size the hyperboles may inflate it, the poet's intensely wrought and over-exploited ideological consciousness will possess it fully, and stretch it until it breaks and disintegrates. Here we have the best example of the incredible extent to which the Chinese poet's consciousness today can be overwhelmed and strained, resulting in the death, or still-birth, of the metaphor.

We have in this article treated examples from only three poets, chosen either for the qualities they possess, or for their great public success which we should not ignore. Thousands, in fact millions, are left out. The large majority of them are inferior, it is needless to say, for the simple fact that among verses of any nation that are currently available to their contemporaries rather than survivals sifted by time, there are always more bad works than good ones. The same case should hold true anywhere in the world today. A point to be made here is that the uniformity of poetic standard, as of everything else in Communist China up to this date, may make our tiny selection more likely to be representative of the main trends, if not of all the varieties in vogue. We do not include Mao Tse-tung's classical verses, a scanty twenty published all told, in our discussion which is intended to demonstrate the general conditions among professional poets. No one else in China today is like Mao as a poet, because no one else is like him as an individual. Over there he is as free as Zeus on Olympus, but it is with the mortal human world we are now concerned.

Incidentally, the three poets we have discussed belong to two generations, one brought up under, and the other adjusted to, the Communist revolution; therefore they may more likely typify large groups of others. If we may seem to have indicated to readers who say they are appalled by Chinese Communist poetry in general, that we have not treated the worst kind (we see no reason why we must) but selected only those of discernible quality or important status, and still these are less than great or even perfectly good poetry, then in fairness we must add that every Chinese poet today reiterates again and again in most self-deprecating terms, in his prefaces or other pronouncements, that he is just experimenting. And what happens in the future no one can tell.

The discussion has been developed around the metaphor and the consciousness, and obtained a view of the somewhat deadening effect on the former by the over-strain of the latter. On this point, however, we do not mean to say that the matter will be permanent, but will remain only so long as the present conditions do not change. We think again of Goethe's remark with which this article started. In the same vein, one might muse, indeed, how much of what has been happening or has been done in the human psyche has really entered into Chinese poetry under Communist rule, though it has been exacting mass poetic production. And how much that has been composed has actually survived government or self-imposed censorship and reached us, though with all the marvellous modern printing and photostating facilities we do see thousands and thousands on paper or microfilm? We can only say on the evidence available that over-strained consciousness in a peculiar condition is producing a peculiar kind of poetry. And that poetry is not freely drawing it sources of energy from, therefore neither is it giving expression and vent to, the individual subconscious and unconscious. As the publicly exhibited consciousness is overworked to annihilate the expression of private individual emotions, the consciousness itself, in fact, tends to become distorted, producing hallucinated results, which are, however, devoid of psychic depth. If the present state of affairs continues, we shall go on getting the kind of single-purposed, mostly showy but superficial and dogma-ridden verse we have been getting. But will this be the only effect? Will not the subconscious and unconscious of the large mass of humanity over there, or what the psychologists call the Id, somehow shape and form itself in some unexpected way—in the individual and in the nation?

The Poetry of Mao Tse-tung

By YONG-SANG NG

> Five poems by Chairman Mao Tse-tung, including "Long March" and "Snow," were recently published in *Combate*, organ of the Cuban revolutionary directorate. *Combate* writes in its footnote: A poet and social activist, Mao Tse-tung has shown himself to the world that he has concentrated in himself rare geniuses. He is a man of great learning and at the same time a brilliant leader of the people and an outstanding poet.
>
> —NCNA-English, Havana, May 7, 1959.

EARLY in 1957, an event perhaps unparalleled in the world of letters was reported from China. A new monthly magazine, *Shih-k'an* (*Poetry*), made its appearance in February of that year, its inaugural issue including a collection of eighteen poems by Mao Tse-tung. The appearance of Mao's poetry was not in itself an exceptional event. From ancient times down to recent decades, Chinese statesmen and military leaders have often displayed talent in the writing of poetry; and it appeared that Mao Tse-tung was carrying on the established tradition of a long line of strong rulers in China who desired to impress the world that they were not only victorious conquerors and vigorous administrators, but also accomplished artists.

Though the publication of Mao Tse-tung's poetry was not unusual, the extent of its dissemination was without parallel in recent history. As soon as the poems appeared in the magazine *Poetry*, they were immediately reproduced throughout China: in all daily newspapers from the authoritative *People's Daily* down to remote local papers on the frontier, and in all periodical publications, whether literary, political, economic, or scientific in nature. They were later also carried in the 1958 edition of the *People's Handbook*, the yearbook published by the *Ta Kung Pao* which is generally regarded as the standard, albeit not official, annual reference work on contemporary developments in China. The same eighteen poems, with an additional nineteenth added later, were duly translated and published in English as *Mao Tse-tung: Nineteen Poems* (Peking: Foreign Languages Press, 1958), the booklet also containing explanatory comment by Tsang K'o-chia, editor of *Poetry*, for the benefit of English readers. In various forms, Mao's poems were widely distributed not only within the Communist *bloc* but even as far away as Cuba and Latin America. A complete translation of all nineteen poems may also be found in the recent edition of

Robert Payne's biography of Mao (*Portrait of a Revolutionary: Mao Tse-tung*, New York: Abelard-Schuman, revised edition, 1961, chapter ten); and other translations, especially of some of the better known pieces are known to exist.

I

Long before 1957, Mao Tse-tung was known to have written poetry, and certain of his poems had already gained circulation and acceptance before the Communist nation-wide victory in China. The official publication of the collection, however, gave Mao new status as a poet. While he had previously been regarded as a revolutionary leader with a flair for poetry, he now became hailed as the official Muse of the Arts in the People's Republic.

Outside China, the applause for Mao's poetry has been less than unanimous, since literary and political considerations have inevitably become intertwined. Many Chinese who condemn Mao's literary efforts as juvenile are at the same time violent critics of his political credo; others who laud his poetry are motivated by a sense of cultural loyalty or by political expediency. The fact that Mao himself is still alive and the effective ruler of his country thus places substantial obstacles in the path of objective examination of his work. And his choice of the classical form, specifically the *tz'u*, as the outlet for his poetic inspiration has made it even more difficult for the general reader to understand his poems fully or to evaluate them realistically.

Since literary stature in China has traditionally been related to scholarly ability, a word about Mao's scholarship may be pertinent as background. Here again, estimates of the solidity of Mao's foundation in classical scholarship tend to vary with the political instincts of the observer. Severe critics view Mao's knowledge of the classical texts as superficial; but none would be so blatantly irresponsible as to dismiss Mao as uncultured or uncultivated. He did have a solid Chinese education in his native Hunan, and he did work as a library assistant at Peking University during a period of great ferment in China's intellectual capital. One Chinese view may be recorded for reference. The venerable Chang Shih-chao, eighty-year-old Hunanese, is acknowledged to be one of twentieth-century China's great classical scholars. A lawyer by profession, he served as Minister of Justice and Minister of Education during the early republican period; in 1949, he was one of the peace delegates sent north by Li Tsung-jen, then acting President at Nanking, to negotiate with the Communists who had then already captured Peiping. Chang Shih-chao has remained in the old capital since, and though occupying no high position in the régime is generally considered an honoured guest of Mao himself, whom he had befriended in earlier days. The statement on Mao's scholarship, attributed to Chang Shih-chao and published in Hong Kong in mid-1961, is as follows:

> "Mao had not read many books. Except for the period in the [Peking University] Library when he read through the *Tzu-chih t'ung-chien* [Ssu-ma Kuang's monumental work on Chinese history], he had not set eyes on very many important Chinese books bound in the traditional form. Of course he is relatively literate as compared with some other high personages who often cannot write the proper characters. As for his classical poems, they are certainly not to be considered seriously [here Chang was said to shake his head repeatedly]. There is a dash of audacity in his poems, but I surely cannot agree with the claim that they are unprecedented in the past, or cannot be equalled in the future." [1]

Mao Tse-tung has selected the *tz'u* form as the medium in which to compose poetry. The *tz'u,* first developed during the later T'ang dynasty, is a song-form originally corresponding to the Western lyric: a verse sung to music. This branch of Chinese poetry reached its highest development in the Sung period, when it became the vehicle for much of China's best poetry. By the Sung dynasty, however, the *tz'u* was less frequently set to music, although the original "tunes" (*tiao*) continued to be used by the poets in setting the form of the poems. These variant tunes, or metrical forms, stipulate the number of lines, the length of cach linc, and the lines which must be rhymed. Furthermore, the precise tonal pattern (even or oblique) for each sound in the sequence is also prescribed, and all first-class poets adhere faithfully to these rigid requirements in writing *tz'u.* (There is more flexibility in the rhyming and tonal sequences used in the *shih,* the basic branch of Chinese poetry.) A *tz'u* may or may not have a subject title. The name of the musical air governing the form must, however, be indicated, though it may have no bearing on the subject and text of the poem. The first collection of Mao's poems published in 1957 are, however, provided with subject titles as well as the required names of the metrical forms employed.

In forwarding his poems to the editor of *Poetry,* Mao emphasised the fact that he had no intention of promoting a revival of classical poetry. His letter of January 12, 1957 to Tsang K'o-chia, which was given the same nation-wide publicity as the poems which it accompanied, stated [2]:

> "Up to now I have never wanted to make these things [poems] known in any formal way, because they are written in the old style. I was afraid this might encourage a wrong trend and exercise a bad influence on young people. Besides, they are not up to much as poetry, and there is nothing outstanding about them. However, if you feel

1 Chiu-yu, "Mao Tse-tung in the Words of Chang Shih-chao," *Wan-hsiang* (Hong Kong), No. 1, June 5, 1961.

2 *Mao Tse-tung: Nineteen Poems* (Peking: Foreign Languages Press, 1958), p. 7.

> that they should be published and that at the same time misprints can be corrected in some of the versions already in circulation, then publish them by all means. It is very good that we are to have the magazine *Poetry*. I hope it will grow and flourish exceedingly. Of course our poetry should be written mainly in the modern form. We may write some verse in classical forms as well, but it would not be advisable to encourage young people to do this, because these forms would restrict their thought and they are difficult to learn. I merely put forward this opinion for your consideration."

Mao's letter is simple and direct, disarming in its candid statement regarding the great influence he wields over the youth of the country, traditional in its formal protestation of modesty regarding the quality of his poetry.

The nature and quality of Chinese classical poetry evade precise definition. In the *tz'u,* form holds an important place in the accepted approach to quality. The most exacting requirements are called for in the metre and rhyming arrangements in a *tz'u,* and critics conventionally demand equal precision in the use of even and oblique tones, not only for the words at the end of the lines but for each word in the poem. Truly, as Mao points out in his letter to the editor of *Poetry,* the form is difficult to learn.

The formal excellence of Mao Tse-tung's poetry can only be established by direct examination of the original Chinese text, since it is impossible for a translation into a Western language to reproduce the required precision of form. The use of a good translation may, and at times does, enable a sensitive critic to make a sound assessment of a Chinese poem. Yet however excellent the translation may be, it cannot achieve exactness in the reproduction of the form of the poem; and the resulting appraisal, however sound, is thus basically incomplete.

Form is definite and precise; allusion, imagery and metaphor are more elusive. The richer the suggestiveness of a Chinese poem, or even of a single line of a poem, the more diverse the reader's interpretations may be as he stretches his imagination in filling the gaps left by the poet. A handy example is provided by Mao's poem, " Yellow Crane Tower," the second piece in the collection of nineteen discussed here. The fourth line in the original reads literally:

tortoise snake grip great river.

Here the subject of the poem is clearly indicated. The Yellow Crane pavilion is on a cliff west of Wuchang, south of the Yangtze (the " great river "). Two well-known landmarks in the vicinity are Snake Hill, near the pavilion in Wuchang, south of the river, and Tortoise Hill (Ta-pieh-shan) in Hangyang *hsien,* north of the river, just opposite Snake Hill. Most readers doubtless conclude that the poet is speaking of these two hills; this view is taken in the translation given in the official Foreign

Languages Press edition. Robert Payne, however, offers a different interpretation. *Vide* his translation of the line:

Stones, snakes, and tortoises grip the river.

Payne further suggests that Mao is referring to high and strangely shaped rocks and that to the Chinese imagination such shorthand effects are almost commonplace, since " their romanticism belongs to the Chinese landscape." Barring a direct clarification from Mao himself, it is impossible for the critic to challenge Payne's interpretation.

Indeed no less an authority than Kuo Mo-jo himself, a recognised poet, has stressed the difficulties of understanding Mao Tse-tung's poetry. In a eulogistic commentary on another group of poems by Mao (the six released in May 1962 which will be discussed below), Kuo says [3]:

> Chairman Mao's poems have been repeatedly steeled so that they are noble in spirit and harmonious in melody, vigorous in tone and yet lovable in their simplicity. They are loved by everyone and recited everywhere. Yet the fact is that not everyone really understands them fully, and not every poem is understood by all.

Kuo demonstrates his point convincingly with one of the poems in the first collection, the seventh in the series, " Loushan Pass." The official translation released by the Foreign Languages Press reads as follows [4]:

Loushan Pass

Cold is the west wind;
Far in the frosty air the wild geese call in the morning moonlight,
In the morning moonlight,
The clatter of horses hooves rings sharp,
And the bugle's note is muted.
Do not say that the strong pass is guarded with iron.
This very day in one step we shall pass its summit,
We shall pass its summit!
There the hills are blue like the sea,
And the dying sun like blood.

This English translation is accompanied by a footnote which was not in the original Chinese version but is directly relevant: " Loushan Pass: a strategic position in the north of Tsunyi County in Kweichow, commanding the immensely difficult road from Kweichow to Szechuan. In January 1935, during the course of the Long March, the Red Army occupied Tsunyi and then crossed Loushan Pass."

The first verse of the poem clearly describes an early morning scene;

[3] *People's Daily* (*Jen-min Jih-pao*), May 12, 1962.
[4] *Nineteen Poems*, p. 16.

the second verse, an evening scene. The question, as Kuo has drawn attention to it, is whether or not the two verses describe events in the morning and evening of the same day. Kuo has verified the distance from Tsunyi city to Loushan pass to be seventy Chinese *li*, or about twenty-four miles, the approximate distance which a marching army might cover in one day over the terrain of northern Kweichow. The poem thus appears to describe the events of a single day, from the early morning when the army started from Tsunyi until the evening when it crossed the pass. The problem, as Kuo points out, is that the first verse —with references to the west wind, the flying geese, and the frosty air— describes a morning in the autumn; the second verse refers to the Communist forces' crossing of Loushan pass which took place (as explained in the note to the English translation) in January 1935 in the dead of winter. Thus it is equally evident that the two verses of the poem do not describe events of a single day. Even in dealing with expressed words and concrete statements, that which appears to be clear may turn out to be complex and uncertain. If the reader attempts to probe further into the poet's state of mind, the range of his imagination, the subtlety of his thought, the majesty of his tone, the ingenuity of his allusions, the task of interpretation is even more difficult, and conclusions may be very diverse.

Probably the single poem by Mao Tse-tung best known in the West is "Snow." Acclaimed as the most outstanding of Mao's published pieces, this poem has been widely translated and frequently cited in biographical writings on Mao. The official English translation, made by Mr. Andrew Boyd, reads [5]:

Snow

This is the scene in that northern land; (1)
A hundred leagues are sealed with ice, (2)
A thousand leagues of whirling snow. (3)
On either side of the Great Wall (4)
One vastness is all you see. (5)
From end to end of the great river (6)
The rushing torrent is frozen and lost. (7)
The mountains dance like silver snakes, (8)
The highlands roll like waxen elephants, (9)
As if they sought to vie with heaven in their height; (10)
  And on a sunny day (11)
You will see a red dress thrown over the white, (12)
  Enchantingly lovely! (13)
Such great beauty like this in all our landscape (14)

[5] *Nineteen Poems*, p. 22. [For the present author's own translation, see page 37 above—Ed.]

Has caused unnumbered heroes to bow in homage. (15)
But alas these heroes! —Chin Shih Huang and Han Wu Ti (16)
Were rather lacking in culture; (17)
Rather lacking in literary talent (18)
Were the emperors Tang Tai Tsung and Sung Tai Tsu; (19)
  And Genghis Khan, (20)
Beloved Son of Heaven for a day, (21)
Only knew how to bend his bow at the golden eagle. (22)
  Now they are all past and gone: (23)
To find men truly great and noble-hearted (24)
We must look here in the present. (25)

The official commentary on the poem by Tsang K'o-chia may serve to summarise the praise lavished on the poem by many scholars and critics, both Chinese and Western. Tsang says [6]:

> The majesty and heroic tone of this poem have hardly any parallel in history. Even Su Tung-po's 'Nien Nu Chiao' [to which we shall have occasion to return later in this article], celebrated for its vigour and grandeur, pales by comparison. . . . That the majesty and beauty of China's countryside should recall the feats of mighty men of old reveals the author's patriotism and admiration for the heroes of old and today. This poem shows a perfect blending of scenery and human figures, past and present. . . . The second verse contains the poet's reflections. There is nothing dry or musty about the historical figures he recalls. Indeed the scene described above serves as an appropriate background for them. The last line is the most significant in the whole poem, one with a profound meaning which deserves pondering. This poem is of the very highest order, both in conception, significance and formal perfection. Its great popularity is entirely warranted.

" Snow " was written about August 1945, at the time of the Japanese surrender, when Mao travelled from Yenan to Chungking for negotiations with Chiang Kai-shek on the settlement of Kuomintang-Communist differences. There is no definite evidence confirming the precise date or method of composition. One prevalent story has it that Mao actually composed the poem while aboard the plane bound for Chungking, his first flight over China. In view of the special demands of the *tz'u* form and the fact that Mao is not a professional poet, this theory is dubious. More acceptable is the explanation that the " exhilarating experience of soaring in the sky, coupled with an intuitive knowledge of history in the making, may have partly accounted for some of his most unusual poetic feelings. An early snow in the northwest may have further heightened his spirits." [7] It appears likely that the inspiration

[6] *Nineteen Poems*, pp. 58–59.

[7] Ping-ti Ho, "Two Major Poems by Mao Tse-tung," *Queen's Quarterly*, Kingston (Canada), LXV, No. 2, 1958, p. 257.

for the poem and a general outline for its composition may well have emerged during the actual flight, but that Mao wrote it later at leisure.

The first section of the poem (lines 1 through 13) offers a vivid description of the expanse of the Shensi-Kansu plain. A straightforward reading of the words as they are is adequate to credit the poet with great powers of observation, masterful use of language and skilful blending of colours. There is no need to attempt to go beyond the immediate context and to seek for possible secondary meanings in the poet's mind. Thus far it is a good poem, well conceived and vigorously expressed.

The second section (lines 14 through 25) proceeds from the poet's description of the natural beauties before his eyes to his recollection of great heroes in China's past history. This method is a common device among classical Chinese poets, the first portion of a poem serving as background for the second, which contains the poet's real message.

The second section does indeed offer much for contemplation. The first two lines (lines 14 and 15 of the poem) are given in the Peking translation as:

> Such great beauty like this in all our landscape,
> Has caused unnumbered heroes to bow in homage.

This is a faithful rendition, the phrase " to bow in homage " (or "to bow deep in admiration," as it is given elsewhere) being a literal translation of the Chinese phrase *che-yao* " to bend the waist." Robert Payne's translation of the second line, however, is:

> Calling innumerable heroes to vie with each other in
> pursuing her.

Here there does appear to be justification for an interpretation beyond the actual text, since the ensuing lines of the poem list men who not only " bowed in homage " but actually conquered the land.

The lines immediately following list some of China's most famous rulers. While the poet does pay tribute to the heroes of the past, he nevertheless finds them all deficient in one quality. They all lack culture. With this general appraisal of these famous heroes, Mao then proceeds to the conclusion of his poem, the climax of his vision. To quote again the words of Tsang K'o-chia, " The last line is the most significant in the whole poem, one with a profound meaning which deserves pondering." The last two lines, as given in the Peking translation, read:

> To find men truly great and noble-hearted
> We must look here in the present.

Robert Payne's version is as follows:

Only today are there men of great feeling.

As Tsang K'o-chia suggests, these lines do have a deep significance which requires pondering. Let us first examine the phrase " our truly great and noble-hearted." The original Chinese is *feng-liu jen-wu.* Students of Chinese literature will identify the source of the phrase in the famous eleventh-century *tz'u* written by Sung Tung-po and mentioned by Tsang K'o-chia in the comment quoted above. Though Tsang states that Su Tung-po's poem, long celebrated for its vigour and grandeur, pales in comparison with Chairman Mao's " Snow," he does not mention that it was in Su's poem that the phrase *feng-liu jen-wu* first appeared.

The poem by Su Tung-po is of course one of the best known in Chinese literature. A *tz'u* composed in the metrical form of " Nien-nu-chiao," it has for its subject title " Thoughts of the Past at Red Cliff." Peking's official translation, as given in the *Short History of Classical Chinese Literature*, reads [8]:

The mighty river flows east,
Sweeping away countless heroes down the ages;
An old fortress on the west
May be Red Cliff where valiant Chou Yu fought.
Jagged rocks scatter foam,
Fierce billows crash on the shore,
Hurling up drifts of snow:
A scene lovely as a painting,
But how many heroes fell here!
I think of Chou Yu that year
Newly wed to Lord Chao's daughter,
Handsome and bold
With plumed fan and scholar's cap,
Laughing and joking as his mighty foe
Was turned to dust and ashes.
Do you smile at me for a sentimental fool,
Roaming in spirit through that ancient kingdom
Though my hair is white before its time?
Life is but a dream—
Let me drink a cup to the moon above the river!

The historical allusion is the Battle of the Red Cliff, where Chou Yu, the great general of the state of Wu (one of the three kingdoms

[8] Feng Yuan-chun, *A Short History of Classical Chinese Literature*, translated into English by Yang Hsien-yi and Tai Nai-ta (Peking: Foreign Languages Press, 1958), pp. 71–72.

which followed the fall of the mighty Han empire) defeated the formidable Ts'ao Ts'ao. The term *feng-liu jen-wu* appears in the second line of the poem, and is translated in the above version as " heroes." " Thoughts of the Past at Red Cliff " is generally accepted as one of the best poems by Su Tung-po. Certainly it contains the qualities—grandeur of style, vigour of expression, majesty of tone—now conventionally attributed to Mao's " Snow." Moreover, even a casual reading of the two poems in the English versions published by the Foreign Languages Press will confirm that, though written in different metrical forms, the two poems do manifest striking similarity in the pattern of craftsmanship, the development of thought, and the capacity to encompass the broad horizons both of history and of the world of nature. Had the later poem been written by a lesser figure than Mao himself, the author might well have been viewed as a plagiarist as far as technique is concerned.

Between Su Tung-po's poem and Mao Tse-tung's " Snow," however, there is a difference, a difference that gives the latter poet much credit. Su Tung-po's great power of imagination has led him to a penetrating recollection of past heroes of China, but he concludes with a sense of self-pity that he himself has not been able to emulate them and deplores his own lack of accomplishment. Mao, while paying due tribute to the ancients, demonstrates enormous self-assurance, considering himself not only their equal but rather their superior, the only cultured hero of the group. With the developments in China which followed the writing of " Snow," culminating in the Communist conquest of the mainland in 1949, the interpretation of the final lines of the poem appeared clear. Paraphrased, they meant that Mao Tse-tung unquestionably viewed himself as the pre-eminent hero of his age in China.

There is, however, some danger that hindsight may freeze the uncertainties of the past into the mould of historical inevitability. It is possible that, at the time of writing, Mao did not exactly have in mind what later interpreters and critics have assumed the lines to imply. When the poem was written in 1945, Japan had just surrendered and China, after much travail, was a victor in the war. But China was Nationalist China led by Chiang Kai-shek, the national leader of the day whether the Communists accepted him or not. And it was to Chiang Kai-shek's headquarters in Chungking that Mao Tse-tung the insurgent leader was going for talks of a peaceful settlement of their differences. Though political friction and intermittent armed conflict between Nationalist and Communist units had marred the later years of the Sino-Japanese war, open civil war was not to break out until the following year. Even conceding Mao's important status in the early autumn of 1945, the conference at Chungking was at most a meeting of the Big Two.

Always aware of the length of their country's past, China's leaders in 1945 might well have looked back at an earlier " Big Two " meeting. The two ancients who met, about the beginning of the third century A.D., were Ts'ao Ts'ao and Liu Pei, both of whom were later to become emperors.[9] At the time, Ts'ao Ts'ao, greatest of the later Han generals, was prime minister of the Hsien-ti emperor; while Liu Pei, who held the courtesy title of " imperial uncle " because he traced his ancestry back to Liu Pang (the Kao-tsu emperor), founder and first emperor of the Han dynasty, was a lesser figure filled with ambition. One evening, Ts'ao invited Liu to a wine-drinking session, and the two discussed the leading personages of the day, attempting to identify those who could properly be called " heroes." Liu Pei mentioned one name after another, but Ts'ao Ts'ao dismissed them all lightly. Finally, Ts'ao Ts'ao made the following statement, one of the best known in Chinese literature:

> In the whole empire, those who can claim to be
> heroes consist only of you and me.

Now compare this statement with the final lines of Mao's poem:

> To find our truly great and noble hearted,
> We must look here in the present.

He might well have said to Chiang at the conference table in Chungking:

> In the whole country, those who can claim to be
> heroes consist only of you and me.

Let us suppose that the talks between Chiang Kai-shek and Mao Tse-tung in August 1945 had not failed completely and that a compromise settlement had led to a Kuomintang-Communist coalition government, which was after all the aim of the talks. Then later critics might well have interpreted the lines as referring to Chiang and Mao together, and Mao Tse-tung might still have been given credit for great intuitive foresight.

II

In the spring of 1962, five years after the publication of the first collection of Mao's poems, another group was presented to the Chinese nation. On this occasion, the official venue of presentation was not the magazine *Poetry*, the honour being given instead to *Jen-min Wen-hsueh* (*People's Literature*), the organ of the Chinese Writers' Union and the

9 Liu Pei became the first emperor of the Shu (or Minor) Han dynasty (221–265). Ts'ao Ts'ao did not actually become emperor himself, but his son Ts'ao P'ei, who usurped the throne to found the Wei dynasty (220–265), honoured him posthumously as Emperor Wu. Indeed he is the Emperor Wu referred to in " Peitaiho," another of Mao's poems in this same collection.

leading literary journal of China, which carried the poems in its May 1962 issue. They were reproduced in the *People's Daily* on May 12, 1962, and other leading newspapers followed suit, though there was less fanfare than in the case of the poems released in 1957.[10]

The new collection consists of only six poems, again in the *tz'u* form. In a brief prefatory note dated April 27, 1962, Mao himself states that these poems were composed while " humming on horseback " during the years from 1929 to 1931. He had completely forgotten them, but since the editors of *People's Literature* had taken pains to assemble them and requested their publication, he had made some revisions and permitted their release. Together with the poems, *People's Literature* also published a long commentary, with annotations, written by Kuo Mo-jo. (It is from the introductory section of Kuo's 1962 article that we extracted above his illuminating study of " Loushan Pass," a poem in the earlier collection, effectively making the point that Mao's poetry, while widely read, is not completely understood.)

One technical difference between this collection and the one published earlier is that while the poems in the 1957 collection all bear subject titles (" Snow," " Changsha," for example), together with their respective metrical forms, no subject titles are given in the present collection. This is the more usual practice, and carries no special significance.

Mao himself says that these poems were composed from 1929 through 1931 while " humming on horseback," truly in the tradition of the mounted conquerors such as Chao K'uang-yin, famed in Chinese history as Sung T'ai-tsu, founder of the Sung dynasty. To the Chinese, Mao's phrase evokes the well-known saying, " A great hero kills the bandits while riding on horseback, and prepares proclamations after alighting from his mount." This is of course a traditional statement stressing the need for a Chinese ruler to be accomplished in both military and literary pursuits, the theme elaborately developed in Mao's poem " Snow." But we must note again that Mao's self-assurance causes him to go one better than the accepted hero in Chinese history, who only turns to his literary pursuits " after alighting from his mount." Mao attends to both war and poetry at the same time.

The publication of this second collection of Mao's poems formed part of the general commemoration of the twentieth anniversary of his talks at the Yenan Forum on literature and art, which was held in May 1942. The May 1962 celebrations were observed throughout China, with the customary re-emphasis on Peking's official literary line, now described as " the combination of revolutionary realism with revolutionary romanticism." The *People's Daily* editorial on the occasion of the anniversary, after the usual review of the history of the talks, the

10 Translations were published in *Chinese Literature* No. 1, 1963.

achievements since their original publication, and an exhortation to the literary world, also calls on cultural workers to increase the variety of literary and artistic production.

As was the case in 1957, the release of more of Chairman Mao's poems in 1962 was intended to serve as a stimulus to greater interest in poetry. On the whole, the 1962 collection appears simpler in form and content. These six poems all refer to the heroic days of warfare in the countryside in Kiangsi, and thus may be said to be truly in the spirit of revolutionary realism. Indeed some of the lines, such as "Thanks to the task force led by Huang Kung-lueh" and "At the front Chang Hui-tsan has been captured in person," [11] rather resemble lines in a Peking opera play, and are readily understood and appreciated by the masses. Realism, however, must now be tempered with "revolutionary romanticism," the quality found in such terms as "heavenly army," "evil mob," "the monstrous roc," and "decaying trees," which are interspersed with such commonplace phrases as "warlords," "workers and peasants," and "leaping forward." This 1962 collection, unlike most poems in the earlier collection which could only be admired from afar by the masses, may in a way be used as actual models for China's proletarian artists; and this seems a marked difference between the two sets.

Of the metaphors used in the set of poems released in 1962, that of Pu-chou-shan in the fifth poem (referring to the capture of the Nationalist general Chang Hui-tsan) is of special significance. The allusion is to the tale of Kung-kung, perhaps the greatest "rebel" in China's legendary history, who, defeated in his bid for the empire, knocked his head against the mountain (Pu-chou-shan), and killed himself. Here Mao Tse-tung himself provides an important note. Quoting the three popular versions of the Pu-chou-shan legend as given in different sources, Mao expresses his personal preference for that given in *Huai-nan-tzu*, according to which the enraged Kung-kung knocked his head against the mountain, "broke down the heavenly pillars," and caused a general transformation of the earth's physical features. The *Huai-nan-tzu* version makes no mention of the death of Kung-kung at the end of his feat. On the basis of this negative evidence, Mao states that Kung-kung did not die but was rather a truly victorious hero, an interpretation at variance with the generally accepted version of the legend which made Kung-kung a frustrated loser who took his own life in despair.

In his commentary and annotation on this poem, Kuo Mo-jo outdoes himself in extolling Mao's interpretation as truly worthy of a great

[11] Huang Kung-lueh (1898–1931) was a Communist commander posthumously glorified by the Party as a martyr. Chang Hui-tsan, commander of the Nationalist vanguard units in the first "encirclement campaign," was one of the more prominent Kuomintang officers captured by the Communists in Kiangsi in late December 1930.

Marxist thinker. Both Kuo himself and Lu Hsün had earlier used this legend in their writings, Kuo in his *Rebirth of the Goddesses* (1920) and Lu Hsün in his *Mending Heaven* (1922). And both of them had followed the accepted view that Kung-kung died. Kuo confesses, " Our understanding was still quite a distance from Chairman Mao's Marxist conception of the universe. Thus we could not at that time see in the legend of Kung-kung the inherent meaning that man transforms nature, man transforms the objective world. Once the Chairman has thus pointed it out, it is like the raising high of a torch in the Chinese world of legends. This will point to a correct direction to be followed in the study of fables and legends, and in the study of ancient history. *I feel that the importance of his notation is not less than the importance of the poem itself.*"

There is yet another possible cause for the publication of these poems in the spring of 1962. All six poems describe incidents in which, despite the debacle of 1927 in China, the Communist military forces were having the better of their engagements against the Nationalist units. It is reasonable to infer, therefore, that Mao was attempting to bolster national morale during the difficult period of reorganisation and readjustment after the termination of the massive Great Leap Forward effort by recounting successful Communist resistance against the enemy, often against overwhelming odds, in the hinterland of Kiangsi during the heroic period of the Communist movement in China. There is a positive note of determination inherent in recalling the time when " the Red flag leaps over river T'ing Chiang, heading toward Lung-yen and Shang-hang " in Fukien; when the focus of practical policy for Mao's men was to " repair the damaged realm, and busy ourselves distributing land "; when an enemy force of two hundred thousand troops entering Kiangsi did not deter the Communists but rather roused " millions of workers and peasants " into action; and when they pursued the enemy for fifteen days over seven hundred *li* of territory.

The two publications of Mao's poetry have thus served several practical purposes: displaying the talents of the Chairman, rousing an interest in poetry as a channel for creative expression, and—in the 1962 case—attempting to revive the morale and revolutionary spirit of his followers to sustain renewed struggle against current difficulties and hardships. Critical analysis of the literary merits of Mao Tse-tung's poetry is inevitably controversial. For the Western student, however, the verses offer a source of new insights into the personality, character and historical ambitions of one of twentieth-century China's most influential and complex leaders. Many of Mao's poems, especially " Snow," and his annotation of the Pu-chou-shan legend, provide useful data for such an inquiry.

Chinese Communist Literature: The Persistence of Traditional Forms

By CYRIL BIRCH

> What pessimistic observers have lamented as the collapse of Chinese civilisation is exactly the necessary undermining and erosion without which there could not have been a regeneration of an old civilisation. . . . The product of this rebirth looks suspiciously occidental. But scratch the surface and you will find that the stuff of which it is made is essentially the Chinese bedrock which much weathering and corrosion have only made stand out more clearly—the humanistic and rationalistic China resurrected by the touch of the scientific and democratic civilisation of the new world.[1]

IF this statement of Hu Shih's is applied specifically to the literary works of the years following 1917, it will be found substantially true. Time and again we shall recognise the basic concerns, the mode of thinking and even some of the literary techniques of the work we are examining to be essentially Chinese in character. What at first glance seemed to be a thorough-going Westernisation of the entire mentality of a writer turns out in fact to be no more than incidental. He has borrowed a set of devices to help him escape from a literary convention he feels as a stultifying dead weight. But his mind is at grips with the central problems of his own life and society as he sees them, and as he writes he appropriates and reconditions even the devices he has borrowed so that they too become assimilated into Chinese literary experience. J. D. Chinnery's study of Lu Hsün's *Madman's Diary*[2] is an acute recognition of this fact. Or we could look at the first sentence of Lu Hsün's *My Native Place* (*Ku-hsiang*):

> Braving the severity of winter, I returned to the native place between myself and which had lain more than two thousand *li* of land, more than twenty years of time.

Nothing could differ more sharply from the opening to the Chinese short story such as we know from the past, with its dating, location and identification of characters deliberately reminding us of the official historiographer. We should have here, we imagine, a first-person narrative in the European introspective vein. Yet *My Native Place* is in fact hardly a

[1] Hu Shih, *The Chinese Renaissance* (University of Chicago Press, 1934), pp. ix–x.
[2] "The Influence of Western Literature on Lü Xùn's *Diary of a Madman*," in *Bulletin of the School of Oriental and African Studies*, XXIII, No. 2, 1960, pp. 309–322.

story at all, though perhaps the finest thing written in modern Chinese. "In its gentle lyricism," as C. T. Hsia says,[3] "(it) approaches the reminiscent personal essay." The opening sentence is indeed exactly the kind of personal reference we find so helpful an introduction to many a classical poem.

My own recent attempts to analyse the metrical patterns of the New Verse of the 1920s, particularly those of Hsü Chih-mo,[4] strengthen my inclination to accept Hu Shih's contention, that "scratch the surface and you will find that the stuff of which it is made is essentially the Chinese bedrock."

Yet the addiction to foreign modes of expression was precisely what drew the heaviest fire of the Communist critics. The "foreign eight-legged essay" was a tendency to be rooted out and destroyed. "Foreign-slanted pedantry and obscurantism must be abolished, hollow and abstract clichés must be discouraged, and dogmatism must be arrested so that a fresh and vivid Chinese style and manner, of which the Chinese masses are fond, may take their place," as Mao Tse-tung said in a speech in 1938.[5] With every intensification of Party control these sentiments are echoed and elaborated: witness Lao She, twenty years later at the time of the Great Leap Forward, on the importance of purity of diction:

> Section six (of what I mean by "foreign eight-legged essay"): speaking in a foreign language. That is, refusing to use language which is there ready for you, but insisting on imitating the Chinese of a foreigner. In Chinese, "backing" is enough for "carry on the back," you don't have to say "carry on the back on the back," because if the thing rests on your shoulder this is "shouldering," if it's under your arm this is "clutching," and there's no risk of confusion. I hope our writers, especially young writers, will go and learn more of the nature of Chinese. The study of classical works can be of great help here.[6]

The "Chinese style and manner, of which the Chinese masses are fond" were embodied in a host of productions which utilised forms resuscitated from popular, folk and local literary traditions. There is no space here even to list the principal new specimens of these many genres, of "oral tales," "quick patter ballads," "drum songs," or of the innumerable types of "local dramas." J. Prusek's *Die Literatur des Befreiten China und ihre Volkstraditionen*[7] covers a wide sampling of the productions of the 1940s. One highly-acclaimed novelty was the *yangko* play, which incorporated the Shensi peasants' "rice-planting

3 *A History of Modern Chinese Fiction* (Yale Un. Press, 1961), p. 36.
4 "English and Chinese Metres in Hsü Chih-mo," in *Asia Major*, VIII, No. 2, pp. 258–293.
5 *Mao Tse-tung Hsüan-chi* (Peking: 1951), p. 497, quoted in Hsia, *op. cit.*, p. 302.
6 "Ta-tao yang-pa-ku," in *Jen-min Wen-hsueh*, No. 3, 1958, p. 2.
7 Published in Prague, by Artia-Prag, 1955.

dance" and various popular song forms into an otherwise spoken drama: the success of the *White-haired Girl*[8] inspired numerous imitations.

The shorter genres, referred to as "literary side-arms," had the advantage of reflecting topical interests with great speed. Sputnik I was launched in October 1957. In November appeared a ballad of the Szechuan "cart-lamp" type with the intriguing title, "The Artificial Satellite Stirs Up the Palace of Heaven."[9] In my translation of the following passages from this piece I try to suggest the homespun quality of the original:

(When Sputnik enters Heaven, the Jade Emperor in alarm consults the various spirits, who confess themselves powerless to deal with the intruder or with the mortals who are responsible for it):

In Magic Mist Hall, commotion over all,
Worthies civil and military consult with each other.
The Jade Emperor summons up the spirits to report:
Should not troops be sent at once to deal with all this bother?

With Father Thunder, Mother Lightning kneels in the Cinnabar Court:
"We've lost our trick of scaring them, I and this my brother.
No use laying on a five-peal thunderstorm—
There they are with lightning-rods to keep them safe from harm."
Uncle Wind, Master Rain next made report:
"Mortals now have weather forecasts, fast and accurate,
And they've planted groves of trees to keep the cloudbursts out."

(Not only can the spirits do little now from their vantage point in Heaven: their earthly representatives are themselves having a thin time of it):

The Kitchen God said, "The more I think of it, the more I feel depressed:
In the past the well-to-do gave me a daily feast,
Even poor people, short of clothes to wear and food to eat,
At all the proper seasons paid their respects at least.
But nowadays, with everyone well-fed and properly dressed,
They've no use for a Kitchen God, they've chased me from my nest."

(Hearing this and other descriptions of the new state of affairs in the Socialist heaven-on-earth, various former residents of earth plan to

[8] Ho Ching-chih, etc., *Pai-mao-nü* (Hsin-hua Book Co., 1949).
[9] Reprinted in *Chien-kuo Shih-nien Wen-hsueh Ch'uang-tso-hsuan: Ch'ü-yi* (Peking: Chung-kuo Ch'ing-nien Ch'u-pan-she, 1959).

return. Each of the Eight Immortals in turn is found a niche in the new society. Li T'ieh-kuai, for instance, whose spirit had to be content with a mouldy corpse for a lodging when his own body was inadvertently cremated, will now have his leg re-set in the People's Hospital. Then):

> Even more delighted was the fairy Ch'ang-o:
> The Palace of the Moon had long been too cold for her.
> Hearing that the moon would be the first objective in space,
> She hung the halls with lanterns, and set out pots of cassia by the gate.
> . . . . .
> But when to the Palace of Nine Splendours came the message-boy,
> Yang Kuei-fei, the Honoured Consort, nearly died of joy.
> Ages ago she'd perfected the score of " Rainbow Jacket and Feathered Skirt,"
> Ready to share with connoisseurs of music here on earth.
> The fairy Ch'ang-o and Yang Kuei-fei whispered their plan to each other:
> Hand in hand they would come among mortals, to find each of them a handsome young lover, a handsome young lover.

Obviously, while conveying a suitable propaganda message a contemporary writer can at the same time get a lot of fun out of elements of the popular tradition of the past. And if we now turn to a writer like Chao Shu-li, who has received as much acclaim as anyone over the last twenty years, it becomes very apparent that he is at his best when he assumes most consciously and consistently the role of the story-teller, in quite the traditional style. It is in accord with this style that he puts himself into direct contact with reader, soon after the start of the *Ballads of Li Yu-ts'ai*[10]:

> Since the war there have been a good many changes in the village of Yen-chia-shan, and as these changes have taken place Li Yu-t'sai has composed new ballads about them. As a matter of fact it was because of these ballads that he got himself into trouble. I thought of saying a word or two about these changes, and copying down a few of the ballads which accompanied them, to give everybody a bit of amusement, and that was how this little book came about.

The story has medium length, a severely limited number of personages and scope of action, and the comic relief provided by the *k'uai-pan* ballads themselves, these last being witty and successful exercises in a folk form. In direct contrast, *The Changes in the Li Family Village*[11]

[10] Chao Shu-li, *Li Yu-ts'ai Pan-hua* (Tientsin: Hsin-hua Book Co., 1949), p. 27.
[11] *Li-chia-chuang-ti Pien-ch'ien* (Peking: Hsin-hua Book Co., 1949).

is a full-length novel, a run-of-the-mill indignant denunciation of landlord villainy. It contains no touch of humour, and covers a broad field of action—the whole political history of a district from 1928 to 1946—without achieving the sweep and movement possible in a good panoramic novel. When Chang T'ieh-so, whose troubles have dominated the first half of the book, leaves the scene to reappear only near the end, unity is lost, sub-plots compete for attention and dullness settles in like a fog.

The same general distinction holds true for his two more recent major works. To quote the cover blurb,

> *Three Mile Bend* [12] is a relatively remote village which is also short of water. To improve the productive environment of the area, the village Agricultural Production Cooperative makes plans to activate the entire village for the opening up of an irrigation channel. Problems connected with the acquisition of land rights for the channel stir up an ideological struggle; and sandwiched into the action are the love and marriage relationships of three young couples. Contradictions and difficulties are extremely complicated and confused, but under the correct leadership of the Party the villagers succeed in overcoming their difficulties, complete the preparatory work on the channel, and by means of this work actively carry out forward-looking education in socialism among the masses.

This book has some of the humour and good humour that *The Li Family Village* so conspicuously lacked, and considerable liveliness of style:

> After this setback [at the village meeting], Always Right (Ch'ang-yu-li) and Spitfire (Je-pu-ch'i) went home pouting so furiously that you could have tethered a donkey to their lips (p. 89).

Chao Shu-li is always fond of proverbs, and sometimes produces a rare one: Muddlehead (Hu-t'u-t'u), when his son wants to set up on his own, thinks, " This lad is just like the ' useless waiter in the teashop—if there's one kettle not boiling, that's the one he'll pick ' " (p. 149).

Furthermore, the " love and marriage relationships of the three young couples " are very interestingly handled: it is odd that the word " love " should be used in the blurb, for except for one brief paragraph (p. 143) there is no evidence of such a bourgeois luxury in the matter-of-fact, practical considerations each of the girls mulls over before picking her mate. Most consistent of all with the hard-headed tradition of peasant marriage, as against the soft-hearted romantic self-determination of the May Fourth writers, is the marriage of Hsiao-chün and Man-hsi, arranged by the matchmaker wife of Huang Ta-nien on a basis of simple mutual convenience (pp. 172–173).

And yet *Three Mile Bend* is a dull book. The " extremely complicated and confused contradictions and difficulties " referred to in the blurb

[12] *San-li-wan* (Peking: T'ung-su Tu-wu Ch'u-pan-she, 1955).

do not become much clearer in Chao Shu-li's presentation. In place of the violent upheavals and shrill indignation of *The Li Family Village* we find here trivialities and gentle persuasion; but the overall effect is the same, of lack of unity, of an author scurrying around breathlessly from incident to incident.

Just as favourably as *Li Yu-ts'ai* compares with *The Li Family Village*, so we might compare Chao-Shu-li's latest story, *Magic Spring Caves*,[13] with *Three Mile Bend*. This new novel concerns the resistance of Shansi villagers to Japanese and marauding ex-Kuomintang troops in the years around 1940–41, and is the most realistic and exciting of the war stories I have read. In telling this story Chao makes his most extensive and most effective use so far of the technical devices of the old story-tellers. By questions to the reader at chapter-ends and elsewhere (" What sort of men were Chang Te-fu and Li T'ieh-shuan? What cave were they going to and what papers were they after? Did Gold Tiger get the message to them? Did they all get away? I'm going to let you have the whole story right now ": p. 8) the author generates suspense, keeps a tight grip on plot developments and deliberately puts the reader right back into the heroic world of the old novels. What we might describe as conventional situations are covered in the old novelists' phrases, *e.g.*, setting off on a journey:

> *Jin-huu i-tzao chii cherng, budaw chy tzaofann shyrhow yiijing dawle jenn-shang.* " Gold Tiger set out at dawn, and had reached town by breakfast-time " (p. 25);

reunion:

> *Tamen jiann Jin-huu laile, tzyhran dush yow jing yow shii, biitsyy-jian wenn charng wenn doan.* " When they saw Gold Tiger had come back, naturally they were both pleased and startled, and he and they alike began to exchange questions on everything that had happened " (p. 33).

Again and again the author captures the perfect concise phrase to sum up a situation:

> *Yn-huu sh syy bujiann shy hwo bujiann ren.* " If Silver Tiger was dead where was his corpse? If alive, where was he?" (p. 35).

A good modern parallelism, reconstructed from old phrases but apt and clear, occurs on p. 95:

> *Sheau-panq niang jiannle jeh leangwey chingnian, yow bei yow shii shii-de sh lao linjiu de erlneu shy-erl-fuh-der, bei-de sh tzyhjii-de Sheau-panq chiuh-shianq-bu-ming.* " When Little Fatty's mother saw the young couple she was both pleased and saddened—pleased because the children of her old neighbour were lost and found again, saddened because her own Little Fatty was still somewhere unknown."

13 *Ling-ch'üan-tung*, Part One (*Shang-pu*) (Peking: Tso-chia Ch'u-pan-she, 1959).

It must be emphasised that clichés such as I have listed are not at all a necessary concomitant of any attempt to write narrative in modern Chinese. One would not find them to anything like the same extent in the pre-Communist " modern " writers, even in those who, like Ting Ling or Ai Wu, continued to write in the Communist period. These phrases appear in the work of Chao Shu-li as the result of deliberate choice.

I am not suggesting that *Magic Spring Caves* is a well-wrought novel simply because it is loaded with story-teller phrases. Simple narrative thrills (Gold Tiger's escape from forced labour and his exploration of the caves with Little Orchid) are an important contribution to success. The propaganda message is so general—it was a good thing to resist the Japanese and the marauders—as to be unexceptionable (unless one was a Japanese or a marauder). There are some fine portraits, as of the old shepherd Li Hung with his countryman's simple delight in mystification: " It was only because of the potatoes that we came here " (p. 98). What I do suggest is that this is no pale imitation of the old-style heroic tale (as *Three Mile Bend* is a pale imitation of a Soviet Russian novel about life under Socialism), but a true descendant of the Chinese narrative line, which draws its strength from the peasant life of North China and could have come into existence nowhere else.

The opening paragraph of the *Caves* describes the topography of the T'ai-hang Mountains in Honan-Shansi, north-east of Loyang. The second paragraph further specifies the locale of the story:

> But I shouldn't gossip so much. The story I'm going to tell you now is a tale from these T'ai-hang Mountains, the events took place there, down at the southern end of the range. There is a canyon there called Magic Spring Canyon. How did it get such a name? Because right at the end of the canyon a spring of water no bigger across than a walnut comes trickling from beneath a jumble of rocks, then after flowing out for a dozen paces or so falls over a ten-foot cliff into a pit in the rock where it collects in a clear pool about a third of an acre in size. In the old days when people were superstitious, whenever a drought came along people would gather here from a dozen miles around to pray for rain, and that's why they called this the Magic Spring. That's how the name Magic Spring Canyon came about.

This passage has several interesting features:

(i) it opens with a phrase (*shyanhuah shao shuo*) similar to that (*shyanhuah shiou tyi*) conventionally used by the prompt-book writers to end a digression (the " digression " in this case being the general introduction of paragraph one). The same phrase is used on at least two later occasions to resume the narrative after an explanatory digression (pp. 97, 99);

(ii) it further enhances the chatty tone of paragraph one, by direct address of the reader and by personal intervention of the author. Compare also the last paragraph of the book:

I really ought to go on writing, but if I do I shall be late for the labour training I should take part in this year, so the only thing is to wait till I've had my spell of training and take it up again then;

(iii) in its explanation of the origin of the place-name which provides the book's title it offers a further example of the type of instructive digression frequently to be found in traditional stories (one might compare, in *Ku-chin Hsiao-shuo, Chüan,*[14] the account of the origin of the name Wu-tang-shan);

(iv) the reference to praying for rain is consistent with Chao Shu-li's perennial interest in superstitions. The beliefs and practices he so loves to describe belong, admittedly, to " the old days when people were superstitious." Often, indeed, he holds up to ridicule those who play on superstitions to exploit the ignorant. Sometimes he gets a good laugh out of this:

One day Chin Wang's father was ill and went to see Auntie Three the Witch to get guidance from the spirits. Auntie Three squatted behind the incense table intoning while Chin Wang's father knelt listening before it. Hsiao-ch'in (Auntie Three's daughter) was only eight then. She was spending the morning soaking the husks off rice. She had put the coarse rice in a pot of water, but when she heard her mother mumbling away she decided the sound was worth listening to, and so she stood by the incense table listening and forgot all about the rice. Before long Chin Wang's father had to go out to relieve himself, and Auntie Three seized her opportunity: " Go and pull the rice out, quick! It'll be soaked through and ruined by this time!" To her dismay however she was overheard by Chin Wang's father, who spread the story about when he got home. Ever after this the jokers of the village, when they saw Auntie Three, would deliberately turn to each other and ask, " Are you sure your rice isn't soaked through and ruined?" (*Hsiao-erh-hei chieh-hun*, pp. 4–5).

Sometimes the tone is gentler, of amused tolerance:

[In *Magic Spring Caves* again, Gold Tiger and Little Orchid, lost in the mountains, find for food the herb " yellow essence," a Chinese tonic herb, traditionally said to turn you into an immortal if you ate it over a long period]: Although we can't claim that our couple became immortals, still they managed to keep their spirits up on it, and in less than a month's time Gold Tiger's leg was well enough for him to walk again (p. 88).

Superstitions are connected with other parts of the novel's locale:

" Why are there so many of these pits?" asked Little Orchid. Old Li Hung explained: " There's a legend says these are ' Poison Dragon Pits,' and there are three hundred and sixty of them, each inhabited by a huge poisonous snake. Only as far as I know, there's not a single snake on this mountain, not till you get out of the mountains over to the east do you get snakes " (p. 92).

[14] *Shuai Lung Wang*, published in collection *I-ko Nü-jen Fan-shen-ti Ku-shih* (Peking: Hsin-hua Book Co., 1949).

—I should mention that the mountain they are on rejoices in the name of Yen Wang Hsiung, " Yama's Bosom."

There is of course a whole category of works of the new literature, especially stories, which continue the attacks on superstition begun by the May Fourth writers. An excellent specimen is the story *The Smashing of the Dragon King*, by Wang T'ieh.[14] The action is as follows:

> The people of the tiny hamlet of Ma-chia-kuai, faced with drought, prefer praying for rain in the old way to fetching water from a spring two miles away, as urged by the new government. The praying is put in charge of an old rogue of a fortune-teller, Ma Yin-yang (" Zodiac Mah "), who arranges incantations and ceremonies in honour of the Dragon King, making meanwhile a sizeable " squeeze " on the sale of incense and so forth. No rain comes, but the villagers are as a direct result of Zodiac Mah's activities involved in a major battle with a neighbouring village. Zodiac is discountenanced and arrested, a government worker comes to organise irrigation, and the village manages to get by until at last the rain does come.

There is a great deal to enjoy in this story. Although the author's whole aim, obviously, is to debunk superstitious practices and practitioners, still it is precisely these targets themselves that provide the colour, life and fun. One begins to feel one would prefer a moderate amount of extortion and fraud to the loss from the village of these picturesque rogues. Witness the sorceress Inkynob (*Mo-tou*—she has lost her hair and disguises her baldness with ink) going into a trance:

> On the western slope of Ma-chia-kuai is a pagoda-tree many years old, and near its roots a little cave in the rocks. Long ago a wooden board was erected here with the inscription " Abode of True Magic," and it was spread about that this was the home of a fairy fox. The tree and the cave had become even more sacrosanct since Inkynob's graduation as a sorceress, and now she had built a small temple beneath the pagoda-tree. She had set up two or three clay idols, and on the altar had placed a gaily-enamelled vase containing a large number of flowers made of red and green paper. No matter how they had to scrape and save for it, the peasants never missed burning a few sticks of incense at this temple on the first and fifteenth of every month. And on this particular afternoon there was more going on at the temple than ever before.
>
> You could see them from the edge of the village, a big semicircle of women and another semicircle of men kneeling in front of the temple. Inkynob was there, looking more spiritual than ever. She shut her eyes and made a series of passes with a pink silk handkerchief. Then she stuck her neck forward like a hen eating corn and began to murmur. Before long the faithful of both sexes who were closest to her began to promulgate her message: " She had a dream last night. She got instructions from the Dragon King. The Dragon King is willing to save the people of Ma-chia-kuai. We have to wait till midnight and then carry an image of the Dragon King a mile to the east of the village. We have to burn incense and kotow, and then shout three times in succession

> for the Dragon King. She guarantees the ground will be soaked within three days."
>
> Everyone was thrilled with the prognostication, and kotowed and gave thanks to Inkynob. The two " novices " knelt close by her and fanned her unceasingly—Inkynob had put a lot of energy into her performance, and it was the dog-days, the beads of sweat from her scalp rolled down and carried with them the ink she had rubbed on, so that her face was streaked with black all over.

It must be admitted that when Inkynob and her partner Zodiac Mah disappear from the action and the cadres take over, the proceedings lose their sparkle: fortunately by then the story is almost ended.

In just the same way, Chao Shu-li gains liveliness and colour from his frequent references to the supernatural, which was after all the most potent constituent of the popular imagination. When Gold Tiger, dumping the corpse of the landlord's " dog's leg " into a pool, cries, " Go and root out hidden grain in the Dragon King's palace! " he recalls a wealth of horror of watery graves (*Caves*, p. 47). Again, popular mythology may substitute for the more recondite resources of classical allusion, now closed to writers. Thus in *Three Mile Village*, the possession of the gift of education is symbolised by a magic gourd:

> Ever since she was a child Yü-mei had heard about the girl who studied magic under a fairy godmother or some such person. When her studies were completed the old dame presented her with a magic gourd which would provide whatever she asked. Yü-mei felt now that Ling-chih (with her middle-school education) seemed to have got such a magic gourd for herself, and she might have had one too but had missed it. (p. 46).

Unfortunately, too few other writers have succeeded in incorporating traditional elements into new work in such a natural and organic fashion. For a clear instance of an unnatural straining after the " folksy " it is instructive to look again at *Wang Kuei and Li Hsiang-hsiang*,[15] a long narrative poem by Li Chi which was greeted with rapture on its first appearance. This poem consists of some four hundred rhymed couplets, with a line of regularly seven syllables, occasionally one or two more, and with almost absolute regularity four beats. This constituent couplet was a folk-verse form current in Northern Shensi, known as the *shun-t'ien-yu*. A writer under the name of Lin P'ing [16] quotes certain *shun-t'ien-yu* he has transcribed, of which Li Chi has received lines verbatim into his poem, *e.g.*:

15 Li Chi, *Wang Kuei yü Li Hsiang-hsiang* (Chung-kuo Jen-min Wen-yi Ts'ung-shu series) (Peking: Hsin-hua Book Co., 1949).

16 In Chou Wei, ed., *Lun " Wang Kuei yü Li Hsiang-hsiang "* (Shanghai Magazine Co., 1950), pp. 63–72.

If for three days I don't see your face
I ask each traveller on the road.
If for three days I don't see your face
I draw your likeness on the wall.

and

Think of you till midnight, can't get to sleep,
After midnight think of you and have to light the lamp.

A feature of these *shun-t'ien-yu,* as of much folk-verse, is what we might call the " detached simile," stated in the first line of the couplet and seldom related in any explicit way to what follows in the second.

The following couplets describing the two lovers were singled out by the critics for their naturalness:

Flower of the lily blossoming red,
Hsiang-hsiang grew into a lovely girl

—and the parallel, a few lines later:

Thickets of willow clustering green,
Wang Kuei was a fine young lad.

Some of the similes incorporate proverbial material in very apt application:

Blind man on dark road, hardship piled on hardship:
What the poor peasant fears is a year of famine.

At other times, though, the poet strains so hard that his effect is artificial or even quite wrong. The following couplet is spoken by the villainous landlord, who is apparently but implausibly referring to himself in the first line:

Smoke from the chimney, soot on the beams,
When I get home that lad will be in trouble.

In the case of the next image, of the leadership of the Communist Party, it is hard to believe that the author actually intended to flatter:

Flock of sheep on the move follows the sheep in front:
In North Shensi has arisen the Communist Party.

—sheep certainly seem to present problems to this poet, as witness the ludicrous instance cited in S. H. Chen's paper. (See p. 53.)

It would be dull to cite too many of the crudities and weak lines of this very long poem. The following are far from isolated:

People don't cry when they aren't upset,
Sheep's-gut face-cloth soaking wet.

or another statement just too simple to stand as valid verse:

> Wang Kuei in winter off to watch his sheep
> Didn't have any clothes fit to wear.

In general, the device of the *shun-t'ien-yu* becomes much too mannered after frequent repetition through eight hundred lines of narrative; also, the metrical scheme, adequate for a short lilting lyric, was never intended to stand the strain of epic proportions.

But I wish to turn rather to two instances of recall of traditional images. The first puts Hsiang-hsiang in the position of Wang Chao-chün or some other heroine of old *tz'u* or drama:

> Watching from her window a wild goose fly south
> Hsiang-hsiang's suffering is more than can be told:
> People say the wild goose can carry a message—
> Take these words from me to the one I love:
> " When you went away, the trees were just in bud;
> Now the leaves have all gone, but still you don't return."

The next passage is quoted by a certain " Chieh-ch'ing " in his review of the poem,[17] and is so striking that one wonders how one failed to be impressed by it on first reading the original:

> Visit ended, Wang Kuei went back,
> Hsiang-hsiang saw him off as far as the ditch.
> " In the ditch is thick yellow clay:
> I'll scrape out a lump of it, shape the two of us,
> Fashion out a you, fashion out a me,
> Make them just as if they were real,
> Break them in pieces, make them again,
> Shape another you, shape another me,
> In your body there will be me,
> In my body there will be you.
> When I've made the clay dolls, when I call,
> Then in a few days you'll come back to me."

Li Chi here places on the lips of his modern heroine the words of a lady who died some six and a half centuries ago:

> Madam Kuan Tao-sheng would often match the *tz'u* poems of her husband [the poet and painter] Chao Tzu-ang [Meng-fu, 1254–1322]. On one occasion Chao, contemplating the acquisition of a concubine, poked fun at his wife in a poem. . . .
> Madam Kuan replied with another poem:

[17] In the collection already referred to, *Lun " Wang Kuei yü Li Hsiang-hsiang,"* pp. 31–32.

You and I two people,
Yet our love so great.
Love so great
Burns like fire.
Take a lump of clay,
Knead out a you,
Fashion out a me,
Then take the two of us,
Break us both in pieces,
Work them out with water,
Knead another you,
Fashion another me,
Part of my clay is you,
Part of your clay is me.
You and I, in life will share a coverlet,
In death will share a coffin.[18]

The reason I had failed to be impressed by the passage Chieh-ch'ing cites from Li Chi's poem was that it was not there: it was excised from the version I first read, which was the most widely-promulgated *Jen-min Wen-yi Ts'ung-shu* edition of 1949. In this version Part II, section 4 of the poem ends with the couplet,

Visit ended, Wang Kuei went back,
Hsiang-hsiang saw him off as far as the ditch.[19]

In the absence of any reference to or explanation of this expurgation the reasoning behind it becomes a matter for speculation. Was the obvious reference to a practice of primitive magic felt to be wounding to the reputation of an enlightened peasantry? Or did an inflamed prudishness blush at the thought of vicarious physical conjunction? Or was the esoteric (and effete?) origin itself felt to bear undesirable connotations? The excision represents an interesting display of some kind of sensitivity, though one is not quite sure exactly what kind. Perhaps the answer is merely that Hsiang-hsiang's display of devotion in this passage was felt to be irrelevant to the progress of her revolutionary love: though in fact it is much more in keeping with such character as she is given in the poem than is the wistful mood of the wild goose image.

T'ien Chien's long ballad *The Carter's Story* [20] was first put out in

[18] Quoted from Shen Hsiung, *Ku-chin Tz'u-hua* (Vols. V–VI of *Tz'u-hua Ts'ung-pien*, printed by the editor T'ang Kuei-chang "of Nanking," 1934, under the sub-section *tz'u-hua*, second section, p. 7b).

[19] Chieh-ch'ing no doubt saw the poem on its first appearance in a newspaper. A 1947 edition contains the passage, but it does not appear in the English translation in *Chinese Literature*, No. 1.

[20] *Kan-ch'e chuan* (Chung-kuo Jen-min Wen-yi Ts'ung-shu series) (Peking: Hsin-hua Book Co., 1949).

1946, the same year as Li Chi's poem. Its length is even greater, some twelve thousand characters all told. The narrative framework is quite similar in that it concerns the overthrow by aroused peasants of a vicious landlord and the liberation of a village girl from his clutches; the girl's father though, rather than her lover, supplies T'ien Chien's hero. But although it received less acclaim, *The Carter's Story* is far superior to *Wang Kuei*. T'ien Chien's success is in the integration of elements from an older popular tradition of poetry into his own highly original mode of diction. In the following passage we can hear how rhythms and reduplications typical of certain classical *tz'u* or *ch'ü* patterns enrich the music of that " drum-beat " verse which yet remains a personal achievement of this poet; we may notice also how he brings a run of lines to a climax by hammering out a proverb into a ringing close:

Naa jy, naa jy	Who could guess, who could guess,
Chyongren-de che	A poor man's cart
Juang-de ley	Filled with tears
Tzay-de chour	Loaded with hate
Haobii gay-de dahwuh	As if it were wrapped in fog
Yow lin-de bawyeu	Drenched with driving rain.
Lan-ni swei shanq che	Though Lan-ni climbed on the cart
Ren yeesh ku	She cried
Che yeesh ku	The cart cried
Kusheng-jy-jong	The girl and the cart
Ren her che	Jolting on
Goenlai goenchiuh	Through the sound of weeping.
Jensh hao nan tzoou	It was so hard to go
Nan tzoou, hao nan tzoou	Hard, so hard to go
Tzoou yeesh chour	Hard, so hard to go.
Butzoou yeesh chour	Sorrow to go
Jensh iuanchour iryh jye	Sorrow not to go.
Chiannian nan geduann!	Truly, a hatred born in a day
	Takes a thousand years to die!
	(pp. 29–30)

Writing some time ago on the topic of " Fiction of the Yenan Period " [21] I described this body of work as deeply indebted to the popular tradition, " but not so much by direct inheritance as by raiding of the family vaults." What I had in mind then, but lacked the space to elaborate, was a kind of deliberate recall of the well-beloved popular classics, practised by the new writers to enrich their own offerings, to conform to the presumably more conservative taste of the broadest public, and no doubt also to soften the shock of the propagandistic message. I can best illustrate this process of " raiding " by considering a favourite type of the *hao-chi*, the " clever stratagem," which is always good for suspense and good for a laugh. This is the stratagem of " bride

[21] *The China Quarterly*, No. 4, October–December 1960, pp. 1–16.

substitution." The *loci classici* we may take as Chapter 5 of *Shui-hu-chuan* and Chapter 18 of *Hsi-yu-chi*. (The former of these old popular novels is favoured above all others as a fountain-head for the sustenance of Communist literary men. Although its outstanding quality is in any case beyond question, certain special factors have contributed to its new eminence. One is the official sanction conferred by Mao Tse-tung himself, who refers to it frequently in his writings.[22] Another is that in stories of the War of Resistance to Japan, the Eighth Route Army when operating in enemy-held territory find themselves in a position very much akin to that of the outlaws of Liang-shan. The intention of the authors of such stories is similar, to establish the type of the champion of the poor, Robin Hood fashion.)

One of Lu Ta's more chivalrous deeds, it will be recalled, is performed one night *en route* to the Eastern capital. He seeks lodging at the farm of an old man, Liu, whose daughter is that very night to be forcibly taken in marriage by a local *tai-wang* or bandit-chief, Chou T'ung. Lu Ta persuades old Liu to let him try his skill at "expounding the doctrine of karma" to the unwanted bridegroom, when he arrives, in an attempt to soften his heart. It is of course rather his head that Lu Ta softens, with his great fists, when the groom creeps at last into the darkened bridal chamber where Lu Ta lies stark naked on the bed in the bride's stead.

The similar episode in *Hsi-yu-chi* relates how Monkey poses as the poor maltreated captive wife of the monster Pigsy. The comic possibilities of the situation are more fully exploited here than in the *Shui-hu* story, but the general principle of rescue is the same.

Now we may look at two (and there are probably more) forced weddings in the fiction of Communist writers. First, a bride substitution in the *New Son and Daughter Heroes*.[23] Hsiao-mei, who is eventually to marry the hero Ta-shui, attracts the attention of the local Japanese commander. Wedding plans are forced on her, but when the groom enters the bridal chamber to claim his rights he finds that the veiled figure he "married" is no pretty young girl but Ta-shui's younger brother, a militia leader. This time the unwelcome groom is neither beaten nor enlisted in a pilgrimage after sutras, but shot dead.

In the novel *Heroes of Lü-liang*,[24] the forced marriage is planned of Mei-ying, daughter of "Second Teacher," a specimen of the enlightened

22 See for example his discussion of tactical retreat, p. 202, in "Strategic Problems of the Chinese Revolutionary War," December 1936, in *Mao Tse-tung Hsüan-chi*, I, pp. 167–242.

23 K'ung Chüeh and Yüan Ching, *Hsin Erh-nü Ying-hsiung Chuan* (Shanghai: Hai-yen Book Co., 1949).

24 Ma Feng and Hsi Jung, *Lü-liang Ying-hsiung Chuan* (two vols.) (Peking: Hsin-hua Book Co., 1949).

poor gentry, to a sergeant of the puppet forces whose nickname is Snake-in-the-Grass (*ti-t'ou-she*, incidentally a good *Shui-hu*-type name). The rescue of Mei-ying is effected by means other than bride-substitution, but I wish to quote at length to illustrate the manner in which the authors re-create the style (if my translation can show this) and narrative technique of the classical models. It may be interesting to note first some closely matching phrases from the *Shui-hu* and *Lü-liang* episodes under consideration:

Shui-hu-chuan [25]	*Heroes of Lü-liang* (p. 58)
Shan-bian luo ming guu sheang " gongs and drums came sounding from the hillside "	*shan-shanq luo ming guu sheang* " gongs and drums came sounding from the hillside "
juangtzyymen du nhiej leangbaa hann " all the farm people clenched their fists, sweating "	*buyouder wohchii leang shooushin hann* " couldn't help clenching his fists and sweating "
itsuh renmaa feiben juang-shanq " a troop of horses and riders raced up to the farm "	*jyy jiann horngx-liuhx itsuh renmaa* " a troop of horses and riders in red and green "
ming-hoangx-de dush chinshieh chyichiang, jinn baa horng-liuh jiuannbair fwuj " all bright-gleaming weapons and pennanted spears, red and green silk strips fastened to each "	*ming-hoangx-de tsyhdau-shanq shuannj horng-liuh tsaechour* " red and green silk streamers tied on their bright-gleaming bayonets "
(*daywanq*) *chyij ipi gau-tour jeuan-mau dah bairmaa* " (the bandit chief) rode a great proud-necked curly-haired white horse "	*Dihtour-sher chyij gau-tour dahmaa* " Snake-in-the-Grass rode a great proud-necked horse "

Here is an abridgement of the *Lü-liang* episode:

> Mei-ying was nineteen *sui* [years old] this year, quick and bright by nature, graceful in appearance. Her old parents loved her as they loved life itself. Now that Snake-in-the-Grass demanded her for his wife, what could they be but anxious and grieved? The problem had (militia leader) Wu worried also. Head down, fingering his chin, he paced the floor deep in thought. After a while he gave a sudden glad cry and said: " What do you think of this way out? "
>
> While he spoke the heads of the four of them stayed together. They all reached agreement, but Second Teacher was still nervous for a while, and his face wore an air of anxiety. Wu thumped his chest and said: " There's no problem. I know some of the men in the engineers platoon. This is the only way! " And Old Man Chang added: " Don't worry. I can manage the go-between part. " . . .

(Old Chang as go-between concludes arrangements for the wedding to take place a few days later):

[25] Tso-chia Ch'u-pan-she edition of the Chin Sheng-t'an version of the novel, p. 64.

Around midday, suddenly gongs and drums came sounding from the hill-side across. Everyone ran out to look and what they saw was a troop of horses and riders in red and green, who in no time at all had entered the village. It was no one else but Snake-in-the-Grass coming to claim his bride. There in front were half a dozen musicians. "Doo-wah doo-wah" went the blowing and banging, and behind came four lantern-bearers and two men with banners, on either side of the bridal sedan-chair. Snake-in-the-Grass rode a great proud-necked horse and wore a gown and riding-jacket, ceremonial head-dress and leather boots. Four policemen, fully-armed, red and green silk streamers tied on their bright-gleaming bayonets, martial and majestic, marched up to Second Teacher's door.

Three shots were fired and the sedan-chair was set down. Snake-in-the-Grass dismounted, and people ready waiting bowed and greeted him and led him in, straight to the main room. Second Teacher himself came to keep him company, and smoked and drank tea and chatted with him, deliberately wasting time. He talked of things ancient and modern, the last five hundred years and the next five hundred years, of things in heaven and things here below.[26] Now Snake-in-the-Grass actually didn't have a single aperture open to admit knowledge (*ichiaw butong*), but in order to make a show of status before his father-in-law all he could do was wiggle his eyebrows in every direction (*jea mei sandaw*) and make some sort of wild reply. It was late afternoon before the wine and the feast were served. Second Master himself offered wine and relatives and friends all in turn came up with a bowl, then K'ang Shun-feng started offering wine, and although Snake-in-the-Grass had a good capacity, with such non-stop drinking it was like trying to dam the flow of a stream, by the time he'd eaten half-way through the feast he already showed signs of tipsiness. The four policemen also had someone to look after them, and drunk wine and guessed fingers, and made a continuous yelling. Not till the time to light the lanterns had come did they set out on their way.

Snake-in-the-Grass wore a cross of red silk, and the bride wore her phoenix head-dress and a red gown, and was carried into the sedan-chair weeping and wailing as though she couldn't bear to leave. By now the gauze lanterns had been lighted, the musicians struck up and the sedan-chair was lifted and carried off. The bride's cousin was escorting her and followed behind the sedan-chair. Second Master watched the party leave and he couldn't help clenching his fists and sweating.

Having drunk so much wine, Snake-in-the-Grass lolled about in his saddle, and the four policemen had drunk themselves dizzy and staggered unevenly after him. On they went until they were entering a copse of birches, when suddenly with a swoosh from among the trees a ball of fiery sparks came flying straight at Snake-in-the-Grass. And there he gave a shrill yelp and fell off his horse, which reared and pranced in alarm. But who'd have guessed it, when Snake-in-the-Grass fell off his

[26] *Cf.* Arthur Waley, *Monkey* (London: Allen & Unwin, 1942), p. 173, Monkey's instructions to Tripitaka on the impending visit of the prince of Crow-cock: "Show him the casket and tell him that there is a treasure within that knows what happened five hundred years ago, and what will happen in five hundred years long hence, and five hundred years between. One thousand five hundred years in all, of things past and present."

> horse one foot stayed in the stirrup, and the horse raced off, right back to Han-chia-shan, dragging him along upside-down behind (pp. 56-59).

From these examples, which could be multiplied almost indefinitely, it is obvious that a concerted drive has been under way for twenty years now to restore to Chinese writing a specifically Chinese appearance, albeit this appearance must harmonise with the popular rather than with the more esoteric tradition of literature. That this drive is not motivated merely by the need for a readier mass intelligibility becomes clear as soon as one considers work in other fields. Historians, anxious to replace the shameful past image of stagnation by that of a dynamic society, have emphasised the part played by peasant revolts. And in the last three years or so there has been a shift of interest towards the establishment of a truly heroic past. Some manifestations of this move have been reported as follows [27]:

> The principal reason for the re-evaluation of Ts'ao Ts'ao is his asserted contribution to *fu-ch'iang*, enriching and strengthening the Chinese nation. And along with the refurbishing of the once-villain Ts'ao Ts'ao has gone a call for the re-evaluation of many others, *not* popular heroes or leaders of peasant revolts, but emperors, generals, statesmen and scholars of the " feudal past "—such as King Chou, the last ruler of the Shang dynasty, the first Ch'in emperor, Han Wu-ti, T'ang T'ai-tsung, and the Ch'ing emperors K'ang-hsi and Ch'ien-lung—on the grounds that they too played " positive " roles in the history of China.

Yet with all its glitter and glamour, the ultimate end served by all this rehabilitation of the " national," the " traditional " is no more than a matter of justifying and glorifying a revolutionary government. The great men of letters of the past would have understood perfectly such a purpose, and each could point out many a cautious eulogist among his colleagues and acquaintances. But a Ch'ü Yuan, a Tu Fu, a Shih Nai-an or a Ts'ao Hsueh-ch'in would never have felt that the heights of truth were to be scaled by adulation of the régime in power or by acceptance of the way the world went.

We end in paradox. The writers of protest of the Literary Revolution, for all their outlandish garb, were heirs to a noble literary civilisation. Their Communist successors have rejected and overthrown the whole concept of what that literature was and meant, but are busily engaged in decking themselves out in its outward forms.

27 Albert Feuerwerker, " Rewriting Chinese History: Interpreting the Past in the People's Republic of China," in *University of Toronto Quarterly*, XXX, No. 3, April 1961, pp. 273–285.

Enthusiast and Escapist: Writers of the Older Generation *

By VINCENT Y. C. SHIH

THE purpose of this article is to show what Communist literary dictatorship has done to some of the writers, who, though not literary giants, had in the past shown some promise in the art of letters.

Limited in time, I shall restrict my discussion to three * writers considered major luminaries during the pre-Communist period: Mao Tun, Pa Chin and Shen Ts'ung-wen. The choice is not made completely at random. Mao Tun, after some vacillation during the last years of the twenties, became increasingly orientated to the Communist line during the thirties and forties; and when the Communist régime was established he became one of the official spokesmen of Mao's view on literature. Pa Chin, who during the pre-Communist days was most of the time dominated by a melancholy mood, and whose ineffectual humanitarian motifs brought the reader only the barest ray of light, emerges after the Communist take-over as one of the most vociferous and enthusiastic propagandists for the new "glorious era." And Shen Ts'ung-wen, an erstwhile non-political writer, seems to have bowed low under the bludgeonings of the Communist effort to reform him. These three men represent three points in a spectroscopic band of the writers in their feelings toward Communism prior to the establishment of the Communist régime. How they have fared since the take-over cannot but be of interest to us, if only to show that under the Communist régime one either conforms or fades away. (This is true politically speaking; from the literary point of view, they all fade away.) Mao Tun gets into his element and becomes the doctrinaire and the arbiter of Communist literary taste; Pa Chin with the uneasiness of a poor relation, voices with zest and gusto the glory of the new state and unceasingly sings the praises of everything he saw while at the Korean front. And Shen Ts'ung-wen, one of the best veteran prose

* As presented to the Ditchley Conference, this article was entitled "Doctrinaire, Enthusiast and Escapist: Writers of the Older Generation" and included a long section on Mao Tun, Chairman of the Writers' Union. In view of the fact that this section also forms part of a longer article on Mao Tun, to be published in a forthcoming issue, we have decided to exclude it from the present article. However, we have left Prof. Shih's introductory paragraph unchanged to show why he selected these three writers.—Ed.

writers, has become almost a total nonentity. The space in between could be filled with a number of writers: Kuo Mo-jo, closest to Mao Tun if not above him; Lao-she, a shade below Mao Tun and one niche above Pa Chin; Ping-hsin, in between Pa Chin and Shen Ts'ung-wen. Many reasons can be adduced to show why it is better not to try to cover the whole spectrum. The most cogent one is: the spectrum would turn out to be only a variety of shades of one solid colour, *i.e.*, from a glowing red to a pale pink, and in the case of Shen Ts'ung-wen, the pink serves only as a protective colour. [The section on Mao Tun followed here.]

Pa Chin, the Enthusiast

Pa Chin has never been oriented toward Communism either in thought or in temperament. His humanitarian individualism, his militant anarchism, his love of freedom to say what he had to say, the impulsiveness and spontaneity with which he expressed his feelings, his determination to expose and attack whoever built their happiness on the sufferings of others, his melancholy mood and general pessimism, his inability to point out with any clarity new ways and directions—all these combined to make it unlikely that he could ever be a good Communist. When in 1949 the All-China Federation of Literary and Art Circles held its inaugural meeting, Pa Chin was asked to say a few words. When his name was announced, he left the meeting in haste. No explanation was offered for this behaviour. In 1950 he wrote "A Letter That Was Not Sent" to the members of that conference, praising them for their part in the building of new China. He said that they were building new China with their blood without showing the air of heroes. While he wrote with ink, they wrote with blood; while he wrote for city dwellers, they brought warmth and light to countless oppressed in the countryside. Thus he would like them to understand that his reluctance to speak was due to a sense of inadequacy on his part. But to us this initial hesitation could mean his shyness about Communism at first, and his self-depreciation later might express the mood of a penitent recalcitrant. After the takeover, Pa Chin became more and more enthusiastic about the new régime; and under its auspices his star has been rising steadily. Today he is a member of the presidium of the All-China Federation of Literary and Art Circles, Vice-Chairman of the Writers' Union, editor-in-chief of *Shanghai Wen-hsueh* and *Shou-huo*, and like Mao Tun, has been a member of delegations to writers' conferences outside the country.

As a writer, Pa Chin's fame rests entirely on his novels. He writes with passion, setting his reader's heart afire and moving him to tears.

Despite all the architectonic defects of his novels, he had a profound influence among the youth. He has been called a humanitarian, showing great concern for the interests of mankind. But his humanitarianism often sinks to sentimentalism because of its ineffectiveness. According to his own account, his stories are vehicles for the portrayal of his emotions. In his novels he lays bare his heart and pours out his feelings before his reader, allowing his feelings to run uncontrolled. He is spontaneous and impulsive, ruled always by his emotions with little regard to organisation. To him thought content is all important, and form is only secondary. He wrote from personal experience, although not all his characters were built on actual individuals. Nearly all his characters are composite portraits with traits drawn from a number of individuals of a common type, persons whom he knew intimately. Once created, his characters tend to attain an individuality of their own, speaking and acting independently of their creator. The range of his subject-matter is rather limited, and this he has explained as being due to the limitations of his own life. At the time of writing his viewpoint was limited to what was familiar to him. His attitude toward the function of literature was in part acceptable to the Communists. He said he used his pen as a weapon to fight his enemy, which he defined as traditional conceptions and irrational institutions which are obstacles to social progress and the development of human nature. He considered all that destroyed the effort of love his enemy; chief among these were the old social and political institutions in general and the large feudalistic family system in particular.

Under the new régime Pa Chin has been accorded respect and honour few non-Communist writers have had the privilege to receive. During the " hundred flowers " period, Pa Chin, lulled into a state of self-confidence by a false sense of security, spoke up. He showed dissatisfaction at being a figurehead as the Vice-Chairman of the Chinese Writers' Union, criticised Party interference in literary activities under the name of guidance, and proposed that art and literature be returned to the people. For a while nothing happened. But a step-child is always a step-child. Lest Pa Chin should forget, Party members in June 1957 took Pa Chin's sympathy for Howard Fast expressed in his " The Tragedy of Howard Fast " as an excuse to accuse him of failure to recognise the enemy and thus to lose sight of his proletarian viewpoint. His proposal to give art and literature back to the people also came under fire. When he acknowledged his mistake and thanked his critics for the lesson he had received, the attack subsided only to reappear in greater magnitude in October the same year. Yao Wen-yuan, a Party critic, singled out the anarchism in his first novel, *Mieh-wang*, for attack; the refrain was picked up by others whose common theme was: Pa Chin's novels are all permeated by anarchistic thought, without a single character worthy of being a strong Communist revolutionary. These initial salvos had all the ominous signs of developing into a major barrage. But miraculously nothing came of them. The reason seems to be that while there was occasional need to use the big stick to keep him in line, Pa Chin, on account of his influence with the youth, was too valuable a symbol to destroy. Pa Chin for his part contributed amply to this amicable solution by self-criticism and determination to follow the orthodox line. This determination was expressed in his 1960 article: "Wen-hsueh yao P'ao-tao Shih-tai-te Ch'ien-t'ou" ("Literature should Run Ahead of Time").[1]

There is one interesting episode in *Ch'i-yuan*, a novel he wrote in 1944, which tells us more intimately his views on novels, writers and literature in general. Li, a writer, is talking to one of his admirers, Mrs. Yao, saying that his books are mostly nonsense. In protest she said,

> "You cannot say they are nonsense. I remember a novelist once said that you writers are doctors of the human soul. At least I for one have taken your medicine. I feel that you have brought together the hearts of men, making it possible for them to understand one another. What you do is like bringing coal to those who are suffering from cold, bringing comfort to those who are miserable."[2]
>
> ". . . I have plenty of leisure in Yao's family. When he is out, I read to while away my time. I have read many novels, translations, creative novels, some by others and some by you—I read them all. These novels open up a new world for me. My world used to be a tiny one: two families, a school, scores of streets. Now I begin to realise that I am surrounded by a huge human world; now I begin to have an inkling of the true human heart. I also begin to see that there is so much misery and suffering around. Now I understand what life is all about. Sometimes I am so elated that tears start to flow; sometimes I feel so sad that I can only smile foolishly. Whether crying or smiling, I always feel relieved after it is over. Sympathy, love, mutual aid—these are not nonsense. My heart and others' are bound together: when they smile I feel happy; when they cry I also feel sad. I find the world filled with so much suffering and misfortune; but in it I see more love. It seems as if I can hear laughter which speaks of gratitude and satisfaction. My heart is as warm as spring. 'To live is indeed a beautiful thing.' I believe you once said this."
>
> "What I meant is: To toil for one's own ideals is a beautiful thing."
>
> She nodded and said, "That's the idea. If one wishes his life to be filled with happiness, with meaning, how can one be without ideals? Long ago I heard an English woman doctor preach in Chinese. She quoted from the Bible: "Sacrifice is the greatest happiness." I did not understand what it meant then. Now I understand. Help others,

[1] Pa Chin, "Wen-hsueh yao P'ao-tao Shih-tai-te Ch'ien-t'ou," *Wen-yi Pao,* Nos. 268, 269, 1960.

[2] Pa Chin, *Ch'i-yuan* (Peking: 1944), pp. 174–175.

give them what belongs to you, make those who cry smile, those who are hungry satisfied and those who are cold warm. Aren't that laughter and those smiles the best possible reward? Sometimes I feel that even trying to be a nurse would do me good, for then I would be able to help those who are unfortunately sick: support this one with my hand, get something for the other, bring medicine for the third, and scatter the fourth's despondency with some comforting words."

"But in thinking of others you should not forget yourself," I interrupted, deeply moved.

"This is not forgetting myself; this is expanding myself. I believe there is such a saying in a foreign book: I see myself in others' laughter and smiles. I find myself in others' happiness, in their daily life, in their thoughts, and in their memories. If one can achieve this, how wonderful." [3]

This is a classic example of Pa Chin's humanitarian sentimentalism, genuine and moving in its youthful immaturity. In 1956 he wrote under the title " Jan-shou ti Hsin " (" A Burning Heart ") to indicate his debt to Gorky. But it is really a portrait of his own intellectual life.

> I like especially Gorky's short stories, and it does not matter whether they were written in his early life or in his later years. In them I clearly feel the heart of the author comes very close to mine, and he is talking to his reader with utmost sincere good will. . . . In all his works the reader is infected with his love and hate. His personality is revealed in them. Without appearing to instruct he makes you feel his love and his hate. The reality, naked reality, which he portrays, comes to life before you, and his personality makes you think, compels you to observe and investigate this reality closely.[4]

In 1948, four years after he wrote his *Ch'i-yuan*, he wrote " T'an Hsiao-shuo," in which he said, " the quality of a novel depends on life-experience, on a fullness of life and a correct understanding and analysis of it." This understanding is not to be had either from reading novels, no matter how many, or from the instruction of a few masters. " Only those who have participated in the revolutionary struggle, who have stood firm on the side of the proletariat and accepted the Marxist world view may be said to understand the secret of writing." [5] He has become completely indoctrinated with the Communist pattern of thought.

His experience as a writer commissioned to paint the portraits of Korean war heroes and the need to vindicate his own viewpoint during the campaigns against Hu Feng and Ting Ling and their groups further conditioned his frame of mind until it functioned very much like that of a doctrinaire. This he exhibited in his criticism of Lu Ling's " Wa-ti-shang te ' chan-i ' " in 1955. He had a preconceived idea about what

[3] *Ibid.* pp. 175–176.

[4] Pa Chin, " Fan-tang Fan-jen-min-te Ke-jen Yeh-hsin-chia-te-lu shih Chueh-tui Tsou Pu-t'ung te," *Wen-yi Pao*, No. 191, 1957. Pa Chin, " Ta Huan-le te Jih-tzu," *Ta Huan-le te Jih-tzu*, (Peking: 1957).

[5] Pa Chin, " T'an wo-te tuan-p'ien hsiao-shuo," PL, No. 103, 1958.

a Korean volunteer or commandant should be according to the Communist pattern; and then applied this pattern in his criticism of Lu Ling's image of the heroes. Lu Ling had written a simple story about a battle fought in a lowland, in which Wang Ying-hung, a new recruit, is sent to take part in the battle. At the moment of his departure, a Korean girl who loves him dearly gives him a handkerchief which he tucked into the front of his shirt. When he is fatally wounded, the handkerchief is soaked in blood. At the moment of death a thought flashes through his mind that he not only dies for his country but for her as well. Deeply touched by the scene, the commandant returns the handkerchief to the girl as a token of love. During the course of narra tion, Lu Ling also made the observation that this love was unrealisable both from Wang's point of view and from the viewpoint of army discipline. Pa Chin, in unison with other critics clamouring to demonstrate the correctness of their viewpoint, began his attack by dubbing Lu Ling's work as based on the petty bourgeois philosophy that love is supreme. He said it reminded him of medieval knighthood stories which he used to enjoy in his teens. However, he said, Wang is a young fighter who has just come from his homeland to fight Americans in Korea, and the commandant is a battle-toughened veteran. How can they entertain and exhibit the thoughts, feelings and actions that characterised the knights in Medieval Europe eight or nine hundred years ago? Furthermore, how can a veteran such as the commandant have any interest in love and waste so much time for it like a petty bourgeois who believes in the principle that love is above everything?

Furthermore, to say that love is unrealisable from the point of view of discipline would imply that the army discipline is ruthless. But in all his experience in Korea, he never found discipline a problem. True, there was a regulation prohibiting the volunteers from falling in love with Korean girls. But in view of these warriors' class-consciousness, this regulation was not a bondage. While in Korea Pa Chin said, he constantly heard high praises of the excellent qualities of Chinese warriors. Certainly when they consider Korean women their own mothers and sisters, they would not even be aware of the regulation, because not even in their dreams do they entertain effeminate feelings such as love. So Lu Ling's description is a deliberate distortion of and insult to the image of the heroes fighting in Korea. Reasoning in a similar manner, he set up Korean women as a type, supported again by his own experience. According to this type, Chin, the Korean girl, and her mother as described by Lu Ling cannot possibly be factual. Finally Pa Chin set about to paint what the image of a commandant should be, and in the process he also showed why it is unthinkable for one in such a responsible position to allow a new recruit like Wang to risk his life on such a dangerous mission. His conclusion:

> The author of this short story considers reality his enemy and hates it. So according to his own standpoint he reconstructs the real life of the people and clothes each of his characters in the story in his own thought, making them speak what the author would like them to speak, and act under his direction. To replace collectivism with the despicable individualism, patriotism and internationalism with the decadent philosophy of liberalism, the thought and feeling of the proletariat and revolutionary warriors with those of the capitalist individualists, and to achieve the purpose of propagating anti-revolution by confusing the minds of the readers regarding what is black and what is white—these constitute Lu Ling's " Lowland Combat." [6]

In passing, Pa Chin defines for us what he considers to be the character of members of the proletariat; they are all honourable, broad-minded and forgiving, simple and honest, loyal and truthful. A hero is described as noble in character and heroic in stature. With this in mind, we have a lead in our study of his Korean war heroes.[7]

Chastened by his experience in the purgatory of 1957, Pa Chin the doctrinaire became an enthusiastic propagandist. In his " Literature Should Run Ahead of the Time," which he wrote in 1960, he expressed joy at seeing the exuberant activity of production heroes who had offered all they had in the building of China; and he exhorted writers, the " engineers of human soul," to toil like any other worker in portraying the heroes in an image worthy of the brilliant stature of these new men. The success of new literature was assured under the intellectual banner of Chairman Mao. Then he went on repeating the Communist clichés: thought reform broadens one's horizon, and sharpens one's sense of urgency about the need for a correct world view. Without a correct world view, it is impossible to obtain mastery over the creative method in the portrayal of new men, the new life and new moral concepts. Neither will it be possible to understand what the main currents in this new life are. He believed that at the moment no writer in China was still reluctant to accept the world view of Marx and Lenin. But, he said, it is not an easy task for one to observe, experiment, study and analyse on the basis of that world view. In order to do these, one should first of all abandon completely one's bourgeois thinking. One must realise that there is still a great deal of this thinking in one's mind, and that it requires a constant effort to uproot it.

[6] Pa Chin, " T'an pieh yu yung hsin ' Wa-ti-shang te chan-i ' " *Ta Huan-le te Jih-tzu,* pp. 109–127.

[7] Concerning Lu Ling, Pa Chin wrote two articles: " T'an ' Wa-ti-shang te chan-i,' " PL, No. 70, 1955: " Tan pieh yu yung-hsin-te ' Wa-ti-shang te chan-i,' " *ibid.* Both are included in *Ta huan-le te Jih-tzu.*

Pa Chin also took part in denouncing the revisionists who believed in showing some defects in the image of the hero, in realistically exposing the darker sides of society, in the freedom of creative activity. We know the Communist answers to all these. Mao Tun before Pa Chin had already done the necessary executioner's job. Pa Chin's allegations here sound like an overplayed, worn-out record. He ultimately attributed the reason for their misconceived ideas to the presence in their consciousness of bourgeois thinking and their desire to distort fact in their attempt to attack Socialism. His defence against the accusation that under the present régime there is no freedom in creative activity is a fair example of his argument. Bourgeois writers alleged that there was no freedom in writing in Communist China, because Chinese writers did not write about flies and garbage. According to Pa Chin, it is precisely this absence of flies and garbage as subject-matter in the Chinese Communist writings that indicates the freedom to write what one wants to. They have the freedom to go anywhere to participate in the life of the people in every aspect of their struggle. The only freedom denied them is to spread rumours and to tell lies.[8] The Communist Party and the Chinese people not only allow them to write anything they want to, actually they encourage them and support them in their creative freedom. As participants in the people's work, what they describe is none other than their own life, the life they share in enjoyment with the characters they create. Through their writings they render service to China's Socialist construction, and foster Communism until it bursts into bloom in the hearts of the readers. This, Pa Chin said, is true freedom, a freedom which, not like that in a capitalist society where darkness and ugliness prevail, is all light and good.[9]

The most interesting part of the article is his self-criticism. It shows his uneasiness after the 1957 encounter and his eagerness to reform and conform. After exhorting " the engineers of human soul " not to fall behind the other workers in the building of new China, and emphasising the need of a correct world view, he subjects himself to a searching criticism. He deplored that he had written very little and that what he did write was poorly done. He was born and raised in a feudalistic family. The moment he got out of this family at the age of eighteen or nineteen, he stepped into a petty bourgeois intellectual circle. Years of living in such surroundings did not give him the courage and determination to strike out on a new path for himself. He read a great deal, not, however, to learn but to satisfy his curiosity. Without any guiding light, the reading did him little good. With all his effort to cast off the old pattern of thinking, he knew that his writings were still permeated by

[8] Pa Chin, " Sheng-huo-tsai Ying-hsiung-men Chung-chien," PL, No. 36, 1952.
[9] *Ibid.*

the old poison without his realising it. He is often criticised for not showing any new path to his reader. His explanation: "In my novels I fail to point out a way for my reader, and this is because at the time of writing I myself had not found a way." The apology he offered for his melancholy mood should be particularly satisfying to the Communists. He said,

> At that time, though I never laid down my pen, I did not have a mind which was scientifically trained, nor did I have any practical experience in revolution; furthermore, I did not have a correct world view, and I had always been separated from the people. All I had was a youthful sense of justice and a pen soaked in passion. I found no way out in my life, neither did I find any way out in my works. Wholeheartedly I sought for light; but in the old society all I found was a profound darkness.[10]

If we remember that in 1948 Pa Chin had already adopted those points which he said he lacked in 1957, we shall realise how non-Communists must have been constantly plagued by the feeling that they were always walking the tightrope, not knowing when they would fall because of the unexpected resurgence of old patterns of thought.

He considers himself more fortunate than many others who did not live to see the triumphant arrival of the new China. The pen which he used to paint misery and suffering may now be used to depict the people's victory and happiness. He said,

> Although I have written little during these years, I have put some of my new feelings on record. In the general happiness of the people of China I have found my own happiness. I shall never forget that particular day: the first day of October, 1949. On that day many comrades and I were present on top of T'ien An Men, listening to Chairman Mao who proclaimed with dignity the establishment of the Chinese People's Republic. As I watched those countless hands wave excitedly in that vast square and the red flags without number fluttering in the wind and listened to the fervent shout of joy, I felt my heart was jumping out of my breast. Only those writers who have suffered long and been deprived of freedom can understand how I felt. It was the first time I ever saw so clearly spread out before my eyes China's bright future aglow and in full bloom. On that day for six continuous hours we hailed with you "Long live Chairman Mao," and for six continuous hours rang back the clear voice of Chairman Mao, "Long live Comrades!" These joyous cries are still ringing in my ears encouraging me at every step I take in my advance.[11]

Yes, only those who have long suffered can understand the unrestrained joyous emotional outburst accompanying the realisation of a dream held in check for as long as one can remember by formidable forces which

[10] Pa Chin, "Wen-hsueh yao P'ao-tao Shih-tai-te Ch'ien-t'ou," *Wen-yi Pao,* No. 269, 1960.
[11] *Ibid.*

had seemed eternal and immutable. In 1955 Pa Chin contrasted the glorious present with the dark past which was punctuated by a series of outrageous and ruthless acts committed by both the imperialist powers and the old régime. His list contains the police of the Shanghai foreign Municipal Government opening fire on helpless people in Nanking Road in 1925, the purge of Communists by the KMT in 1927, Japanese shelling of common people's dwellings in Shanghai in 1932, and their levelling of Chapei in Shanghai in 1937. He also remembered the insults and indignities the helpless Chinese had suffered at the hands of both their own people and foreigners. Then he asked: Is it possible that people who have suffered these and many other indignities could ever dream of a day such as today? Today, he said, a new China had come into existence with a future as glorious as the Chinese wished to make it; today with the conclusion of the first Five Year Plan the state had achieved numerous triumphs; as a result one found the sandy land of days of yore turned into ten thousand *ching* of fertile land, checkered by irrigation canals and framed in rows of willow trees, symbolising the success of industrialisation, a success made possible only by the whole-hearted contribution of all the people.[12] Enthusiasm such as this has become part and parcel of Pa Chin's emotional life.

Pa Chin's literary career during the first years of the Chinese People's Republic consisted of a number of journalistic reports about the Korean front. In his "Chung-hsin ti chu-ho" ("Congratulations from the depth of my heart")[13] he gave an account of his thoughts and feelings during his visits in Korea. For many years, he told us, he had been learning how to observe and how to experience life; for many years he had thirsted to know the people, especially the new people. His visits to the Korean front gave him the opportunity to do so. The image one formed of the heroes from actual participation in their life was vastly different from the image he conjured up without the benefit of actual experience. While in Korea he was given every chance and assistance to observe and live with the volunteers in all aspects of their life. He became acquainted with their battle experiences, their ideas, their feelings and aspirations. To them he reported the progress China had made in her construction. Living among them, listening to their stories, stories of stoic fortitude and unbelievable heroism, he achieved a sense of comradeship, a feeling of belonging. "We are all members of the same family." Wherever he went he met with people who lived by the principle: "One man suffers to make the thousand enjoy happiness." Their unselfishness and patriotism obviously moved him deeply. "Every day I felt some motivating force pushing me, a

[12] Pa Chin, "Ta huan-le te Jih-tzu," *Ta Huan-le te Jih-tzu,* pp. 109–127.
[13] Pa Chin, "Chung-hsin te chu-he," PL, No. 49, November 1953.

feeling driving me, a kind of love that burned in my heart." Thus he felt that he had to express these feelings in order to regain peace of mind. At a moment like this, he began to write.

The stories he wrote in this period may be considered his worst. We may recall the revisionists trying to make the point that to tell a writer what to write is to make a liar out of him. With all Mao Tun's effort to prove otherwise, Pa Chin serves unwittingly as a forceful case in support of it. In his zeal and enthusiasm to portray Korean war heroes in their perfection, he tells us some fantastic tales, which nobody in his right mind could take seriously. His portrayal of the warriors is a monotonous catalogue of manly virtues and his accounts of Korean women and children read like chronicles of angels, completely devoted to the volunteers. War prisoners taken by the north enjoyed club privileges, playing games and attended by waiters liveried in white; while down south prisoners were treated like animals. The following are some of Pa Chin's tales. In support of the accusation of American germ warfare, he said:

> We saw with our own eyes how the American imperialists spread poison and dark design over Korea. At seventeen degrees below zero we saw germ-carrying flies lay eggs on the snow; we saw piles of dead fishes dropped on mountains; we saw thousands of fleas caught from the land covered with snow; we saw dead rats infected with plague; and we also saw germ containers of all shapes and forms dropped from American planes. . . . There were also leaves covered with germs wrapped in gauze, poison-infected crows and magpies, germ-carrying flies, mosquitoes, pork, foxes, and other strange things unrecognisable to us.[14]

Of all his stories, that of Chang Wei-liang is perhaps the most fantastic. Chang, a reformed peasant, was blown up by an enemy mine while performing his duty; both his left arm and left leg were seriously wounded.

> He looked at his left leg. The wound had been dressed. His torn uniform was bloodstained. His wound hurt terribly. Now he recalled how he dressed his own wound. He was trying to pull a handkerchief from his pants' pocket. It was in the left pocket. He made an effort to pull it out. Along with it came a piece of broken pelvis bone about two inches long. When he saw the blood-covered bone, his heart froze. He thought, "I am through." He hesitated only for a moment, and immediately pushed the bone back in place, in spite of the pain. Then he applied first-aid and dressed the wound.

He crawled ten days and nine nights back to his camp, without food and water. During that long ordeal, he crawled through the enemy's fire and got out of range, crawled under barbed-wire fences, using

[14] Pa Chin, "Sheng-huo tsai Ying-hsiung-men te Chung-chien," PL, No. 36, 1952.

his teeth to cut the wire, pulled out the ignition mechanism from three mines with his teeth, and used three branches to form a raft to carry himself across a brook, with his left hand and left arm on it and his right arm and leg used as paddles. Meanwhile, his wound had got worse, and pus started to flow. Flies covered his body and there were maggots everywhere. His source of inspiration was his loyalty to Chairman Mao, to his country and to his people.[15]

The story of Huang Wen-yuan is a little less fantastic, but not more likely. Huang was on a surprise attack mission with a few of his comrades. His clothes caught fire from enemy fire. Fearing to betray their position and thus cause their mission to fail, he remained rigid and endured stoically, allowing the fire to burn him to death without making a move. His last words to his comrades: "For my country I have given my all. I am unable now to complete the mission my superiors have entrusted to me. Take my weapons and fulfil the mission."[16] His devotion and source of inspiration was again Chairman Mao.

The story of Ts'ai Chin-t'ung expresses similar unlikely stoicism. One day performing his duty as sentry, he singlehandedly disposed of scores of enemy soldiers attacking his position. His left wrist was broken; his forehead, his right leg, and his stomach were all hit by bullets. Part of his intestine had been torn out. Grinding his teeth in pain, he pushed in the intestine, and brought his broken left wrist over and put it on the wounded stomach. In this condition, sometimes crawling and sometimes walking on his knees, he managed to cover a few miles, crossing a river on his way, to reach his camp.[17]

All his heroes are patriotic, brave, stoic, noble in character, always thinking of others, of their country, and of course, of Chairman Mao, and never for a moment giving a thought to themselves. Even members of their families were always confident of their victory, and prepared to accept whatever happened in the cause of the state. Their letters to their sons and brothers in Korea were always full of encouragement and optimism, urging them to put their country and people first; no private feelings ever found their way into these letters.

As one looks at Pa Chin's portraits of the Korean heroes one cannot help but wonder if he was not ridiculing them under the guise of cajolery. On second thought this does not seem likely, unless Pa Chin is completely unaware of the Communist inability to tolerate satire. From the strong feelings he expressed on National Days, feelings which were most truly genuine, we have no reason to believe that he was not sincere in his portrayal. The only explanation we can offer is that he

15 Pa Chin, *Ying-hsiung te Ku-shih* (Shanghai: 1953), pp. 12–51.
16 Pa Chin, "Huang Wen-yuan T'ung-chih," PL, Nos. 45–46, August 1953. The story is also included in the *Ying-hsiung te Ku-shih*.
17 *Ying-hsiung te Ku-shih*, p. 65.

was working under strain, with the Communist directives acting as constant reminders of what he should write. It is even possible that he was truly sincere in what he wrote, a natural result of an unnatural and deranged mind. Not that I consider Pa Chin's mind particularly deranged.[18]

Few works Pa Chin wrote in later days during the first years of the Communist régime can be described as literary. A few short pieces by him were published in the novel section of *People's Literature*. Two deserve our attention: " Huo-ming-ts'ao," (" Life-giving Herb "),[19] and " Ming-chu ho Yü-chi." [20]

" Huo-ming-ts'ao " and " Ming-chu ho Yü-chi " are really one story in two parts about two children brought together by the Korean war. Chin Ming-chu's father was killed in battle while his mother was wounded during a raid. P'o Yü-chi's father was taken captive, and her mother lost her life in an air raid. The author, quartered in the house of Ming-chu, was deeply drawn to him and his little friend Yü-chi. He watched them dance and play and listened to their songs, enjoying their love and confidence, which every volunteer uncle inspired in the hearts of every woman and child in Korea. In their conversation the author found out the story of sadness that darkened their innocent young lives. He also watched sadly their innocent quarrel over the fate of Yü-chi's father; Ming-chu, wishing him dead because a captive could live only if he was willing to be the enemy's running dog and death would vindicate him; and Yü-chi, hoping with all her innocent heart that her father was still alive. To resolve this situation, the author offered to tell them a story.

Two children, Chang and Li, set out in search of sunlight to escape the deprivation heaped upon them by landlords and government clerks. They had often dreamed of a land free from landlords and free from government clerks, a land where

> mountains are covered with beautiful flowers and everywhere is filled with songs of joy; a land where the sun will not set and the barns are always full; a land where everyone has a clean roof over his head and every child goes to school to study. And where each face shines with smiles of happiness. . .[21]

They met with all sorts of difficulties on their way, but never for a moment did they lose heart. Then one day Li fell and hurt himself and was about to die. Chang was told that on the mountain top there was some herb which had the power to revive the dead.

18 We are told that writers who came back from the Korea front were kept for two months in a camp in Tientsin where they were thoroughly briefed as to what and how to report to the people.
19 Pa Chin, " Huo-ming-ts'ao," PL, No. 80, 1956.
20 *Ibid.*
21 Pa Chin, " Ming-chu ho Yü-chi," PL, No. 85, 1956.

> If he transplanted it and fed it with his own blood and waited until its leaves turned red from blue and then pounded them into pulp and placed the pulp in the mouth of the dead, the dead will become alive again.[22]

Chang did what he was told, watering the plant with his own blood which flowed from a hole he bored in his leg. When Li woke up from his coma, he found Chang lying by his side, ghostly white from bleeding.

The second story, "Ming-chu ho Yü-chi," took place during his second visit to Korea, about half a month after the signing of the truce. We find Ming-chu and Yü-chi about to be separated as the war ended. In the narrative, apart from an occasional mention of war brutalities, the war has receded into the background. Yü-chi had hoped to become a dancer when she grew up; but, according to Ming-chu, she had to give up that hope, because her left foot had been hurt during a raid. Yü-chi, however, was still confident of her future. To show that she was right, she joined a group of children in their dance, only to fall down in the middle of it, subtly suggesting that a young hope had been dashed to pieces as a casualty of the war.

Their conversation inevitably turned to their impending separation. To console them, the author told them another story about two friends who, forced by circumstances, became separated. Wang fell in love with a daughter of a parvenu. Conscious of his newly gained status, the girl's father interfered and forced his daughter to marry into a rich family. Unable to remain in the familiar surroundings without being constantly reminded of his sorrow, he decided to leave the locality. His friend Chou told him at the moment of his departure:

> "We shall meet again. Let's agree that ten years from now we shall meet at the head of the River Yü in the capital." Then Chou added, "If we are married and have children, let us bring them too."[23]

At the appointed hour, Chou, who was married and had one son and one daughter, came to keep his appointment, although his wife tried to dissuade him. But Chou was certain that Wang would not fail him. They were at the head of the River Yü at the appointed time, which was twelve noon. There was no Wang. But about ten minutes or so later, a boy approached him and inquired if he were Chou and handed him a telegram, addressed to Chou to be delivered to the head of the River Yü on a certain day and at a certain hour. The telegram said, "I am sick in a certain hospital in a certain city. Sorry for not being able to meet you at the appointed hour."

22 *Ibid.*
23 *Ibid.*

These two stories are undoubtedly much superior to anything Pa Chin wrote about the Korean front. Wang's tragedy has always been one of Pa Chin's constant themes. There is no laborious effort to impress people with what he has to say, and the atmosphere of the stories is infinitely more peaceful and calm. Even the propaganda elements—the utopia, the Sun, the turning from blue to red, the feeding of the life-giving herb with blood, selfless sacrifice, while still not very subtle, are vastly more refined than hailing Chairman Mao and the Party in undisguised barbarousness. The style is simple and the language unburdened with the exaggeration that marks his Korean narratives. The war remains only in the background, and life has assumed its normal pace, enlivened by children's songs and dance. There is no further need of grandiloquence in the portrayal of simple country life. The author himself seems to have regained some of his former humanitarian sentiment. The themes of childish love and friendship have a restorative effect on the spirit after one has plowed through so many variations of heroism, bravery, loyalty, and sense of responsibility.

In 1961 he wrote " Chün-chang ti Hsin " (" The Heart of the Army Corps Commander "). In this story, Pa Chin tried to depict the intangible feelings and thoughts of the commander as well as his external exploits. He is successful in bringing the commander's mind into relief without saying too much about it. But in every other respect, it is as dull and true to the Communist form as his other war propaganda stories.

In 1958 Pa Chin made up a plan according to which he was going to write. Not many creative works have come of it. [Mao Tun had a good excuse for not writing.] What does Pa Chin have? But the answer to this question may be irrelevant. Excuse or no excuse, both Mao Tun and Pa Chin could have the same reason for not writing creatively. [Mao Tun has found his calling.] Pa Chin, too, perhaps, has found his—an enthusiastic propagandist.

A further and more cogent reason was revealed in the May 1962 issue of *Shanghai Wen-hsueh,* where Pa Chin came out very strongly against the interference in literary activity of small groups of people who, according to him, turned up from nowhere the moment anyone opened his mouth or picked up his pen, with a hoop in one hand and a club in the other, the hoop to trap people with and the club to hit them on the head with. Because of this interference, fear was generated in the minds of many writers, including himself. He deplored the fact that he had not written much, but at the same time he felt uneasy in realising that he actually felt fortunate in not having written much. Like so many other writers, his main concern was not what he could achieve, but how to avoid faults. This fear of exposing oneself to the fault finders paralysed all creative impulse and forced all writers to act cautiously. He then urged his fellow writers to gather enough courage to throw off this fear in order to write creatively. In an apparently sincere and serious tone, he declared: "I must do some serious writing and attach importance to writers' courage and sense of responsibility. . . . Writers of new China in particular, should be concerned with more important things than merely avoiding faults."

Pa Chin brought the article to an end by an eulogy to Mao Tse-tung's literary views, and expressed the feeling that lacking courage and a sense of responsibility was an indication of one's failure to follow Chairman Mao's direction.

Shen Ts'ung-wen, the Escapist

Shen Ts'ung-wen, one of the best writers in modern China, had virtually ceased to write under the Communist régime. To his bewilderment he, who had come from a farmer's family and in all his writings had shown an intense interest in the life of the people closest to the grass roots, was singled out for attack by the Communists, while many others whom he knew to have more reason to be against Communism were basking in glory as members of the supposed coalition government. It is true that he he had not shown any very great sympathy for Communism, but neither had he written anything that would endear him to the old régime. As a matter of fact, some of his writings during the war were not allowed to see the light of day. He could not understand why the Communist régime, among whose literary figures were Ting Ling, his friend, and Ho Ch'i-fang, his pupil, would not tell him what to do. Instead, they used threat and intimidation, under the strain of which he became a nervous wreck. At one time he even attempted suicide.

Without being informed, he was dropped from Peking University, where he was professor of Chinese literature, and was made a copyist in the Palace Museum. At first he resisted the effort to make him confess; he also refused to attend thought reform class either at the North China University or the Revolutionary University. But no Maginot can withstand for ever the relentlessly persistent attack from all possible avenues; we find him in 1950 submitting to the Revolutionary University, ready to have his thought reformed. According to Mah Feng-hua's observation, he did not appear greatly changed.

In 1956 he was reported to have written his confession in which he acknowledged that he had made no contribution to Communism and in thought and temperament he tended toward liberalism, and that he believed that the thought reform would not do him much good, because he was too far off the standard set by Mao Tse-tung for the intellectuals.[24]

His work in the Palace Museum must have offered him just the kind of reprieve that kept him sane. It is not likely that he could escape political involvements completely, but there must have been moments when he experienced the same thought and sentiments which characterised the intellectuals during the Wei and Chin dynasties. While those intellectuals indulged in wine and metaphysical talks, Shen lost himself among the treasures that took hundreds of years and the resources of dynasties to accumulate. The Palace Museum is indeed a wonderland for an escapist who would like to become oblivious to the cold world around. We find him working hard and earnestly at compiling a history of Chinese ceramics and Chinese textile designs. In 1957 a beautiful volume on Chinese textiles came out with Shen as its chief editor.[25]

After seven years of watching, the Communists must have discovered that gentle Mr. Shen, whom Kuo Mo-jo had previously characterised as " Fen-hung se ti tso-chia " (Pink writer; " Pink " in the sense of " romantic "), could not have done any harm to the Communist cause. In 1957 he was reported to be a member of the Chinese Writers' Union That year also saw the publication of a volume of Shen's selected works.[26] The importance of this event cannot be minimised, even though the selection was obviously made under restrictions. It means that the Communist régime again found Shen to be of some value to them, and if he continued to be gentle, he would be allowed to do what he could best do. It is indeed a great tribute to Shen Ts'ung-wen that he could remain calm and serene at a moment like this. He did not burst forth with any grandiloquence in gratitude and praise of the great bounties of the régime. Even in the preface to his selected works he was timid and reserved. He passed in brief review not only the development of his own literary career, but also the development of modern Chinese literature with some of its weaknesses. After the May Fourth movement, he said, too few writers realised the political function of literature and so there was no one who could give literary activity the right kind of leadership in co-ordinating it with social movements.

He recalled how difficult it was for him, with all his knowledge of the classical literature, even to find a job to support himself. Fortunately from life he had learned " not to lose heart in the face of any

[24] Mah Feng-hua, " Huai-nien Shen Ts'ung-wen Chiao-shou," *Tzu-yu Chung-kuo, XVI*, No. 3, February 1957. This is a moving eye-witness account of Shen's life during the first years of the Communist régime, the basis of my account given here.

[25] Shen Ts'ung-wen, Wang Chia-shu (ed.), *Chung-kuo Ssu-ch'ou T'u-an* (*Chinese Textile Designs*) (Peking: 1957).

[26] Shen Ts'ung-wen, *Shen Ts'ung-wen Hsiao-shuo Hsuan-chi* (Peking: 1957).

difficulties, and never to feel concerned." [27] And then almost casually he said, "With similar attitude, I took care of *hsueh-hsi* (study) the year before last under the most trying and painful circumstances." [28]

The following may sound like self-criticism; but a careful reader cannot fail to see that sense of pride and dignity between the lines.

> . . . Some part of my language is uncouth, and the other part shows a mixture of the vernacular and the classical. In my stories facts are mixed with emotional and imaginary elements. Such a lack of purity and simplicity is due to my experiment of student exercises. The range covered under my pen is rather broad; but the subject-matter I know best is still my homeland watered by one thousand *li* of the Yuan River, the people and events in the districts and villages along the bank of the river. Their love and hate, sorrow and joy, the way of life and pattern of feelings, all have their distinct quality. As I was born and raised in such surroundings, my life is inseparable from them. During the last twenty years China has gone through a most trying ordeal, a period in which radical changes have taken place. Many of my former Peking friends and my colleagues in schools have been victims of the revolutionary and resistance wars. Many others either died a natural death or have had other plans. By nature I am obstinate and conservative. For over twenty years, my main activity has been short story writing. . . . On the one hand the changes taking place in our society are so fast and radical, and on the other hand the pattern of my life is so narrow and devoid of change, not to speak of my conservative and obstinate thought, that it is natural that my work should fall behind social reality. Like a student in a school, I should be detained in my class for ever.
>
> Even during the eight years of the war of resistance, I did not write anything of value. When the great social change took place and all people were liberated. I who had already been out of step with the needs of the old reality was, as could be expected, unable to follow. Thus I stopped writing and it has remained so for eight years. Because of my change of calling all day long I spend my time among thousands of textiles, ceramic pieces, lacquer work, jade and artistic designs. This new task which I have just learned deals mostly with the history of our material civilisation, and its function is to serve the needs of the people's production. The deeper I get into the field, the more I feel my inadequacy. In a situation such as this, my friends may still remember what I wrote, but I have almost completely forgotten them.[29]

Only in passing did he say "Our country under the correct and firm guidance of the great Communist Party, and through the effort of millions and millions of people has assumed a new appearance." And he hoped that in the future he could renew his literary effort to sing praise to the great achievements of New China.

27 *Ibid.*, "Preface," p. 3.
28 *Ibid.*
29 *Ibid.* pp. 4–5.

As time passes, we find Shen freer in his praise of the Communist régime. Not that he wrote much like Pa Chin, but the little he did write bore witness to this statement. In 1959 in memory of Chin I he wrote:

> After the liberation of all China and the establishment of the people's government, our state entered into a new age in history, and literature and art also entered into a new age in history. In order for the principles pointed out to us by Chairman Mao in his talk at Yenan to be realised, literature and art should be oriented toward serving the political interests of the workers, the farmers, and the soldiers and the proletariat. All artists and writers in the nation have enthusiastically responded to the great call, courageously throwing themselves into the great furnace of the revolution, taking part in land reform, three- and five-anti campaigns, resist-America and help-Korea campaign, thought reform, and the anti-rightist campaign.[30]

Even these words of praise do not tell us very much about the inner feelings of Shen Ts'ung-wen. In 1959 these expressions had become worn-out clichés, vastly different from the same kind of expressions used by Pa Chin in the first years of the new régime. In the case of Pa Chin, there is ample reason to believe that he was genuinely enthusiastic; in the case of Shen, all we can assume is that the phrases have become a manner of routine expression, not intended to carry any genuine emotions.

[In discussing Mao Tun we have observed the resurgence of classical literature, both in thought-content and form, of which the supreme example was set by Mao Tse-tung's poetry.] Shen Ts'ung-wen must have welcomed this as another easy route of escape. His interest in material civilisation, aroused while working in the Palace Museum together with his love for classical literature, produces in him a desire to bring written literature and artifacts and physical objects unearthed through archaeological excavation together for mutual validation. In 1961 we find him discussing with profound classical scholarship the problems involved in bringing the two together.[31] In this article not only the subject-matter is classical, even the language used is dominated by classical elements. On October 21 and 24, appeared another article about " The Beard," criticising Wang Li's article " Lo-chi yü yü-yen? " (" Logic and Language ") in which Professor Wang discussed the history of the beard. Shen pointed out that Wang was not accurate in his interpretation of some ancient texts, and his conclusion was therefore not warranted. He suggested that if the concrete physical objects and

[30] Shen Ts'ung-wen, " Tao Chin-i," PL, No. 121, 1959.

[31] Shen Ts'ung-wen, " Ts'ung ' Pu-p'a-kuei te ku-shih ' chu T'an tao Wen-hsien yü Wen-wu Hsiang-chieh-ho Wen-t'i " (" From the commentary to ' Stories about not fearing Ghosts ' to the Problem of Uniting Literature and Artifacts "), in the " Wen-hsueh Yi-ch'an (" Literary Heritage ") section in the *Kuang-ming Daily*, June 18, 1961, p. 4.

artifacts had been used to check against the written records, mistakes like these could have been eliminated.[32]

At the end of 1961, as a member of the Chinese Writers' Union, he was sent on a mission to various points of interest in the nation. Whatever the purpose of the tour it could not be anything but political. At Chiang-kang-shan, the cradle of Communism where a famous battle was fought, he composed two poems in the old classical five-word-line form. In the first poem he recalled the " Peach Garden " utopian seclusion of the place implying that the existing government was then as ruthless as the Ch'in. He told us how he shared the simple difficult life of the rustics and in reading again Tu Fu's poetry experienced the same kind of frustration that that great poet experienced several thousand years before. Then came the great revolution, which engulfed Ching-kang-shan in its path. The Red Army, champions of the people, won their hearts during their short stay. Now that the ruthless Ch'in had been destroyed, all people, old and young, are enjoying their life of happiness and satisfaction.

> It's the end of the year when I come
> With a heart as warm as spring.
> Moved deeply by the relics of old,
> I sing praise to the new.
> Government is for the people,
> Directives are to be found in Mao's works.[33]

The political tone is just as strong and obvious in the second poem. This is what one would expect. But the emphasis on the need to absorb the old heritage affords him an escape route even where political interest is the strongest. He expresses those political ideas in an old form, a form which lends its hoary nature and hence some dignity even to a theme as unpromising as glorifying the Red Army.

In the same issue of the *Jen-min Wen-hsueh* are three other poems in the same classical form, with, however, themes which can be only distantly related to the present, and then, only in a general way. In " Hsia-shan hui Nanchang t'u-chung " (" On my way back to Nanchang from Ching-kang-shan "), his journey reminded him of Wang Ts'an's " Teng-lou fu " and Tu Fu's " Pei-cheng." The floating clouds and geese migrating south called up Wang Po's " T'eng-wang-ko hsu." True he touched on the great success of the communes; but if all reports about the communes are not entirely false, and he must have seen the result, his feelings could not have been very sincere, for in his concluding stanza we find him thinking of Po Chü-i, Ou-yang Hsiu and Wen

[32] Shen Ts'ung-wen, " Ts'ung Wen-wu T'an Ku-jen te Hu-tzu Wen-t'i " (" Discussion of the Problem of the Beard of the Ancients on the Basis of Actual Objects "), *Kuang-ming Daily*, October 21, 1961, p. 4 and October 24, 1961, p. 4.

[33] Shen Ts'ung-wen, " Ching-kang-shan Ch'ing-ch'en," PL, February 1962.

T'ien-hsiang, none of whom is closely related to the Communists. Chü-i's poetry may have suggested a concern about the welfare of the people; but by implication, he would be censuring the present régime, and his poetry would have to be interpreted as a satire, which no one in his mind would think of using against the reigning Communist power. However, it is not entirely impossible that Shen did mean his poetry to be a satire. He might have learned of the stupidity of Communist censors whose sensibility was not too subtle. We are told that Chou Li-po, a prize-winning author, got away with his damaging remarks against Communism in his *Shan-hsiang Chü-pien* (*Great Changes in a Mountain Village*). At any rate his next poem had again to do with Po Chü-i, and he also refers to T'ao Yuan-ming. The last two lines:

> In their poetry they show love for the people,
> And in the people's heart they are deeply enshrined.

may again be read as a satire against the powers that be.

In form Shen comes very close to Tu Fu in style, with some elements of the vernacular language of the country folk, which Tu would not have objected to. Apparently he has mastered the prosody as well as the language. In Shen we may have lost an excellent short story writer, but we have in the process found a poet and scholar, an exchange that need not be a loss to the world of letters.

In portraying [Mao Tun], Pa Chin and Sheng Ts'ung-wen as [Doctrinaire], Enthusiast and Escapist I may have done injustice to all of them. This, however, I shall leave to the reader to judge. To me they offer a picture, though of necessity an incomplete one, of what one can expect under the Communist literary dictatorship.

Heroes and Hero-Worship in Chinese Communist Fiction *

By T. A. HSIA

I

A READER in the United States of America or Great Britain may have great misgivings when he opens a book of fiction from Communist China. He is painfully aware of the conditions under which the book is written. He knows that thought control in Communist China means not only a set of taboos but also a strict order to write about certain subjects in a certain manner. With little effort he can guess the plot which rushes on to actual victory or victory imagined. And there is the other side to the " struggle," which is always wrong and bad and doomed. He knows what characters he is going to encounter: the familiar ugly face of a landlord, the aspiring workers, peasants, and intellectuals who unite to follow the leadership of the Communist Party, and the waverers who somehow have to make a choice between the good and the evil—shadows of the types which, he remembers, dominated proletarian literature in the 1930s. Oversimplification is always an insult to intellect; and the insult becomes all the more unbearable if things are simplified not merely because of the writer's ignorance but, as the reader suspects, from an intention to deceive. Of course, the reader does not have to suffer all this if he can help it. But the book in his hand may be useful as source material for some kind of research, a social document or a storehouse of Communist jargon. So in the name of research, he doggedly reads on, with little expectation of pleasure or stimulus for thought. He is prepared to be insulted and to be bored to death.

Such apprehension was my own experience when I began to read some of the better advertised Communist fiction. I cannot boast that I am an unbiased reader, since my feelings are not at all favourable to the Communist régime. I used to think that literature in Communist China had died with Hu Feng, the last man under the régime who had something sensible to say about literature and the courage to say it. Now with Hu Feng and his " clique " smashed like a gang of criminals, and especially after the withering of the " hundred flowers " in 1957,

* This article was written while I was working as a member of the Modern Chinese History Project of the University of Washington.

I never suspected that anything worth reading would come out of Communist China except, of course, materials for the use of research.

My fears are confirmed in numerous instances where wooden characters talk jargon in a series of roughly sketched struggles set to the ideological pattern. It is sickening, too, to see that the three entities—the masses, the Communist Party, and Mao Tse-tung are so often confused. But now and then, I must confess, I have been attracted to things which I never expected to be there : a characterisation with some traits not prescribed by ideology, an ambiguous situation that permits a non-Communist interpretation, and the narration of an incident sustained not so much by the weight of dogma as by the force of dramatisation. What fascinates me particularly are the terrible truths about the Communists themselves, truths usually disassociated from Communist literature, but which are now told in an oblique way, and quite honestly, too, by some Communist writers. So, to my great surprise, I have discovered that there are novels from Communist China that make interesting reading.

It should be noted that some of the novels are also remarkable from a technical point of view. Superficially the reader might get the impression that technical proficiency has little to do with ideology or that it may be even used to embellish ideology. There are perhaps novels which are ideologically "correct" but technically brilliant. But such an impression is wrong, for the art of fiction is not compatible with ideology. Where ideology restricts, art frees; where ideology generalises, art discriminates; where ideology simplifies, art complicates; where ideology lies, art tells the truth. The real hero in Chinese Communist fiction today is the novelist himself who asserts his individuality not by an open revolt against ideology, but by his devotion, even in his limited way, to art. He who tries to sell art to ideology is attempting the impossible. It can only result in the weakening of ideology.

Mr. William Empson's remark about proletarian art is pertinent here. "To produce pure proletarian art the artist must be at one with the worker; this is impossible, not for political reasons, but because the artist is never at one with any public."[1] Or, in a word, pure proletarian art is either non-existent or not art.

Of course, a person can refuse to be an artist and he can still serve some cause. The Communist propagandist, for instance, enjoys the notorious liberty to ignore art, though he, too, writes. He can concern himself solely with how people *should* talk, act and think according to their "classes" in their society. But the moment he takes the trouble to study how they *do* talk, act and think, he is studying life

[1] William Empson, *Some Versions of Pastoral* (Norfolk, Connecticut: New Directions, 1960), p. 15.

and life is always bigger than ideology. There are an unlimited number of people, things, events and relations that contradict ideology or that ideology simply does not account for. When a writer persists in reducing his personal study of life to words, he is deviating from ideology. Apparently he is dealing with mere technical problems of writing, but actually he is struggling with the eternal problem of the relation between life and art. Inevitably, though perhaps only dimly, he will also see where the Communist Party and its ideology belong in this great world. A story-teller in Communist China who begins with a dissatisfaction with the run-of-the-mill work of his colleagues, or with his own earlier works, may be tempted by the ambition to tell his story well, to give a more " lifelike " reproduction of people and action as he sees them. But he will then be vexed by the complexity and subtlety in life which, as a mere propagandist, he does not have to bother about. He can still surrender himself to ideology and content himself with a bad novel. But if he wants to write a good novel, within the limits of his freedom of expression and the limits of his talent, he will end in venturing into grounds where he is responsible only to himself. His narration which, by the force of political reality, has to satisfy the demands of ideology, but which, owing to his ambition, has now also to satisfy the demands of art, will eventually burst out of the bounds of the formula within which he would otherwise live happily. He has swallowed a monster, which is art. His book will be kicking with a life beyond the control of ideology.

It seems that not all the powers of censorship can repair the spot where the seam bursts or kill the life in a novel. Many a novel has been published which is not completely in conformity with ideology. It may even provoke thoughts that are dangerous to the Communist régime. But do not think that censorship has relaxed in Communist China or that another " hundred flowers " movement is really under way. The truth is that there is a domain over which censorship is powerless: the domain of mute, individual criticism. Reading, like writing, is an individual affair. To some extent each reader can form his own judgment about a book. A totalitarian government can force him to read a book, but it cannot make him accept it. Or he may accept it for reasons of his own which may be entirely different from the official ones. No censorship is yet so equipped as to determine how many levels of meaning a novel may possibly have. In Communist fiction, ideology supplies the outline for the struggle and the victory; it also forms the substance of the speech made by " model characters." But a novel is supported by a large number of details. Some of the details do fit into the ideology, but some others do not. These details, we may guess, come from the author's personal observation of life.

Not only the details have their meaning, but they may form into a pattern or patterns and thus acquire another meaning. So the more abundant and more lifelike are the details found in a novel, and the greater their variety, the richer is the meaning which the book yields. Unlike a slogan, a song or a polemical essay, where meaning can be kept clear and simple, a novel is not a sure tool for propaganda. Not even the novelist himself is always aware what profundity he has touched or what dangerous thoughts he has aroused, if he ever tries to portray life as he personally sees it. Superficially, he still speaks for Communism, but each little detail in his book may become an ironical comment on the general theme. And the accumulation of such details may defeat his purpose entirely.

Take, for example, the two books by Chou Li-po,[2] *Hurricane* (1949) and *Great Changes in a Mountain Village* (1958).[3] Both of them have received high praise from the Communist press, but their full significance is yet to be explored by a non-Communist critic. Both are stories from " their " side about the Communists' control of the peasants, but few books on the same subject from " our " side can match these in the depth of understanding and the stark truth about the terror of the Communist system. *Hurricane,* which won a Stalin Prize in 1952, is divided into two parts. The loosely constructed second part, about the mopping-up operation of the " land reform " movement is not so interesting as the first which concerns the destruction of a " local despot " (bad landlord). From the very beginning, the landlord is at the mercy of the Communists who arrest him, put him up before a mass trial, and then release him. Then he is again arrested, again put on trial, and again set free. The Communists, who could stop this mental torture and dispose of him without too much ceremony, are postponing his death because they are creating a force aiming at the destruction of something much bigger than the life of a landlord : the basis of Chinese society. They are working hard to fan up mob fury which leads to the lynching of the man some 200 pages after his first arrest—200 pages of fast action, precise scheming and mounting tension. They revive old memories of hatred, spread gossip, put words into the peasants' mouths, give them a false image of themselves, encourage their hostility and subject them to regimentation. And they are doing all this with a self-assurance, cynicism, tenacity and persuasiveness which may be said to be diabolical. The evil deeds of the landlord in this

2 Chou Li-po was born in 1908 in Hunan. Further biographical information about him is found in " Editorial Notes," *Chinese Literature* (CL), No. 1, 1954, pp. 165–166. According to a Japanese source (*Gendai Chugoku Jimmei Jiten,* 1962), Chou Li-po joined the Chinese League of Left-wing Writers in 1934.

3 *Pao-feng Chou-yü* (*Hurricane*) (Peking: Hsin-hua Book Co., 1949), two vols. *Shan-hsiang Chü-pien* (*Great Changes in a Mountain Village*) (Peking: Tso-chia Ch'u-pan-she, 1958).

book belong largely to the past and are therefore retold, but what the Communists are doing in the name of revolution is dramatised. Since retelling is not so vivid as dramatisation, a thinking reader is left to draw his own conclusion about the Communist system while he is being told how urgently the elimination of the "bad landlord" is required.

The theme of *Great Changes in a Mountain Village* poses a more subtle problem for the novelist to solve: how to justify the Communist Party when the self-styled champion of the proletariat begins to expropriate the peasants. Here violence is out of place, since the struggle is no longer between the "revolutionary" and "counter-revolutionary." As the story opens, the landlord's rule has been overthrown and the current "mass movement" is about the establishment of the "co-operatives." The plot concerns the Party's effort to persuade the peasants to give up their land which will from now on be "collectivised." The "middle peasants," the richer survivors of the land reform movement, who are well aware of their insecurity under Communism, do not create so much trouble as is required by ideology. The trouble comes rather from the "poor peasants," who, now enjoying a higher social position because of their original proletarian status according to the official classification, use every possible means known to the rustics, short of an open clash with the Communists, in order to preserve what little was given to them only a few years earlier. So there begins their struggle, half-comic, half-pathetic, with the persuaders—the smiling but tough cadres and the loquacious activists. The Party's position is defended by jargon ("private ownership" v. "collective ownership") and promises of a happier future; it is also supported by the implied threat of the use of force. The threat is real, but the reasoning is false and feeble, so far as its function in the drama is concerned. The reader will remember how each of the peasants resists in his stupid and ineffectual way. Some perform moronic antics reminiscent of the fabulous Ah Q. The episode of one old peasant (Chap. 15: "Love for His Land") is particularly touching. Ch'en Hsien-chin, an experienced farmer, originally a "poor peasant," and brother to a Communist killed in the war, kneels down on what is still *his* land and sobs secretly when he realises that he has to give in.

The Party wins in the end, of course, but it is not clear how. On page 255, the villagers are still far from being convinced. A panic sets in on a night when they go out in mass, including the very old and the very young, to protect their trees from expropriation. They succeed in denuding the hills, as more than one thousand trees are cut down. Thus they suffer losses, but at least the trees won't go to the collective. Then, on page 270, only fifteen pages later, the co-operative is established, ostensibly with the consent of the majority. As a pure propagandist, Chou Li-po is hardly convincing with his hurried account of the transformation of the peasants' "political awareness," while he describes their resistance at greater length and with far more precision. But as a propagandist at war with the artist within him, he perhaps can do no more. An anti-Communist novelist would be tempted to put in a melodramatic scene of armed revolt; but the cruel fact of submission, so poignantly rendered by Chou Li-po, is a more powerful accusation of the terrible reality in Communist China. An equally important truth is that greed still rules the human heart where Communism rules the society. For among the peasants who grab as much as they can before they lose the collectivisable part of their property are also those who were once made to "struggle" against the landlord.

Anti-Communist novels can indeed be as silly as Communist novels. A story about the peasants' heroic revolt against the Communists does not necessarily tell so much about Communism or about human nature as do the two Communist novels I have just mentioned. No one has ever called Chou Li-po an anti-Communist, and probably he is not one. But of two things we are sure : first, he is a conscious artist (an example of his painstaking effort : the dialect he uses in the first book is a Manchurian variation of Mandarin which is very different from the Hunanese in the second); and, secondly, he has studied, with close observation and imaginative sympathy, life in Chinese villages under Communism. An honest account of the happenings he sees there can never square with ideology. Few writers are absoutely honest, but Chou Li-po has done a remarkably honest job, considering the conditions under which he lives and writes.

Leslie Fiedler's remark about "*No! In Thunder*" is meant for the writers in "our" kind of society. How true it is for the writers in the Communist society is yet to be proven by time :

> It has not always been necessary for the writer to be aware of his denial; his work will do it for him anyway, if it is honest work. Indeed, at certain periods in the past, it seemed almost better that the writer deceive himself as well as his contemporary audience about his intent: that Dickens, for example, believe himself to be glorifying the purity of woman and the simple heart of the child, while giving us in fact his mad, black-and-white nightmares, in which things live the life of men; and men perform with the lifeless rigidity of things. In the same way, Dostoevsky could think himself the apostle of a revived orthodoxy, and Samuel Richardson considered his essential task the defence of bourgeois virtue. . . .[4]

[4] Leslie A. Fiedler, *No! In Thunder* (Boston: Beacon Press, 1960), pp. 8–9.

Obviously, Chou Li-po lacks the intensity of Dickens, Dostoevsky or Richardson. His field of vision is diffused and fragmentary but it is gratifying to find a Communist writer with an individual vision. His study of the oppressed and bemused masses in *Great Changes in a Mountain Village* remains not an affirmation, but a denial of the Communist system. The outline of *Hurricane* fits facilely into the framework of class-struggle, but the sordid facts of the struggle point rather to the cruelty and falsehood inherent in the régime. The cruelty and falsehood are brought out with exceptional clarity in *Great Changes in a Mountain Village* where the peasants discover the truth about their new masters against whom, alas, they are now powerless. It is only to be regretted that they do not discover the truth about themselves.

II

I have paid my compliments to Chou Li-po because I want to demonstrate an observation that not all Chinese Communist novels are equally bad. Many are bad, some are less bad, and a few others, like the rare example of *Great Changes in a Mountain Village*, succeed in irony where they fail as propaganda. For the rest of the paper, I shall take up the subject of heroes and hero-worship as illustrated in the two novels *The Song of Youth*, by Yang Mo,[5] and *Red Sun*, by Wu Ch'iang.[6]

Before I go on with my discussion, it should be pointed out that heroes are not necessarily a prominent feature of every Chinese Communist novel. In *Hurricane*, for example, the "enemy" is so weak that he provides little opportunity for either the Communists, who are manipulators, or the activists, who are tools but who think they have become masters, to display their heroism. *Great Changes in a Mountain Village* is almost a novel without a hero, because here the oppressed peasants hold the stage, while the local cadres play the Western game of poker, crack jokes, take things easy, when there is no "mass movement" afoot, and occasionally strike a threatening attitude. The girl cadre "sent down" from above is merely efficient in her execution of the orders. Her only sacrifice seems to be her temporary separation from her lover for the sake of her duty to introduce "great changes" to the mountain village. She has a revolutionary

[5] Yang Mo, *Ch'ing-ch'un Chih Ko* (*The Song of Youth*) (Peking: Jen-min Wen-hsueh Ch'u-pan-she, Revised edition, 1960). I have not seen the unrevised edition which was probably published in 1957. A partial English translation of the novel is serialised in CL, Nos. 3–6. 1960.

[6] Wu Ch'iang, *Hung Jih* (*Red Sun*) (Peking: Jen-min Wen-hsueh Ch'u-pan-she. Revised edition, 1959). I have not seen the unrevised edition published in July 1957 by the China Ching-nien Ch'u-pan-she. *Red Sun* is available in an English version, translated by A. C. Barnes (Peking: Foreign Language Press, 1961).

past, but by 1955, when her story takes place, many revolutionaries have become bureaucrats.

In spite of their being weak in heroic themes, I hope my analysis of Chou Li-po's novels will be relevant to the following discussion if it has succeeded in elucidating certain ideas regarding the triple relations between life, art and ideology. The novels by Yang Mo and Wu Ch'iang are heavily peopled by characters whose hard and bitter struggles helped to spread the Communist revolution at the time referred to, in the 1930s and 1940s. They are the so-called heroes, to whom the Communist Party owes its victory. Characters like these did, in fact, exist, otherwise the Party could never have won so much ground. The type seems familiar. Unlike the muddle-headed peasants who annoy the régime, though a variety of them is exquisitely delineated in *Great Changes*, the hero has definite, bold qualities, well known to both author and writer. The creative job for the Communist novelist seems to be easy. With little thought he can fulfil his duty as a propagandist while creating a rather entertaining story of adventures and heroic deeds. In many respects, the Communist hero can even look like the hero in American Sunday comics: in his manly features and physique, his loyalty to his friends, his ferocity towards the enemy, his kindness to the weak, his coolness while facing danger, and his selfless bravery. In addition to these are the necessary qualities of a Communist: that he talk and act correctly according to ideology and that he must admit and correct errors if any are pointed out by a better comrade or by some member of "the masses." Again superior to his Western counterpart, the Communist hero is not a reckless lover. When he loves a girl he means it, though, of course, his true love is always the Party. With his disciplined manliness, he seldom falls into the clutches of a bad woman, about whom Communist fiction is generally reticent anyway.

The above generalisations apply to *The Song of Youth*, a "passionate" work, according to a review in *Chinese Literature*, an English magazine, published in Peking.

> Each time I open this novel, it starts a train of memories and carries me back to my young days. A number of the characters in *The Song of Youth* are strongly reminiscent of people I know, so that I seem to see their faces and hear their voices again, to witness again their stirring, heroic fights. . . .
>
> The central figure is the heroine, Lin Tao-ching, a typical character who reveals to us how the petty-bourgeois intellectuals of the thirties in China gradually turned towards revolution. Tao-ching's mother, the daughter of a farmhand, was raped by the landlord and then made his concubine, so though Tao-ching is brought up in the landlord's home she is ill-treated and despised. As she grows up she

enjoys no happiness and her step-mother tries to use her to win connections with powerful Kuomintang officials. . . .

The Communists in this novel—Lu Chia-chuan (Lu Chia-ch'uan) Chiang Hua, and Lin Hung—are well drawn, too. Qualities they have in common are a readiness to sacrifice themselves for the interests of the whole people, nobility of spirit in struggling to realise the high ideals of Communism, and infinite courage and shrewdness in their fight against the reactionary rulers, their class enemies and the enemies of the nation. Though Lin Hung appears in a few pages of the book only, she leaves us with a clear picture of a woman Communist. In prison she inspires two other girls by her experience; and before her execution she cheerfully gives them as souvenirs her cardigan and comb. Details such as these make a deep and lasting impression. . . .

To my mind, the most important quality in a revolutionary writer is this revolutionary passion (*i.e.*, revolutionary passion as evinced in Lin Hung). Of course, aptitude and keen powers of observation are important, too. But more essential is the proletarian outlook, a strong sense of responsibility to the revolution, a firm revolutionary stand and deep class consciousness. A work permeated by such feelings, even if technically imperfect, can make a strong appeal. This is the case with *The Song of Youth*. It may be rather loosely written, but each character is alive and pulls at your heart-strings. For we cannot fail to be moved by Lu Chia-ch'uan's and Lin Hung's heroic martyrs' death, to sympathise with Lin Tao-ching's groping for the truth and her fate, to feel concern over Wang Hsiao-yen who has taken the wrong path and worked against the revolution . . . With genuine feeling the author praises all that is progressive, the revolutionaries and labouring people, the awakening of intellectuals and their search for truth; at the same time she pitilessly lashes out at all that is backward, the counter-revolutionaries and exploiters, the intellectuals who are decadent. Sentiments like these, expressed through art, become a mighty force to stir readers.

As we have noted, *The Song of Youth* is the author's first novel. Like many other works by new Chinese writers today, it is full of turbulent life and strength and covers an important historical period. This is an indication that novel-writing is entering upon an age of great vitality.[7]

The above is a piece of literary criticism which excuses technical imperfections but extols revolutionary passion and the power to " pull heart-strings." The review, however, does not promise much; it may have even a repulsive effect on those prospective readers who ask for less sentiment, for less discrimination between " the progressive " and " the backward," and for stronger evidence of intellect in the novel. In the way it is recommended, the book seems to confirm one's fears about " revolutionary romanticism."

According to the author, she lived through many of the experiences that are ascribed to Lin Tao-ching in the book. If she improves on

[7] CL, No. 6, 1960, pp. 138–141.

the model it is that she makes the heroine more proletarian than she herself is :

> My personal experience in life has determined my choice of Lin Tao-ching as the heroine of the novel. Lin Tao-ching is not myself, but her life contains the elements of my own life. My family was similar to the family of the great feudal landlord to which Lin Tao-ching was born. My father also resembled her father. He raped Hsiu-ni, who drowned herself after she became pregnant. The difference is that I was not borne by Hsiu-ni (but Lin Tao-ching was).[8]

So Lin Tao-ching has her birthright to revolution, because she was the daughter of a peasant girl who was the victim of a landlord's carnal desire. Though apparently a petty-bourgeois intellectual, she is at heart (*i.e.*, inherited from her maternal side) a proletarian. Chang Chia-ch'ing, another revolutionary from a landlord's family in *Keep the Red Flag Flying* (a novel by Liang Pin),[9] also proves his birthright by producing a victimised proletarian mother. In fairy tales, the hero's royal blood will assert itself in spite of the fact that he appears as a vagabond or even as a beast. In Communist myth, it is proletarian blood that predestines a hero's noble qualities.

The growth of Lin Tao-ching in the novel is therefore a process of the purification of her blood, or the realisation of her " proletarian " self. When she has read some Russian novels, she makes this self-analysis : " I am a landlord's daughter, but I am also a farm-labourer's daughter. In my person there are both white bones and black bones " (p. 249). Her wish for the withering away of the " white bones " is realised when after much adventure which she regards as heroic, she is permitted to join the Communist Party.

The three Communists in the novel are free from such worries for, at least in the eyes of Lin Tao-ching, they have already become one with the working-class. Chiang Hua is a college student who calls himself a worker because he began his career as a printer's apprentice and has worked as a coolie and a coal miner. Moreover, his father was a printer. Lu Chia-ch'uan is a village school-master's son, but from his childhood he came under the influence of Li Ta-chao (one of the early leaders of the Communist Party) who preached

[8] *T'an-t'an Ch'uang-tso Ch'ang-p'ien-hsiao-shuo ti T'i-hui* (*Talks on Comprehensions [Experiences] of Novel-writing*), a collection of five essays by Liang Pin, Yang Mo, Wu Ch'iang, Ch'ü Po, and Feng Teh-ying (Shanghai: Shanghai Wen-hsueh Ch'u-pan-she, 1958), p. 11. Yang Mo's article was originally an interview, published in *Chung-kuo Ch'ing-nien Pao* (*Chinese Youth Newspaper*), May 3, 1958.

[9] Liang Pin, *Hung-ch'i P'u* (*Keep the Red Flag Flying* is the English title given in CL, No. 1, 1959) (Peking: Jen-min Wen-hsueh Ch'u-pan-she, Revised edition, 1959). In my opinion, Liang Pin's book is quite original and daring in its study of Communist heroism. It is also superior to both *The Song of Youth* and *Red Sun* in the use of language. I plan to make it the subject of a lengthier study.

Marxism in his native place—Loting, Hopei. Lin Hung, who considers the prison as, and literally turns it into, a "Marxist-Leninist college," received her earlier education in Soviet Russia. Their examples of single-minded courage and determination fill Lin Tao-ching with great admiration.

The reader who expects well-rounded characterisation will be disappointed to find that these and other Communists in the book are not sufficiently differentiated. With one or two exceptions—the "bad" Communists whom I shall discuss later—they have more categorical qualities than individual qualities. They all seem so good, but they are all "flat." This superficiality, an obvious weakness, is nevertheless, essential to the structure of the novel. For the story is written, for the most part, from Lin Tao-ching's point of view. And she is too "passionate" to ask more than superficial questions. *The Song of Youth* is *her* story. Even the characters she admires, the Communist heroes, cannot be presented except through her imperfect understanding. They appear to live in danger, to be fighting for something, and to evince certain attractive qualities which she cannot penetrate. They also talk too profoundly in their jargon about the principles of revolution and the analysis of the current political situation. All the Communists in the book are indeed surrounded by an air of mystery. But their mystery fascinates Lin Tao-ching. As a woman in love, she perhaps can tell the difference between her first Communist lover—Lu Chia-ch'uan who soon vanishes from her life—and her second Communist lover—Chiang Hua, who seems still very alive at the end of the book. But as a pursuer of Communist truth, she must obviate this difference. One man or the other, a Communist is always a Communist first and an individual second. The more sincerely Lin Tao-ching (or Yang Mo) pours out her heart, the more beclouded her vision becomes. Her story is eminently lacking in perspicacity, nice differentiation, and common sense. As passion blinds the author-heroine, it repels one kind of reader as it attracts another.

But in its very vagueness and superficiality, the reader discovers the meaning of *The Song of Youth.* If he does not find much about the other characters, he is at least given a full study of the heroine who is the most interesting character of the book. It is unfortunate for Yang Mo, the propagandist, that for her story, she has to adopt the point of view of a woman of limited mental capacities. Her passionate story necessarily involves a criticism of that woman's sentimentality, ignorance and addiction to day-dreams—or what is usually summarised as Bovaryism. All the people she blindly worships and all the heroic qualities she admires contain an element of self-contradiction: for they are seen through a mind which is, to say the least, naïve. Since her passion is strongly for the affirmation of the ideology, the awareness on the part of the reader of her limitations qualifies or even negates it. Thanks to Yang Mo, the reader is constantly kept aware. The meaning of *The Song of Youth* is not so simple as a reader susceptible to romantic effusions might think.

Given her passionate nature, Lin Tao-ching does not seem to bother much about the theoretical problems of Communism. She reads and listens, but it is doubtful how much she understands. In her discussion with Chiang Hua, she expresses the view, accepted by many in the 1930s, that the Communist Party is interested only in the formation of a united front against Japanese imperialism. She is corrected by him; he declares :

> " Revolution in China will never succeed without the leadership of the Communist Party. The truth is the same with the anti-Japanese war. The Communist Party will not only participate, but also assume the leadership. Tao-ching, do you understand the meaning of leadership?"
>
> Chiang Hua becomes excited when he reaches this point. His gloomy eyes shine with a brightness, appearing at once passionate and profound. Tao-ching has been listening, fascinated. A feeling of adoration, spontaneously grown, suddenly makes her feel very happy. She pours another glass of water for Chiang Hua, and she drinks a few mouthfuls too. Then she leans on the table, her big eyes shining, and says:
>
> " Chiang, how glad I am to meet you here! So little do I know, indeed, my understanding is never perfect . . . [dots in the original]. You must help me from now on. Which college did you graduate from? Since when have you become a revolutionary?" (p. 256).

Here Yang Mo is certainly to be complimented for subtlety. Note how deftly Lin Tao-ching parries the question about " leadership," one of the most important questions to a Communist, but a question too abstract and remote for her feminine mind. Note also how with her girlish archness, she leads the conversation to his personal life in which she is really interested. It is obvious that she does not understand; but the more profound truth revealed here is that, while confessing her worry about her imperfect understanding, she does not really care to understand. She is simply fascinated by the man who overwhelms her with the appearance of superior knowledge and conviction, whose personal history is a mystery, and who also happens to possess sexual attraction for her. Her " adoration " and " happiness " are induced by the light in his eyes which attracts her with much greater force than the " truth " in his statement.

Lin Tao-ching's apparent concern about politics in juxtaposition with her actual unconcern (or her interest in something else) is a subtle use of irony which even a passionate writer like Yang Mo cannot avoid in her dramatisation. Irony, however, can be more bluntly conveyed. All through the book there runs a second theme which at once supports and contradicts the main theme of a petty-bourgeois intellectual's search for her revolutionary self. The second theme is a romantic woman's search for a heroic life. It supports the main theme, because a Communist is expected to perform heroic deeds so long as they further the cause of Revolution. But the two are also contradictory because individual fancy and individual ambition threaten to destroy the meaning of revolution as it is given in the novel. When Lin Tao-ching expresses for the first time her wish to become a Communist, she is questioned by Lu Chia-ch'uan:

> Let me ask you this. You did a great deal of running about; you are dissatisfied with this and disdainful about that; you are depressed; you are suffering—but for whom is all this? For the labouring masses, or for yourself? Now you want to enlist in the Red Army, join the Communist Party and become a heroine . . . [dots in the original]. But please think it over. Is it your motive to deliver the people from the floods and fires? Or is it to satisfy your own fancy—your heroic fancy so that you may run away from your humdrum life? (p. 120).

A sharp reminder of her weakness, a solid lesson in revolutionary education the above piece is; but obviously Lin Tao-ching does not spend much time in thinking it over. After Lu Chia-ch'uan is thrown into prison, she writes him a letter which contains this sentence :

> When I think that my life will become like yours, full of legends and mythological tales, how joyous I am! (p. 232).

It is still the humdrum life that she wants to run away from. But she has forgotten the lesson she has received; otherwise she would never put in such a silly ejaculation, to pain her mentor, to make him think how little improvement she has made. For in the prison he has pains enough. She believes that she is passionately in love; but she is also intoxicated by her own heroism when she writes the letter which she does not know how to deliver. It is perhaps true that a hero-worshipper worships only the image of herself.

Later she is involved in a riot in a village. Though she is not yet a Communist, her name is on the wanted list. However, she escapes under the escort of a farm-labourer, a true proletarian. Oblivious of the danger, she is lost in her meditations, while running in the fields under a cool, starry, summer night (described in a style which a schoolgirl might think pretty but which perhaps tells exactly the kind of observation Lin Tao-ching might make):

> . . . the atmosphere, so heady yet so refreshingly intoxicating, and then, the life of revolutionary struggle, so much like a legend; all this looks exceptionally enchanting in this unusual night; it gives a special kind of aesthetic satisfaction (pp. 347–348).

She has her adventure now, but then she remembers her error and smiles at her " petty-bourgeois sentiments."

She is now conscious of her weakness, but this is perhaps an incurable weakness. After she has joined the Communist Party, she confesses to Chiang Hua:

> " I was thinking how it is that I can become what I am today, that I can realise my ideal—to become a glorious fighter for Communism. Who makes all this? It is you ; it is the Party. (p. 593).

Her " heroic fancy " is fulfilled at last. It is significant that she believes she *has* become a " glorious fighter."

So the two themes are united: Lin Tao-ching has found both revolution and heroism in the Communist Party. The question now to be asked is how the Communist Party is rendered in *The Song of Youth.* In my opinion, here the Communist Party fulfils the image of a revolutionary party; by revolutionary party I mean a political party composed of a number of dedicated but otherwise mysterious human beings deeply engaged in a conspiracy to overthrow a government. That was the nature and function of the Chinese Communist Party in the 1930s. For instance, the Communists used the united front as a slogan but actually tried hard to seize " leadership." That was one way that the conspiracy worked. And because of divided authority in the Party, the conspirators also fought among themselves.

The Song of Youth " covers an important historical period "—roughly, from the Mukden incident of 1931 to the students' patriotic movement of 1935—a period when the Chinese Communist Party, according to its official history,[10] was under the domination of the so-called " Leftist Doctrinaires." " Leftist Doctrinaires " are bad enough in the eyes of Party orthodoxy, but Yang Mo makes the Leftist Doctrinaires in her book even worse. A leftist doctrinaire may remain a loyal Communist, but Tai Yü, the leftist doctrinaire in the book, becomes a spy on the payroll of the Kuomintang after his release from prison. Thus he becomes the villain. It is his power over another woman character, Wang Hsiao-yen, that makes the reviewer in *Chinese Literature* feel so much concern over her virtue.

Wang Hsiao-yen, daughter of a college professor (a " progressive " one), is a quiet, nice girl, a foil to the more vivacious Lin Tao-ching. She has her revolutionary dreams too, but her lover happens to be the " bad " Communist Tai Yü. She is kept ignorant of his villainy until the end of the book, but the reader is aware of it all the time, being helped by the novelist's omniscience. So the question—will virtue

[10] For instance, Hu Ch'iao-mu, *Chung-kuo Kung-ch'an-tang ti San-shih-nien* (*The Last Thirty Years of the CCP*) (Peking: Jen-min Ch'u-pan-she, 1951), pp. 34–39.

succumb to the temptation by hypocrisy?—may keep him on tenterhooks.

As I have said, the Communists in *The Song of Youth* are mysterious figures. As secret agents working under the " White " régime, they are compelled to lead a surreptitious existence and to make sudden appearances and disappearances without the necessity to explain why. They are on guard about their real intentions and they even hide their real identities. That they all assume pseudonyms suggests that they lead double lives, one in the open and the other in the dark. It is not easy to tell whether a name a person is known by is his real name or his pseudonym. For instance, Lu Chia-ch'uan is a real name; Chiang Hua is a false name; Lin Hung is real, Tai Yü is false. To penetrate the mystery about their life is beyond the mental powers of Lin Tao-ching, who luckily does not need to make this intellectual effort. She listens with her wide-eyed innocence and believes wholeheartedly. Life for her is easy, so far as her relationship with the Communists is concerned, for her lover happens to be a " good " Communist in whom she can place implicit trust. Chiang Hua impresses her with his talks about Marxism. Though he is mysterious about his movements and though he casts suspicion on one of his comrades (Tai Yü), no suspicion about him (Chiang Hua) is ever aroused in her trusting heart. When he declares his love, she accepts him. And she becomes happy in the consummation of her wishes. There is, however, no such good luck for her friend Wang Hsiao-yen. She, too, meets a Communist who talks with apparent profundity about Marxist theory, who quotes Marx verbatim, who impresses her with his importance in the Communist Party, who is mysterious about his movements, who casts suspicions on his comrades —and she trusts him. When he declares his love, she accepts him. But she barely escapes the worst misery that a Communist novelist can think of. For Tai Yü turns out to be a " bad " Communist.

So *The Song of Youth* is the romance about a lucky little girl who, instead of rising from rags to riches as she would do in a capitalist society, wins her independence from her landlord father's house and happily joins what she regards as the proletarian revolution. The lucky little girl—ideology does not matter here—also wins the right man in the end. The story of the Communist Cinderella, who attains the best she can wish for in life, would be much simpler in meaning except for the sinister presence of Tai Yü. Indeed, in his mystery, his way of talk and his expressed conviction he bears such a strong resemblance to Chiang Hua that the reader wonders whether there is a way for a woman trembling on the verge of romance to tell the difference between a " good " Communist and a " bad " Communist, or between a good *man* and a bad *man*. Wang Hsiao-yen's episode is a strong reminder of the fate that might befall Lin Tao-ching who receives her Communist lover (or someone who declares himself to be a Communist) with no less candour. It is impossible for her to check, for a Communist is his own authority about his past. Besides, the girl needs his " help " so badly, as we have seen in the dialogue between Lin Tao-ching and Chiang Hua. A Communist who talks volubly can be anything—leftist doctrinaire, rightist opportunist, a Trotskyite, or even a traitor to the Party. But so long as his life is anyway full of " legends and mythological tales," he will have his appeal to the girl's heroic fancy.

In introducing a " bad " Communist, Yang Mo's intention is perhaps to " lash out at the counter-revolutionaries," as well as to provide melodramatic interest, but she accomplishes an effect to the contrary. She calls attention to the superficial attraction of a Communist and the hero-worshipper's inability to tell a " villain " from a " hero." With all her enthusiasm to serve ideology, the author, however, is finally caught in the structure she has built up for her novel. Ideology demands a positive hero, but such a hero has no place in her world of vague impressions and hazy understanding. When passion becomes the core of a moral life, even heroes and villains may lose their distinction. For passion is not the faculty to recognise, far less to discriminate.

Yang Mo, a victim of passion herself, can, at her dramatic best, put in such a criticism of her heroine: " The girl is possessed by Marx's ghost! " (p. 369). Such a remark is harmless, since it would afford Lin Tao-ching great satisfaction to learn that she is really losing her " white bones " if she has won the reputation of becoming thus possessed. But the remark is only partially true, since Lin Tao-ching, though under a spell she surely is, is possessed by other things, too. To reduce this spell to words would require a more subtle, more precise, and more lucid prose than Yang Mo is capable of; it perhaps calls for the genius of a Flaubert, whom I do not expect to find among Communist novelists. But in the creation of her heroine, she cannot help discovering the truth about her. She discovers even the terrible truth about the difference between appearance and reality, since the world Lin Tao-ching lives in is a world of appearances. Inhibited by ideology and limited, perhaps, by her talent, Yang Mo does not attempt to or does not know how to incorporate her discovery into a proper form of fiction. But though not well-organised, her discovery is there, to give her novel a deeper meaning.

III

Revenge is a theme which is not fully developed in *The Song of Youth*. The Communists in the book cry for revenge (pp. 401, 454) when they are taken to the execution ground, but their comrades ignore this appeal in their pursuit of the united front against Japanese imperialism. The reader, if he is familiar with the history of the Chinese Communist Party, knows that an alliance with the " enemy " proved to be a more effective way of carrying out the " revenge." But revenge is not built in the plot of the novel. The reader not so familiar with the history may be impressed by the logic of the leftist doctrinaires, Tai Yü (pp. 552–553) and Wang Chung (p. 608), whose opposition to a policy of " capitulation " seems to have originated from a stronger feeling for their dead comrades. Their logic remains cogent even though they themselves are, in fact, as the author assures us, traitors to the Communist Party.

Red Sun, the other book I am going to discuss, is firmly built upon the logic of revenge. A Communist army was defeated by the 74th Division of the Central Government army in the late autumn of 1946; it revenged itself by the annihilation of the same division at the battle of Mengliangku in May 1947. How the Communist soldiers take the defeat and effect the revenge is the main theme of the book.

A war novel, *Red Sun's dramatis personae* reads like a long list of " heroes " from the army commander down to the soldier of lowest rank. There are also some women and some peasants who assist in the Communist war effort. They are conscious of their heroism, which is never vague or ambiguous in meaning, as is the heroism in Lin Taoching's mind. Here " hero " is a title of honour officially conferred upon a deserving soldier. For instance, Yang Chün, a section-leader later promoted to platoon-leader, was made a Hero not long after he joined the army (p. 264).[11] And the title of honour can be shared by a multitude in the " hero section," " hero platoon," and " hero company " (p. 421). Unblushingly " hero " is on everybody's lips:

> " You know what? These men are *real* fighters; Heroes! They are real heroes!"
>
> From his happy, excited expression and his ringing voice one could tell quite unmistakably that this army commander had what is called " joy in his heart and laughter in his eyes." The heroic deeds of the men under his command were making him experience the joy and happiness of a commander (p. 213. Barnes, p. 259).
>
> This mainstay force is a most distinguished Hero-unit. It's part of the New Fourth Army, one of the mainstay regiments of the New Fourth Army, and very famous. . . . Our militia in the River Sha District is a militia of heroes with a glorious record of struggle. Tomorrow night we shall join forces with the mainstay force, our elder brothers, and capture Machiachiao! . . . . (p. 379, Barnes, p. 468).

[11] Page number refers to the 1959 revised edition of *Hung Jih*. Where English translation is cited, I use A. C. Barnes' version.

Women in this book have a definite reason for hero-worship. Here is a rhapsody from an army nurse:

> But *he's* a hero! He fights the enemy hand to hand with a bayonet! He climbs city walls nine or ten feet high and hurls himself on the enemy! He swims across wide rivers in the ice and snow. . . . (p. 307. Barnes, p. 378).
>
> The secretary of the River Sha District Committee of the Communist Party was Hua Ching (Hua Ch'ing).
>
> She longed to throw herself into the heat of the struggle, and the record of struggle of the heroes claimed her admiration; her spirit had been drawn by the brilliance of the War of Liberation, she had been infected by the heroic temperament of Liang Po, who she loved with all her heart, and she had been stimulated by the great victory at Laiwu (p. 361. Barnes, p. 444).

Liang Po, the deputy commander of the victorious army, wins the woman's love by his "heroic temperament" or soldierly virtues. His bravery, like the bravery of others in this book, is believable, since here war is real war, not a shadowy hide-and-seek.

Red Sun is a manly book. Men dominate the book as one military action after another leads inexorably to the climax of the battle at Mengliangku. Wu Ch'iang writes in manly style, too, straightforward and at a fast pace. His meaning is not obscured by the fantasy and mystery which hangs like a veil over the heroes of *The Song of Youth*. Indeed, the two books are remarkably dissimilar in their treatment of heroic themes. Here is the final scene of the students' demonstration in *The Song of Youth*:

> "On one side there is the holy task; on the other there is depravity and infamy." Suddenly this sentence rings in Tao-ching's heart. Meanwhile, right before her eyes—in the midst of the tumultous masses, the thousands and tens of thousands of people—there appear, one after another, the faces of Lu Chia-ch'uan, Lin Hung, Liu the Big Sister, the "Aunt," Chao Yü-ch'ing, and Chiang Hua, too, who was recently hurt but who only a moment ago flashed past her like a comet; then, unaccountably, the wolfish face of Hu Meng-an (a Kuomintang official), the bloated, yellow face of Tai Yü, and the glinting small eyes of Yü Yung-tse (her first husband) all flash by. Crowds that would move the mountains and agitate the seas, the gunshots in the distance, the flow of fresh blood, the spirited songs—they all come up before her, surging like sea-waves. To her weakness is now added over-excitement and fatigue; she feels a fainting fit and she almost drops to the ground. A girl student by her side holds her up with force. They do not know each other, but they are now tightly locked in an embrace (p. 621).

Fluid and fragmentary impressions, incomplete impressions (of a face instead of a person) (note also that the Communists do not have distinct features), the general confusion of sensation with illusions—all of these conveyed in loosely-constructed sentences—indicate that a hazy mind is at observation. Lin Tao-ching's fainting fit and her falling into the lap of a complete stranger are significant details which bring out her frailty, her trusting nature, and her need for support, qualities which not only characterise her personality but which have to reappear to leave their final imprint on the scene of the "tumultuous" mob.

Red Sun ends on a quite different note. Its last scene is a tableau quite impressive for mass, height, and solidity:

> . . . As the army commander and political commissar, many of the unit commanders, and the heroic fighters of the Red Flag Platoons and the Red Flag Sections stood erect on the highest point of the summit of Mengliangku, towering in magnificent isolation in the Yi-Meng Mountains, and looked down at the hills spread at their feet with wide eyes that flashed like the eyes of a hawk, they made a brave picture of greatness and nobility and unity (p. 543: Barnes, p. 671).

What the reader misses here is the intimacy of an individual mind, or even the immediacy of Lin Tao-ching's confused sensations. The scene (or the replica of a colossal monument) is imposing, but it is too stiff, too remote and too cold. The heroes look as if they were planted there. Anyway, it conveys the uncomfortable feeling of posing before a camera; it lacks feeling; it lacks depth. It is the picture of an attitude.

But the tableau in the concluding scene is not an irrelevant detail. It stands rather as a recognition of the hero as a poser. This recognition, which comes out in a magnificent symbol, clarifies the meaning of the book while it redefines the meaning of heroism. After several hundred pages of adulation and hero-consciousness which turns the Communist Army, as it were, into a Mutual Admiration Club for the Heroes, the artificiality of heroism in *Red Sun* must have become obvious. There is no surer way of debasing heroism than to multiply heroes. Wu Ch'iang the propagandist may be still trying to keep up the norm for heroism, but Wu Ch'iang the novelist can only succeed in calling attention to the commonness of his heroes, since there are so many of them. But commonness is not the distinctive mark of the heroes in *Red Sun*; their distinctive mark is artificiality. The Hero is made by the army command or the Communist Party. To be a Hero thus becomes an uneasy task, since he has to satisfy the demands made on him by his superiors and comrades. A Hero who tries hard to keep his title would be the most pitiable hero one can think of. I wonder whether any hero, or anyone who aspires to be a hero, has ever been rebuked in such terms as a company commander in *Red Sun* is by the army commander:

> It's quite natural that you should be glad that we've won a battle and destroyed the enemy. But I never expected you to choose this way of

> showing how glad you are! Look at you! Look at the way you've been drinking! You have done very well as a company commander, two Hero sections in your company, and more than a thousand prisoners to your credit, and from the way you conducted yourself in the fighting you've every qualification for being made a Hero. But judging from the fuddled state you're in now, you're heading for a fall! You don't look fit to be made a Hero! I don't think you've even got very good qualifications for being an ordinary company commander at the moment! . . . (p. 217, Barnes, p. 264).

The poor fellow may deserve the rebuke in the context, but to throw the term Hero right into a would-be hero's face and to use it as a weapon of persuasion and threat is the worst indignity that cynicism can perpetrate on heroism.

A hero is of course not necessarily a Hero. (The Chinese term *ying-hsiung* stands for both the Hero as a title and the hero as a person distinguished for selflessness and valour in the novel.) The soldiers in *Red Sun* perform feats of great courage, but a more important fact which Wu Ch'iang has brought out unmistakably is that they are not always given the chance to display their heroism. For here every military action is the result of deliberate manipulation. The heat of battle is generated from cold calculation. Hot-tempered soldiers are placed under command, discipline and other restrictions. The soldiers advance or retreat on orders. They are despatched to the first line; they are held back to the rear (while their grumbling is disregarded); they are ordered to reach a certain spot within a fixed limit of time. They do not always know where they are sent; they seldom know why; they are sometimes anxious to learn what is happening on the other fronts—but strategy is not their concern. The most courageous soldier can only do the part that is assigned him. His scope of activity is limited; his range of knowledge is pitifully small. Even Shen Chen-hsin, the army commander and therefore the leader of the group of " Heroes," has to rely on the commander-in-chief (Ch'en Yi) and the deputy commander-in-chief (Su Yü) for decisions on the movements of his army. But Ch'en Yi and Su Yü do not appear in the book except as two code numbers (501 and 502) and the voices on the telephone to which only a few high officers are privileged to listen. And far higher up, there is Mao Tse-tung, seemingly the source of infallible wisdom, the architect of grand strategy, and the producer of victory. Under the hierarchy of command, not only soldiers become small parts of a great whole, but even revenge, the *leitmotif* of the book, loses much of its sweet taste. The soldiers under Shen Chen-hsin's command, the reader is told, take their defeat at Lienshui bitterly, regarding it as a personal injury, and are determined to have the satisfaction of revenge. But their " revenge " is planned and directed by someone remote and invisible. When they are kept in the dark, they suffer from frustration, but theirs is only to obey and to wait. The heroism of Captain Ahab would be seriously compromised if the *Pequod* were remote-controlled by a radar station which gives directions to a fleet of whaling-boats to assist him in his hunt for his enemy Moby Dick.

In the final image of *Red Sun*, the Communist soldiers stare into the mountains with eyes like hawks'—but sometimes they have to transform themselves into hawks:

> The orders of Field Army Command—Commander-in-Chief Ch'en, Deputy Commander Su and Deputy Political Commissar T'an—are that our Army shall fly there! Fly! Got that? They want us to grow wings and fly there! *They want us to turn into hawks*! Our regiment's position will be at the extreme front of the army, the closest to Mengliangku, the hawk's head and beak! (p. 393: Barnes, p. 485).[12]

So the Communist Army, and every soldier in it, is looked upon as a big bird of prey, trained with care, and released only at its master's will, to accomplish his orders. When the same regiment was not permitted to join the battle at its initial stage, its commander, Liu Sheng, fretted at his inaction rather like a chained hawk:

> Evening was drawing in by the time Liu Sheng saw the signal. He felt that a depressing closeness had settled on the room and on his mind, so he turned his slow steps toward the banks of the Sha.
>
> The current was swift through the tumbling, tossing waves. On a leaning, collapsing tree on the river bank there was a pair of birds whose names he did not know, with grey plumage, keeping up a continual harsh chatter at him. These two birds and their voices produced in him a feeling of revulsion, as if they were mocking him for the way his hopes of battle had been dashed (p. 380: Barnes, p. 469).

Liu Sheng's regiment is finally used at the most crucial sector in the battle-line. However, he does not see victory, for he receives a fatal wound. Dying, he says these last words to his comrade: " Fight a good fight. . . . Be *obedient* to the Party. . . . See the revolution through to the end! " (p. 507: Barnes, p. 626).[13] His command is now passed on to Chen Chien, the political commissar. When the new commander goes to battle, his gait is the strut of a small man suddenly made " great "; is typical of a self-conscious " hero." His attitudinising seems comically out of place under the given circumstances.

[12] Barnes' version omits " They want us to turn into hawks."

[13] For " Be obedient to the Party," Barnes' version has " Be loyal to the Party." The sentence in Chinese is " *T'ing tang-ti hua* "—literally, " listen to the words of the Party."

> Chen Chien, who had been infused with strength by the sacrifice which had been made by his comrade-in-arms and now had a double responsibility as regimental political commissar and acting regimental commander, strode out of the little room with bold, buoyant steps and with the noble (*heroic* in the original—*ying-hsiung*) bearing that he always had and that now showed even more clearly, and set out once again for the leading positions where the fight was raging to begin his work of directing the next stage of the battle (p. 510: Barnes, p. 630).

Perhaps this man is not conscious of his "heroic bearing," but anyhow he is conscious of the "strength" derived from his comrade's sacrifice. A significant fact about *Red Sun* is that its characters are prone to strike an attitude of heroism even when they are compelled to accept a minor, unheroic role in the great game of war. The cold facts of war, the physical reality concerning which Wu Ch-iang is meticulous in detail, do not call for, and often forbid, a continual display of heroism. Heroism is to be consummated only in a supreme moment. A man who walks like a hero while anticipating action is only a silly, vain, and ridiculous figure. In depicting the "heroes" as he knows them, the author can hardly avoid giving the hint that heroism is so easily mocked by a poser, a victim of grandiose illusions or, what is particularly relevant here, by a product of that process of political education known as brain-washing.

Red Sun, with its superficial characters, is a superficial book. Burdened by an overabundance of heroes the author has difficulty in differentiating between them. The reader is not led into the consciousness of any individual character for more than a few pages, and then not much is to be found there. Their training as soldiers and as Communists has made or is about to make them uniform. They are incapable of thought, feeling, and attitudes beyond a very narrow range. What bothers the reader is the clarity with which Wu Ch'iang views his "heroes"—the superficial clarity of a war correspondent who was "there," but who saw only what he wanted to see. His style, marked by a journalistic brilliance, hardly does his subject justice; certainly not more than Yang Mo's hazy, impressionistic style does. For heroism is a profound, awesome subject, to explore which one needs the austere discipline of a Conrad or the daring primordial imagination of a Melville. Yang Mo, infatuated herself, is not the person to study the infatuation. Wu Ch'iang while piling praises upon his "heroes," is not aware of his infatuation either. He admits his book is inadequate in the characterisation of the intellectual cadres.[14] This is certainly true, and is perhaps a real loss to the reader. The intellectual cadre may not necessarily entertain rebellious thought, or

[14] *T'an-t'an Ch'uang-tso Ch'ang-p'ien-hsiao-shuo ti T'i-hui*, p. 16. Wu Ch'iang's article was originally published in *Wen-yi Pao*, No. 19, 1958.

ponder over the meaning of life in the face of sudden death, or the meaning of heroism. But such a character might at least provide a fresh point of view, some sensibility not yet entirely encased in attitudinisation, a little independence from the infectious obsession with heroism, a little awareness of that infection, and some statement of self-knowledge about " the dread in the soul," such as is made by Ishmael in *Moby Dick*:

> I, Ishmael, was one of that crew; my shouts had gone up with the rest; my oath had been welded with theirs; and stronger I shouted and more did I hammer and clinch my oath, because of the dread in my soul. A wild, mystical, sympathetical feeling was in me; Ahab's quenchless feud seemed mine. With greedy ears I learned the history of that murderous monster against whom I and all the others had taken our oaths of violence and revenge.[15]

As it is, *Red Sun* is largely supported by action (which alone might commend a novel to a reader in either capitalist or Communist society) and a series of studies of an attitude. But Wu Ch'iang goes farther than that. Ever since the day, he tells us, when he saw the dead body of General Chang Ling-fu, commander of the 74th Division, he was obsessed by the thought that he had a story to tell. He wanted to write a novel about the " glorious battles " and the " heroic " characters who participated in them. For years, and for many sleepless nights, he was thinking of them and studying their possibilities as materials for a novel.[16] When the book was finished, he had done a painstaking job. Yang Mo, according to herself, is a laborious writer, too, but she is mainly concerned with revolutionary passion. The problems of writing were more complex for Wu Ch'iang:

> I always keep this in mind that I shall not follow my own heart's desire by contradicting either the laws of life in the objective world, or the nature and will of the characters. But neither should I abandon the freedom that I have a right to enjoy by allowing myself to be restricted by the natural state of life and men so as to be enslaved by the natural life and the natural man.[17]

There is much quibbling in the above passage, so it may need some explanation. What he means by " freedom " may be either plain freedom or his willing conformity to the official doctrines about writing (*e.g.*, " socialist realism " with emphasis on the people's " aspirations "). " The laws of life in the objective world " are the laws of Marxism-Leninism. " The natural state of life and men " is perhaps a state not

[15] Herman Melville, *Moby Dick*, Chap. 41.
[16] Author's preface to the Revised Edition, p. 3.
[17] Wu Ch'iang, " Hsieh-tso *Hung-jih* ti Ch'ing-k'uang ho I-hsieh T'i-hui " (" The Conditions Under Which I Wrote *Red Sun* and Some of My Comprehensions "), *Jen-min Wen-hsueh* (*People's Literature*: PL), No. 1, 1960, p. 125.

yet " retouched " by ideology, and open to the study of any sensible human being. To be realistic in the portrayal of such a state he regards as " enslavement." The quibbling is painful, since evidently he feels the conflict between " freedom " and " enslavement." He does not like to abandon himself altogether to ideology. He has his private considerations which he knows are dangerous but which he cannot get rid of. He is aware of the oppression of ideology, but he cannot shut off reality.

It is perhaps never his intention to mock at the mockery of heroism, but it is technically impossible for a novelist working within a realistic framework to present such an over-abundance of heroism and make it look authentic. With his caution against the " enslavement " to " the natural state of man," Wu Ch'iang, perhaps, never tries to explore the subtle difference between what a man pretends to be and what he is. But, writing from his personal experience, he inevitably brings up the facts of Communist manipulation, facts that the Communist Party does not feel it necessary to suppress. One of the memorable scenes in the book is the ritual of the initiation of twelve soldiers into the Communist Party (held simultaneously with the funeral service of Liu Sheng). The ritual is held in the black depth of a newly captured cave, on the eve of the decisive assault on the summit of Mengliangku. Many soldiers of the company attend, all deeply awed, and fired with great enthusiasm. It is a moving scene in itself, mysterious, solemn, and terrible, a re-enactment of the myth of the rebirth of heroes.

> The singing, sad, angry, confident, powerful, low and vigorous, echoed round the gloomy cave for a long time before gradually slipping away outside the cave towards every summit and valley of the whole of the Yi-Meng Mountains (p. 515: Barnes, p. 636).

But all the spell is broken if the reader remembers what took place about sixty pages earlier. There, two political commissars were talking about the preparations for just such a drama:

> " Oh! That's good," said Pan Wen-tsao [head of the regimental political department]. " In the past we've tended to be rather conservative about developing Party members, something of a closed-door policy, but the Field Army Political Department and the Army Political Department have issued a directive that we should develop Party members on the firing-line and have new members taking the oath of loyalty on the firing-line. We must pick out some of those who are courageous and sincere and willing to study and absorb them into the Party. The reason I've come to see you is in actual fact to discuss this subject."
>
> " It's what we've been intending to do," said Lo Kuang [political instructor to the company], and he proceeded to give Pan Wen-tsao an account of the members in the company branch and of those fighters whom it was intended to develop into Party members.

> "Just 'intending' is not enough. You must investigate the loyalty of cadres and fighters to the Party in the line and develop the best elements of Party in the line. This is an important link in the chain of increasing our fighting power and ensuring victory. We have not been sufficiently aware of this point in the past" (p. 469: Barnes, pp. 577–578).

The bureaucratic jargon ("policy," "directive," "develop," "investigate"), the mechanical terms ("absorb," "link," "chain"), and the tone of self-assurance about the Party's control over the fighters get into proper focus the mystery and poetry that is to ensue in the "oath-taking on the firing-line." After the author, inadvertently, I supose, has supplied this behind-the-scenes dialogue, what might be the "rebirth-rite" becomes, in the reader's mind, a witches' Sabbath.

Wu Ch'iang was born in 1910.[18] Whatever he published while he served as a member of the Chinese League of Left-wing Writers in the 1930s is not known to me. His only other known works are the two novelettes published in 1953 and 1954, *He Raises High the Shining, Bright Carbine*, and *The Horse Breeder*.[19] *Red Sun* is his first novel. Yang Mo was born in 1915,[20] and *The Song of Youth* is her first novel. Both authors are middle-aged now, but both have distinguished themselves as writers only in recent years: *i.e.*, after 1958, the year of the Great Leap Forward in Communist China.

There is no evidence to disprove that the two authors are supporters of the régime; but as novelists, they seem to maintain a private vision. Their books got published and met with acclaim in Communist China, probably because they satisfied the censorship by the amount of slogans, proletarian pep-talk and political "analysis" they loaded into their books. But a critic in the non-Communist world should not be misled by the "loaded passages" he finds there. If a novel is to be studied as a novel—even if it is published in Communist China—its meaning is inseparable from its structure and form, its metaphor and symbolic pattern, and the rhythm and colour of its language. If it contains a "world-view," the world-view is not necessarily represented by the passages where the author is trying to be "correct." Numerous passages, indeed, could be quoted, even from these two novels alone, to show how Chinese writers have surrendered their souls. But if there is still some sign of bewilderment left in them, some sign of ambiguity or mental reservation, it becomes apparent that the surrender is not total. And to my knowledge, totalitarianism does demand total surrender. This statement of mine, of course, is not to be interpreted as

[18] A biographical sketch of Wu Ch'iang is found in an appendix to the English version of *Red Sun*. Another is found in the Japanese magazine *Daian*, No. 10, 1961.
[19] Wu Ch'iang, "Hsieh-tso *Hung-jih* . . . ," PL, No. 1, 1960, p. 118.
[20] A biographical sketch of Yang Mo is found in CL, No. 3, 1960, p. 3.

an apology for totalitarianism; I only want to show the indomitability of the human soul, and, in particular, of the artist's soul.

Yang Mo and Wu Ch'iang are writing under very difficult conditions; but their "world-view"—so far as my partial analysis can illustrate, since I am dealing with "heroes and hero-worship" only—is interestingly and encouragingly individual. In his study of the battles fought in Kiangsu and Shantung in 1946 and 1947, Wu Ch'iang goes as far as to discover some "heroic" qualities in his enemy, General Chang Ling-fu, commander of the 74th Division (p. 529). It seems that Wu Ch'iang never attempts to prove that the Communist victory at Mengliangku was due to "the tide of history," though I wonder how the proof would ever be made, either by a novelist or an historian. The Communists won the battle for a very simple reason: their enemy made mistakes and they knew how to take advantage of his mistakes. This comes out clearly in Wu Ch'iang's narration.

If there were a tragic hero in *Red Sun*, it should be the feared, hated, intrepid and proud Kuomintang general, Chang Ling-fu. I shall cite a few lines of dialogue between him and his chief-of-staff:

> "For another thing, sir, you've fought ninety-nine battles right out of a hundred in your time but this time you've fought wrong" (said the chief-of-staff).
>
> "And where have I gone wrong?"
>
> "In trying to fight single-handed and in over-confidence" (p. 529: Barnes, p. 653).

The fall of an ever-victorious general—a modern version of Hsiang Yü or Kwan Yü—and that owing to his egotism and over-confidence, or what the Greeks called *hubris*—is a theme for a tragedy. Wu Ch'iang, of course, will never be the person to write it. But, at least, he has suggested the possibility.

Communist War Stories

By LI CHI

MODERN Chinese literature, which I date from the deliberate new beginnings made at the time of the May Fourth movement, is distinguished by its conscious effort at Europeanisation, which is in itself a catchall term embracing a whole assembly of themes and techniques, images and linguistic features taken and adopted from the vast literature beyond the seas and vaguely and often incorrectly designated as European. To be European was in fact simply to be non-traditional Chinese.

As an art form not formally recognised by the traditional Chinese literary world but privately or even surreptitiously cultivated by literary men (although story reading and story recital had enjoyed a large audience for over a thousand years), modern Chinese fiction is, if anything, more than any other branch of literature, a product of Western models. It is no exaggeration to say that Chinese writers were overwhelmed by their encounter with the immensely rich and varied output of what is generally called Western fiction.

One branch of fiction, war fiction, arrived latest on the scene, and, when it arrived, in the early autumn of 1937, it caught the writers bewildered and unprepared.[1] It is true that for decades before 1937, the Chinese people had known very little of peaceful days, yet an all-out war on which the fate of the whole nation depended, did not come until the summer of 1937. The onset of all-out war produced a world of difference. In an incredibly short time, the period before the war seemed as remote as generations ago. The whole scene of life changed. In the literary world, the indignant shaking of fists writers indulged in at the indecision of the government appeared suddenly like the beating of ineffectual wings in a void belonging to a bygone age. It is true that a year previously, in the summer of 1936, the Chinese Writers' Union had been formed and had put forward the slogan "Literature for National Defence," and that a rival group, headed by Lu Hsün, had brought out the slogan, "Popular literature for the National Revolutionary Struggle," but even in those days the writers

[1] This is speaking of the situation in general in 1937. As a matter of fact, novels dealing with Japanese invasion in the north-east were written and published in the early 1930s. The most successful of this group, namely, Hsiao Chun's *Village in August* (*Pa-yueh te Hsiang-ts'un*, 1935), had a tremendous influence on later writers of war stories. However, in the autumn of 1937, when all-out war suddenly confronted the people, it caught most writers unprepared.

who issued those slogans were more interested in altercations among themselves than in producing a literature to serve the purposes stated in their proclamations. Now in 1937, the question of popularisation demanded immediate solution. Each writer who desired to serve the cause of fighting the war was confronted with the problem of how he could in his writing reach the largest number of people and instil in them the urgency for resistance.

It was then that the literary tradition that had been building up since May Fourth was taken up for serious scrutiny and re-evaluation. There is no denying that although well nigh two decades had elapsed since the 1919 May Fourth movement, the literature produced by that movement had failed to reach a large public. What was the writer to do now so that he could reach the largest possible audience, an audience which hitherto had not registered the least interest in this new literary trust? The Chinese Writers' National Anti-aggression Association, at its formation in Hankow on March 27, 1938, proclaimed that writers should, " like the troops using their guns in the front, use their pens to stir up the people, to protect the fatherland, to pulverise the invader and to win the victory." It also called on writers to " go down to the countryside and to serve the armed forces." [2]

A more powerful directive came from Mao. In his speech " The Position of the Chinese Communist Party in the National Struggle," October 1938, Mao made this statement on literary work: " The foreign eight-legged essay must be banned, empty and abstract talk must be stopped and doctrinairism must be laid to rest to make room for the fresh and lively things of Chinese style and Chinese flavour which the common folk of China love to see and hear. To separate the content of internationalism from national forms is the practice of those who understand nothing of internationalism; we on the other hand must link up the two closely. In this matter there are within our ranks serious mistakes which should be conscientiously corrected." [3]

This is a clear injunction that writers must not follow the trend of Europeanisation which was part of the May Fourth tradition. That this is an important Communist literary stand may be seen from the words of Mao Tun, who, as late as 1960, found it necessary to quote these words again and expound their meaning. Mao Tun says in his report to the Third Conference of the All-China Federation of Literary and Art Circles: " These words of Chairman Mao were not directed solely to literary creation, but all the same they were a most important directive

[2] Quoted from Liu Shou-sung, *Chung-kuo Hsin Wen-hsueh Shih Ch'u-kao* (Peking: Tso-chia Ch'u-pan-she, 1957), Vol. 2, pp. 12–13.

[3] Mao Tse-tung, *Selected Works* (New York: International Publishers, 1954), II, p. 260.

for literary creation. They were the first resounding attack on the ill winds that had been blustering on the literary stage since May Fourth and they showed the broad highway to the literary worker who was wavering at the cross-roads." [4]

Thus war fiction, unlike the other branches of modern literature, did not start along the lines of Europeanisation, but was given the task, from the beginning, of searching for a tradition of Chinese writing which could adapt itself to modern needs. That form was to be at once acceptable to the large uneducated public and adequate to handle modern warfare with all its complexities. Mao's hint at " national forms," which gave rise to a protracted storm of controversy, need not concern us here; it was, so far as writers in Yenan were concerned, a most welcome and clear direction they were glad to hear and follow. Unlike the veteran writers of the May Fourth period, most of the writers in Yenan were young people more eager to produce stories and plays than to engage in debates about literary theories and traditions.

In 1942, at his talks at the Yenan Forum, Mao gave a more detailed plan to the writers regarding standpoint, attitude, audience—which was to be made up of workers, peasants, soldiers and cadres—and, finally, study.[5] A careful framework, then, was drawn for the literary workers and all that they had to do was to fill out that framework with particulars, each according to his ability, experience and understanding.

Mao's literary programme was obviously planned according to three exigencies of the moment: (1) the powers of comprehension of the peasants in the Communist-controlled areas and of the party cadres; (2) the interests of the Party and the war of resistance; (3) the training of the " literary workers " many of whom had made only short incursions into formal education.

The war with Japan was not the only war which produced a crop of war stories. Since 1937, there has been a series of three wars, each following the other in a descending scale of urgency. Following the war with Japan, the civil war between the Communists and the Kuomintang and the Korean War each produced its crop of war stories. From the fact that the directions set down by Mao, with some modifications, served also to guide the literary worker of the latter wars, it might be expected that the three groups of war stories would bear a sisterly resemblance to one another. Yet this is not entirely the case. War stories about the civil war and the Korean War, indeed, bear a sisterly resemblance, but the stories written during or immediately after the war

[4] Mao Tun, *Fan-ying She-hui Chu-i Yueh-chin ti Shih-tai, T'ui-tung, She-hui Chu-i Shih-tai ti Yueh-chin!* (Peking: Jen-min Wen-hsueh Ch'u-pan-she, 1960), p. 20.

[5] Mao Tse-tung, *Selected Works* (London: Lawrence & Wishart, 1956), Vol. IV.

with Japan form a group by themselves. We will therefore examine them in two groups.

True to the injunctions laid down by Mao, war stories of the first period, like those of the two later periods, are as much an exercise in the craft of fiction as an exercise in fulfilling a political commitment. If reading one or two of this group of stories is refreshing because of one's interest in a gripping theme or in the swiftly paced narrative, reading a dozen or two more of the same reveals the unattractive nature of set pieces cut to a pattern. One finds the same representative types appearing in scenes whose differences lie only in their geographic situation and circumstance of the moment. One can safely anticipate the resourceful Party member outwitting the enemy by his intelligence and bravery. The landlord, who is uniformly a traitor, may be given an opportunity to reform, but his confessions are to prove mere subterfuges and he is eventually lost beyond redemption. There is at least one scene of torture where the grim endurance of the high-minded Party member or the defiance of the village people under Communist leadership are depicted in sharp contrast with the Chinese traitor's cowardly treacherousness in administering torture or carrying out other orders of their Japanese masters. While the landlord is a lost soul, the poor man who has wavered or erred is usually given a chance to repent and reform. One may indeed feel that much of it is real; still one also cannot but feel that reality is not allowed to suffuse a whole novel.

A helpful aid to an insight into all three groups of stories are the prefaces and postscripts supplied by many writers. Stories are not infrequently revised, often more than once, for improvement both from an artistic as well as from a political point of view. Writers do not take pains to hide the fact that situations are contrived according to prescribed patterns. This, incidentally, explains the current favourite practice of co-operation of authors in writing stories. Now that individualism is condemned, collaboration is not only natural but desirable, as joint effort can better perfect a shared goal.

Yet, in spite of the restrictions imposed upon writers, the best war fiction of this period is distinguished by a freshness of presentation, sincerity of purpose and fine characterisation seldom found in the stories of the later two periods. First of all, in repudiating the May Fourth tradition, the primary concern at this time was to lay aside the so-called "Europeanised grammatical construction." There is no denying that one chief reason why the literature of the May Fourth movement failed to interest a large public is that writers adopting a new style often did not write in the syntax of ordinary Chinese discourse. Wang Li, devoting a long chapter in his *Theories of Chinese Grammar* [6] to Europeanisation

[6] Wang Li, *Chung-kuo Yü-fa Li-lun* (Shanghai: Commercial Press, 1944), Vol. II.

asserts the class character of this syntax, which he correctly observes, did not belong to the Chinese people as a whole. Hence, in 1938, the immediate task the writers set for themselves was to use the syntax of ordinary discourse. Under Mao's encouragement that they should live with the people and learn their language, they took a lesson in the discipline of language which the advocates of the *pai-hua* movement never took, by mingling with the troops and the people and thus learning to reproduce in their works the idiom of the particular place they wrote about. The success they achieved was something new at this time, as their style was not a reversion to the old vernacular style of novels like *The Dream of the Red Chamber* and *Lover-Heroes*, nor a straining after " European " syntax, but the use of a living idiom of a certain district. Writers such as Ting Ling and K'ung Chueh are not themselves northerners, yet their conscientious effort at learning proved fruitful in their use of dialects, which is lively and unexaggerated. As most war stories of this period are concerned with people in small villages in the north or northwest, the use of local dialect is as helpful a part in producing the atmosphere of a place as the use of local colour such as the *yao-tung* (caves) that serve as dwellings for the people there.

Some writers allow themselves to be a little more high flown. Some of Shao Tzu-nan's short stories are written in the old popular vernacular style, but parts are close to doggerels. The opening lines of *Yen Yung-t'ang Gains Life after Nine Deaths* [7] are a good example:

> You, you may attack with water, attack with fire, shoot me, behead me; I am a—boiling will not soften, hammering will not flatten—a tang-tang bronze pea!

Following the doggerel, the narrative begins with the ballad technique of interlocked sentences: "This story occurred at Nan-wo-k'ou on the banks of Yao-tzu River. This Yao-tzu River is . . . ," etc.

This kind of style might not be suitable for the more sophisticated war stories of later days, but it is appropriately tailored for telling an heroic story of folk nature to a humble audience.

Secondly and more importantly, this was still during the period when Mao's injunctions were allowed some freedom of interpretation. New China at this time was still a vision and not a reality. Hence writers were, on the whole, more free and spontaneous in the treatment of their materials and themes.

Several of the stories of this earlier group may be discussed because of structural interest or interesting characterisation. Structurally, the *Heroes of Lü-liang* [8] is the one that follows closest the old popular stories

[7] Shao Tzu-nan, *Yen Yung-t'ang Chiu-ssu I-sheng* (Shantung: Hsin-hua Book Co., 1947). This passage is borrowed from a play in *Yuan-ch'ü Hsuan* (*A Selection of Yuan Drama*), most likely a play by Kuan Han-ching.

[8] Ma Feng, Hsi Jung, *Lü-liang Ying-hsiung Chuan* (Peking: Hsin-hua Book Co., 1952).

of episodic nature. The structure of the *Water Margin*, one of the most popular stories of this type, owes its origin to the recital of stories. Before the *Heroes of Lü-liang* appeared in book form, it was published in the newspaper *Chin-sui Ta-Chung Pao* in instalments, relating stories of a selected group of heroes produced in the Fourth General Assembly of Heroes of the Chin-sui Border Region. The work started, therefore, as a series of individual stories linked only by the same group of characters. They were also recited to enthusiastic illiterate audiences. Later, when the authors were preparing them for publication in book form, they incorporated materials they had gathered from other sources into a novel of eighty chapters. The preface to the fourth edition recapitulates the history of its composition and apologises for the looseness of its structure.

Admittedly the structure of the *Heroes of Lü-liang* is loose, yet the sequence of its episodes is not purely accidental. Beginning with a brief narration of the fate of the area after the Lu-kou-chiao incident, the story really begins in 1942, when the enemy raids the village and captures a number of the villagers. From that point on, development of the militia and the power of the people govern the sequence of incidents. Lacking as it does a structural plan to which details are subordinated, careful attention has been paid to achieving a climatic conclusion in the arrangement of the episodes. Some outstanding incidents, such as the felling of the well-beloved forest to defeat the enemy's plan of railroad construction and escorting peasants close to the strongholds of the enemy to carry out spring planting and autumn reaping are done with exceptional power and give meaning and significance to the story.

In technique the writers borrow freely from traditional stories, especially the types of practical jokes played upon the enemy: the use of women as wiles, men disguised as women to trick the enemy, springing surprise attacks upon the enemy in the dead of night, planting of a secret agent in the heart of the enemy's premises, the use of a secret tunnel under the ground to reach an otherwise inaccessible place, are familiar tricks to the people and are used with unconcealed delight.

Another revival of an old device in all three groups of war stories and in which the *Heroes of Lü-liang* fully shares is naming characters according to the roles they play in the story. It is an old practice to give characters names whose meaning or sound (by means of punning) indicate their traits of character. There seems little doubt that this device is especially effective in recital of stories, as the audience enjoys hearing a character wearing his personality on his sleeves. The most popular names of heroes of towering strength in the new war stories are Shih-chu (Stone pillar) and T'ieh-chu (Iron pillar). In *Heroes of Lü-liang*, the Communist leader is called Lei Shih-chu (Thunder Stone pillar); the old man who sacrifices his own life to save the people of the whole village is called Chang Chung (Chang Loyalty). Other characters whose names tell their own tales in this work are K'ang Ming-li (K'ang Understanding reason), K'ang Chia-pai (K'ang Ruins home), and K'ang Shun-feng (K'ang Goes with the wind).

The *Heroes of Lü-liang* is one of the most successful war stories, and rightly so. Its indebtedness to a traditional form is not the only feature which makes it popular with the unsophisticated public. It is in conception and execution the most harmonious with peasant taste and comprehension. The story, the most important thing to every lover of fiction, is here the dominating interest. The characters are given a superficial individuality for ease of identification and the episodes are told with so much animation, vividness and warm sympathy that even if the reader wants to protest against some of its exaggerations he is bustled along with such gusto that he is left no time for anything but to follow. Mass strength, to use a Communist term, is represented at its best here. The intrusion of the Party, more conspicuous towards the latter part of the book, is, on the whole, subdued. Apart from a few places where the Party steps in to pronounce its lessons, which are dispatched in a few lines, the characters remain more or less the same merry, ignorant, but earnest and resourceful country people that they are to the end of the book. Chang Yu-i, who, in a moment of anger, speaks out in chagrin against the Party member: " You are intellectual elements and you have culture. I do not understand polished talk. If you want apology, you go and apologise. I may at least withdraw from the Militia! It is a business that risks your head. Don't think that anyone must do it," seems to remain complacent with his ignorance at the end of the story, so different is he and his fellows from the ambitious climbers described in other stories.

The other outstanding and also very popular novel of this period, *New Lover-Heroes,*[9] resembles the *Heroes of Lü-liang* in that it also deals with the war years in a small village; in most other respects, however, the two form a contrast with one another. The dominating interest of the *Heroes of Lü-liang* rests in its masterful narration of a variety of episodes, its warm and sparkling idiom and the tenor of urgency enwrapping the whole story. In *New Lover-Heroes*, the reader's interest is from the beginning absorbed by the leading characters, who, as the story unfolds, are shown to be highly self-conscious characters developing towards a definite goal. The episodes in the story are interesting enough, but they are subordinated to the main theme of the story, which is a

[9] K'ung Chueh, Yuan Ching, *Hsin Erh-nü Ying-hsiung Chuan* (Shanghai: Hsin wen-yi Ch'u-pan-she, 1952).

portrayal of the transformation of ignorant but highly alert and resolute villagers into exemplary cadres. Unlike the militia men in the *Heroes of Lü-liang*, they cast off their ignorance and illiteracy in no time. The young hero, Ta-shui, an illiterate at the beginning of the story, grows rapidly in knowledge and intelligence when he is trained to be a cadre. Before the story is half-way over, he has advanced so much in outlook that his first query about the girl whom his father proposes to betroth to him is to ask if she can read; and on his father answering in the negative, he says he does not want a girl who cannot read.

In construction, the reader is first struck by a superficial resemblance between the two novels, as both adopt the old device of division by chapters. The *Heroes of Lü-liang*, indeed, is contented with rather wholesale adoption of the episodic form of fiction. *New Lover-Heroes* uses chapter division, but it weaves a carefully planned plot in which unity and climax are achieved by paralleling the protagonists' development in ability and strength with the expanding scope of conscious resistance. In the use of chapter headings, too, one finds a contrast between the two works. Following the conventional device, the chapter headings of the *Heroes of Lü-liang* are balanced couplets of seven, eight or nine characters and their phrasing is like that of couplets used as chapter headings in second-class popular stories, which are very different from the elegant phrasing of those that appear in such novels as *The Dream of the Red Chamber* and *New Lover-Heroes*.

New Lover-Heroes introduces something new, and is adapted for the appreciation of the cadres who have only recently become culture conscious. Each of its chapter headings consists of a short phrase stating the subject of that chapter followed by a proverb, a folk saying, a few lines of Communist poetry or the injunction of a Communist leader, such as Mao Tse-tung or Chu Teh, to foreshadow the atmosphere of or comment on the content of, or give a clue to the significance of, that chapter. Here are a few examples:

Chapter 2 The Communist Party

Stars follow the moon,
People follow the Communist Party

—People's saying

Chapter 10 Sleeping on ice

No wavering in the midst of hardship

—Chairman Mao's saying

Chapter 13 Venturing into the tiger's lair

Without entering the tiger's lair,
How can you obtain the tiger's cub?

Chapter 16 Love and Hate
Fiery red is the blooming pomegranate tree,
I love you and you love me;
Young people are as numerous as fine sand,
Why do you love only me—

—Folk song

Chapter 20 Victory
Courage, courage, and again courage!

—General Chu Teh's words

In the use of language, although both novels make skilful use of dialects, a greater concern for artistic representation and a desire to produce something new distinguish *New Lover-Heroes*. The *Heroes of Lü-liang* revives an old mode of story telling and uses a modern living dialect, but it does not disdain borrowing verbatim some old clichés loved by old vernacular writers. One finds there such expressions as: " The four gendarmes were so scared that the wine [they drank] had all evaporated into cold sweat " and " Capped with a goose feather and you are not aware that it is light; weighted with a mill and you are not aware that it is heavy."

K'ung Chueh, one of the two writers of *New Lover-Heroes,* is a native of Soochow, trained at the Lu Hsün Literary Academy during the first years of the war. He has given an account of his painstaking efforts to master the local dialects of the north-west.[10] His use of dialect in the novel is indeed a remarkable success, but he does not content himself with just using dialects. In the narrative part, his style is different from that of the old vernacular novels, because it has absorbed in its fluent style, points of Western grammatical construction which in category might belong to what is called Europeanisation, but which mingle easily with the Chinese syntax and are not incongruous but produce a delightful sense of newness.

In his Yenan forum talk Mao stressed the two-fold purpose of popularisation and elevation. The latter was designed for the cadres, who, as he said, " are generally better educated than the masses, and art and literature of a higher level are entirely necessary to them." The *New Lover-Heroes* is a novel answering that demand, a point which Kuo Mo-jo is careful to bring out in his preface to the novel: " Cannot all men learn to be like Ta-shui? Cannot all women learn to become Yang Hsiao-mei? It does not matter if you are mediocre, backward, or even illiterate and ignorant. If only you have been awakened, seek progress, are possessed of the spirit of self-sacrifice, and faithfully practise Chairman Mao's ideology then you can become a pillar of the new society."

[10] *Chung-hua Ch'uan-kuo Wen-hsueh I-shu Kung-tso che Tai-piao Ta-hui Chi-nien Wen-hsien* (Peking: Hsin-hua Book Co., 1950), pp. 436–445.

The story *Yen-su Crag* [11] contains a character interesting not because it is a success in characterisation but because it is a failure, a failure which illustrates an aesthetic truth: the incompatibility of the demands literature makes on a writer and the commitments of a writer who dedicates his efforts to one ideology.

This character in *Yen-su Crag* is Chang Lo-shan, the powerful landlord. Differing from most other landlords who are almost invariably described as entirely despicable and wicked or very cowardly, Chang Lo-shan is impressively drawn as a man of strength of character. Yen-su Crag, it is said, is an almost inaccessible mountainous village and therefore has always enjoyed the freedom of those outside the pale of the law. In this place Chang is the uncrowned king and his every word is law. He not only has wealth, but has control over a band of over a thousand men fully equipped with ammunition, rifles and light machine guns. When war comes, this isolated village is also affected. First a battalion of the Central Army, retreating from Nan-k'ou, decends upon the village and starts to give the people trouble, but they are buried alive by the villagers. In 1938, when the enemy carry out their extermination campaign, the villagers indeed find that they are not the match of the enemy, but they tolerate them for only one night, for during that night they launch a surprise attack and so force them to retreat after daybreak the next day. Then, the political workers of the Eighth Route Army hear of this extraordinary village and they send two of their men to find out about it. These men are detained right away, but, after a long talk with Chang, they convince him of the invincibility of the Eighth Route Army and the need to resist Japan; so he promises to co-operate with them and hands over to them his men and weapons. His appearance is drawn in this manner:

> The door opens. The man standing outside is Chang Lo-shan. He wears a fur-lined gown of old bronze colour with a swastika pattern. A long beard hangs on his chest, a dappled pepper and salt. High cheek bones make his eyes look slightly sunk, but they bristle with spirit. Although close to sixty, he is extraordinarily hale and hearty. In his left hand he holds two walnuts, which he leisurely rolls. The airs of one who has lorded over the place in the past are not one whit abated.

This man who has lorded over the place by sheer force of character and who at the time the story begins is said to be unabated in his airs, collapses, just as ignominiously as all the other landlords, before the intimidations and temptations of the Japanese. His behaviour contrasts on the one hand with that of Chang Hsiao-kuei, the head of the village, who is a Party member and dies a martyr's death, and on the other hand with that of the Japanese soldier, Katano. Katano is deeply

[11] Chou Erh-fu, *Yen-su Yai* (Shanghai: Hsin-hua Book Co., 1954).

moved (and no doubt reforms as a result) by the generous treatment he receives from the Eighth Route Army, and he can be so moved, because, as is suggested by a Communist officer, he must have come from the worker-peasant class.

The portrayal of Chang is unconvincing because the writer shows that soon after he presents that character he becomes uncertain as to what he should make of him. From the manner in which Chang is introduced in the story, it is obvious that the writer intends to produce a landlord of a different calibre from the stock ones. In the process of writing, however, he must have discovered that this creation would lead him to contradict a Communist formula. In order to save himself from falling into that error, he patches it up by giving him the orthodox role reserved for a man of his class. If the inconsequentiality of the end makes the reader wonder why he started in the way he did, he should soon realise that a writer who has thus committed himself cannot afford to follow the development of a character logically and hence cannot but suffer creative failures.

Another interesting character from the war stories of this period is a creation of Ting Ling's. After Ting Ling had gone to Yenan during the war, she published in the newspaper *Chieh-fang Jih-pao* the sketch of a manager of a co-operative, as a result of which Mao Tse-tung congratulated her for making peasants and workers her subject matter. Ting Ling produced her best work during these years and created a number of characters distinguished by her regard for sensitive and truthful representation. In the character of Cheng-cheng in her short story, "When I was in Hsia Village," [12] she has created a woman character unique in conception and yet which is not without its prototypes in Chinese history. Cheng-čheng is a village girl who, after having fallen into the hands of Japanese troops, spent a year moving with them from place to place. On her return to her own village she is regarded as a hero by the young Communist worker who says that she has been working among the Japanese for over a year. To A-kuei, the woman Communist worker who accompanied Ting Ling to the village, this young girl is an object of infinite sympathy. To most other people of the village, especially the women, she is intolerable except for the fact that her presence among them throws into sharper relief their own chastity; to her own mother and other members of the family she is an innocent victim of circumstance, but still a humiliating presence for the family. The girl herself is the only one who views the whole unfortunate episode in her life in its true perspective. Open-minded and open-hearted, warm-natured and sensible, she

[12] Ting Ling, *Wo tsai Hsia-tsün ti Shih-hou* (Peking: Jen-min Wen-hsueh Ch'u-pan-she, 1946). This story is also included in *Yenan Chi* (1954) in which a few added sentences depict Cheng-cheng as working against the Japanese rather more consciously.

finds no need for sympathy or cause for shame, yet because of her unfortunate experience and ruined health, she refuses to marry the man whom she has loved and who still loves her and wants to marry her. After an unhappy stay at home, she decides to go to the city, where she is sent to get medical care so that she may avail herself also of the opportunity to study.

The traditional Chinese attitude towards the woman who has lost her chastity, whether voluntarily or otherwise, has always been contempt or pity, and that attitude has proved, among all the deeply imbedded false attitudes, the hardest for the Chinese to discard. Ting Ling makes a keen observation in the following passage:

> Sometimes she [Cheng-cheng] paused in her talk. At this time, she would look at us, perhaps trying to find some reaction in our faces, but perhaps she was just thinking about something else. Obviously A-kuei was suffering much more than she. Most of the time A-kuei was silent, sometimes she would say a few words, words intended merely to convey her infinite sympathy, but when she was silent, it was even more obvious that she was horror-stricken at what Cheng-cheng said, that her soul was crushed, that she trudged over the sufferings Cheng-cheng had gone through.

Here is the contrast between A-kuei, the woman who is bound by the age-old view, a view which you might say, refuses to be released from the narrow range dictated by tyrannous tradition, and Cheng-cheng, the woman who rises above it. Cheng-cheng is a new woman worthy of the aspirations of a new culture, and reminds one of Shelley's lines in *Prometheus Unbound* singing of the women who were

> From custom's evil taint exempt and pure;
> Speaking the wisdom once they could not think,
> Looking emotions once they feared to feel,
> And changed to all which once they dared not be,
>
> Act III, Scene 4.

The general impression given to one by the second group of war stories may be summed up in the one word " hollow." Indeed, the sense of unreality they exude is sometimes so strong that if history and our own memory did not assert their authenticity, the reader well might wonder if these stories were about actual wars.

An initial comparison of the stories of the first group and those of the second group yields a few contrasts in the materials available to the story writer. The scope of the last two wars was obviously much narrower than that of the conflagration that lit up numerous spots of the country at the same time during the war with Japan, and they did not affect so deeply and uniformly the people of the whole country. The potential raw material for fiction in the latter two wars may thus be said to have been poorer. The colourful guerrilla and militia were largely replaced by regular or at least well organised troops. With the withdrawal of the Japanese army there were no longer those forts which featured so eventfully during the war with Japan. Gone also are the scenes of torture and the many episodes of courage and narrow escape. And yet, the absence of these colourful incidents cannot account for the hollowness of the war stories. In place of what had passed into history, other pressing problems that were stirring enough came to dominate the later wars. In so readable a book of war stories about the Kuomintang and Communist struggle as *War Flames Ablaze Everywhere*, by Liu Po-yü,[13] one finds vivid descriptions of the intense cold of the north-east where troops cross rivers in temperatures of well below zero and stirring descriptions of vigorous fighting and the accomplishment of numerous heroic deeds. Indeed, in the novel *Fire Flames are at the Front* [14] on the same subject, by the same author, the presentation of the theme of the difference between the north and the south and the sufferings of the northerner when he first comes to the swampy, humid, mosquito-infested mountainous areas of the south, which have proved to be the undoing of famous historical expeditions, is done with sympathy, humour and understanding. The Korean war story that has the delightful title of *Three Thousand Li of Rivers and Mountains*,[15] by Yang Shuo, is strewn with short delightful sketches of nature and glimpses of Korean life. Thus it seems that the hollowness of the war stories of this group cannot be attributed to poverty of raw material since each war has its own background and its typical crop of incidents. The wonder is that in spite of some commendable writing among them, they do not possess the spark of life so essential to a piece of true art.

Searching a little further beyond the question of the raw material of war stories, we are faced with the problem of the value of war fiction. In connection with this, one should consider a notable phenomenon of the war years. As the war with Japan dragged on, the theme of war became appallingly dull to many people. Some literary men in Chungking felt this and in newspaper articles called for writings on themes other than that of the war. The feeling seems to have been that war was an interrupting and, therefore, an alienating force in life, and that war literature contained nothing better than propaganda.

War, admittedly, is an interruption of peaceful living, yet it is, no less than peaceful living, a phase of life, and anything that illuminates a

[13] Liu Po-yü, *Chan-huo fen-fei* (Shanghai: Hsin-hua Book Co., 1949).
[14] Liu Po-yü *Huo-kuang tsai Ch'ien* (Peking: Jen-min Wen-hsueh Ch'u-pan-she, 1952).
[15] Yang Shuo, *San-ch'ien Li Chiang Shan* (Peking: Jen-min Wen-hsueh Ch'u-pan-she, 1953).

phase of life has a place in literature. This accounts for the enduring popularity of outstanding war novels, Chinese as well as Western.

The fault, then, does not lie in war literature itself but in the handling of war material, which is determined by one's concept of war. If a war story gives a picture of the history and struggle of a people, of the things in which are mirrored the pride and happiness, the grief and humiliation of a people, war fiction should be able to achieve as enduring greatness as fiction of any other kind.

The comparative success of the best war stories of the anti-Japanese war period not only does not stem from their propaganda value, but also does not come from the colourful and stirring episodes themselves. It comes from that spirit of earnestness which, as all reflections of life must, pervades the episodes narrated in the stories. They illuminate, spotty and one-sided though they may be, the picture of the life of a people locked in a struggle with an enemy within their gates. Notwithstanding the propaganda purpose and the extolling of physical strength as the chief virtue, war is shown as a force that men have to grapple with and try to do without.

Reckoned by the degree of violence in fighting and display of heroism, stories of the civil war group are not one whit behind those of the earlier group. Still, what linger in one's memory after reading the best of them are floating scenes of vivid description against a background of make-believe. Even when viewed purely from the purpose of propaganda, one wonders how effectual such propaganda can be when it is administered in an atmosphere of such palpable unreality.

The background for the change in the tenor of these stories may largely be sought in the shifting of emphasis by expounders of Mao's literary ideas. After the overall victory of the Communists in 1949, the great theme of the day, says Chou Yang in his *Thoroughly Carry Out the Literary Lines of Mao Tse-tung*, is that of " giving expression to the great theme of patriotism." " Literature," says Chou, " should first of all set forth the advanced personages among the Chinese people, represent the great strength of the Chinese people and the Chinese Communist Party, their superior wisdom and heroism. . . . Literature should help the people to sweep clear the inferior psychology engendered by the humiliating position long borne by the people, and to build up a national self-respect appropriate to the great Chinese people and the national position we occupy today. It should strengthen people's faith regarding their own great strength and bright future. It is a pity that our literature has not been able to fully accomplish this. It has not been able fully to represent the strength of the Chinese people who have ' stood up '; its characters often have not stood up, in their 'spiritual attitudes'; some are even described as stooping and bent." [16]

Another point of emphasis is "revolutionary romanticism." Mao Tun says: "Under the ideological leadership of the Marxist-Leninist world outlook, we have united the truth-seeking spirit of science and the heroic ambition of ceaseless revolutionism, and, standing on the height of Communism, we reflect both the reality of today, and also, with infinite enthusiasm, with grand and optimistic tunes, and with full and dripping pens, sing the praises of the budding state of tomorrow that is born on the foundation of today's reality. In other words, we sing of all the teeming and lively new things. We remain reflectionists, but we do not reflect passively and negatively; on the contrary, in high and dashing spirits, we employ Communist ideology to throw into brighter and sharper relief, the tomorrow that is budding in the reality; that is to say, we want to give reality a positive influence so as to push today all the more quickly into tomorrow. This is the union of revolutionary realism and revolutionary romanticism." [17]

Basically, underlying the exhortation to portray patriotism and to unite revolutionary realism with revolutionary romanticism are the old precepts for eulogy and exposure and propagandistic exaggeration that have been the preoccupation of the writers all along. The difference is that with the confidence and pride newly gained from the establishment of a Communist régime, it was believed, it seems, that intensified efforts at exaggeration would reap an even greater harvest in strengthening the people's belief in their own invincibility and superiority. During the Japanese war days, the central lesson writers aimed at learning was enrichment of personal experience through getting to know life at first hand and the adoption of literary forms acceptable to the masses. Now, with the shifting of emphasis to racial superiority in the name of patriotism and pushing today the more quickly into tomorrow in the name of the union of revolutionary realism and revolutionary romanticism, writers do nothing but distort and misinform the reader about real life. Literature becomes burdened with an amount of make-up beyond its capacity to bear. Thus, while reading the best war stories of the earlier period, we are able to enjoy, with a certain amount of tolerance, what we know is exaggerated presentation, we find the over-stepping of bounds in the exaggeration of the stories of the second group wholly falsifies the impression the writer wants to create. The following is an example of what a commander-in-chief is said to think of his troops: when they were making their last rehearsal [crossing the Yangtze], the

[16] Chou Yang, *Chien-chueh kuan-ch'e Mao Tse-tung ti Wen-yi Lu-hsien* (Peking: Jen-min wen-hsueh Ch'u-pan-she, 1952), p. 81.
[17] Mao Tun, *op. cit.*, p. 65.

commander-in-chief arrived. He was very much satisfied with what he saw. These warriors, he thought, have gone far, far beyond what may be described by the mere word 'bravery.' They are actually creators of the science of victory and representatives of high wisdom." [18]

This is the general vein in which those to be eulogised are spoken of. Every military officer and every common soldier is a perfectly saintly model of his class, and if he is not yet he is on his way to it. Admittedly this is not reality, but it is hailed as representing the budding tomorrow in today's reality, a union of revolutionary realism with revolutionary romanticism. Speaking of romanticism, which also came, it is said, from Mao Tse-tung, one may compare a line of his poetry, "The six hundred million of the sacred land are all Shun and Yao" [19] with the hyperbolic passage quoted above. Mao's line is not only good, but powerful. In poetry, the millions being all saints is a bold suggestion of potentiality, such as was suggested by a Sung Neo-Confucianist, whereas the literal-mindedness of a military officer's evaluation of his troops in such terms is plainly unthinkable.

The result is that war, the gravest of all human activities to any man of sense, is, in the hands of these romantic writers, shorn of all its gravity and grim reality. Instead, it is, in these stories, treated as a sporting occasion. The responsibility of the able military leader is to rouse the spirit of his troops by manipulating the human instinct for vainglory. The following is a dialogue between a superior military officer and a lower one:

> Ch'in Ming lowered his eyes, cigarette in hand and asked, after a long thoughtful pause: "How are the workmen? Can they adapt themselves to this type of fighting?"
>
> Wu Cheng said: "Genuine gold fears no beating. After all, they are of the proletarian class, so there is no problem; only some of them seem a little below par in feeling."
>
> Ch'in Ming asked thoughtfully: "Have you stirred up their zeal?"
>
> Wu Cheng said: "Haven't I! Every Party member is in the front, producing the effect of leadership."
>
> Ch'ing Ming sat up, extinguished his cigarette on the edge of the brazier and said: "This is correct. There is something more. You should universally stir up the new heroism of the people under the leadership of the Party members. Have you been able to do that?"
>
> Wu Cheng said nothing.
>
> Ch'in Ming glanced at him and said: "You should know, heroes are not born, they are cultivated. In every man's chest is buried a seed of fire, with something noble hidden in it. All that you have to do is to give it a stir," and, as he said this, he took up the fire tongs and gave the fire a shove, at which crackling spots sputtered brilliantly from the fire, and he continued: "Every man can shine, every man can be a hero.

[18] Hai Mo, *T'u-p'o Lin-chin Chiang* (Peking: Tso-chia Ch'u-pan-she, 1954), p. 176.
[19] A line in one of two poems by Mao, *People's Daily*, October 3, 1958.

Why don't you launch an over-all movement for merit establishment? It is only through the movement of merit establishment that workers may get the honour that is their due." [20]

By means of such manipulation, war comes to be regarded as a great game in which each soldier pins his day-dreams on gaining honours for himself on the battlefield. The obsession of each soldier should be, it is hinted, " How brave am I?" " Can I win a medal in this battle?" " Can I be made a Communist Party member, maybe right on the battlefield?" The following is a dialogue among soldiers just before action:

" Director! Watch me! Let the Party test me to see if I am qualified."
" Comrades, the opportunity for our regiment to be regularised has arrived!"
" Have you got your next month Party membership fee ready?"
" It is in my small pocket; if I am no longer here you will hand it in for me!"
" Mine is in my cap. Remember!" [21]

In the famous epistle the Han general Li Ling sent to Su Wu, he said his troops " looked upon death as welcome as returning home." It seems that this is the kind of spirit the story writer wants to bring out in his soldiers, but one wonders if Li Ling would, were he brought back to life, identify this frivolous and juvenile spirit with that of his troops. It is owing to such an attitude given to the troops that no amount of bitter fighting and feats of courage described later on can save a story of this type from being false and unreal.

These war stories can boast of having carried out the Communist programme of creating a standardised human product. They have, in fact, carried it out so well that after reading a number of these stories, the reader does not retain in his memory any distinctive characters such as Ta-shui and Hsiao-mei, even though reading about the latter in *New Lover-Heroes*, one is aware of the writers' deliberate restraint so as to avoid giving to them too much prominence. One does not even find a creative failure as Chang Lo-shan, because there is no longer room for a writer to make such a mistake. Thus, these writers, in their effort to help push forward the policy of collectivism, both in life and thought, have reduced literature to an instrument of pure, formal propagandistic teaching.

Before we conclude, it might not be irrelevant to take a retrospective look at old Chinese war stories to see if Communist war stories are influenced by them in any way besides their general debt to traditional fiction spoken of above. An outstanding connection between the old and new groups is the appearance in new war stories of types of characters

[20] Yang Shuo, *op. cit.*, p. 105.
[21] Hai Mo, *op. cit.*, p. 189.

reminiscent of familiar old types. One type is the loyal but recklessly courageous fighter. This is a favourite type with old writers and readers. The guilelessness of these characters is a preliminary that wins the goodwill of their readers while their lack of forethought and excessive zeal for fighting usually provides either fun or exciting feats of daring. Wu Sung and Li K'uei in *Water Margin,* Chang Fei in the *Romance of the Three Kingdoms* and Niu Kao and Wang Kuei in the *Story of Yueh Fei*[22] belong to this group. In Communist war stories, we still meet with a modern version of this type in the shape of a militia man or a common soldier.

Two other types that are not so popular but figure nevertheless in the older war fiction are the old fighter who refuses to admit that he is old and the young lad who is eager to be a fighter. The prototype of the former type may be found in Ma Yuan, the Han general, who, at the age of 62, demonstrated his fitness as a soldier on his horse so as to win the emperor's consent to let him lead an army to suppress a rebellious tribe in the south. An outstanding example of the young boy anxious to be a fighter is found in the story of Yueh Fei, in which his son Yueh Yun, when still under the age of ten, is said to have begged his father not to kill all the Tartars so that he might have a chance to kill some when he grew up. The approbation of physical courage implied in these stories agrees eminently with Communist policy. While it is assuming too much to maintain that the Communists took their examples from the older war fiction, it is noticeable that they produced characters of the same type, particularly the lad who is eager to get enlisted before he is of age.

In other respects, the difference between ancient warfare and modern warfare must be responsible for much of the differences between the stories. In ancient warfare, the outcome of the struggle depended both on strategy and the fighting skill of individual warriors. The battlefield was a place for display of magnificent equipment and the personal prowess of combating generals. They, the generals and warriors, are the central figures and the listener's or reader's interest was chiefly monopolised by descriptions of their heroic bearing and skill. The completely different character of modern warfare and the Communist attitude to it have changed all that. Regarding central figures in Communist stories, Professor Birch has very aptly said, the peasant has been "led from his place in the wings, where he waited to perform briefly as buffoon or potential bandit, to the centre of the stage as a dramatic figure in his own right."[23] The peasant coming to the centre of the

[22] *Shuo Yüeh ch'üan chuan,* popular Ching edition of the story of the Sung General Yueh Fei.

[23] Cyril Birch, "Fiction of the Yenan Period," *The China Quarterly,* No. 4, October–December 1960, p. 11.

stage in his own right is indeed an achievement of Communist fiction. Thus, in war stories it is the militia man and the common soldier who have become central figures. In 1960, Mao Tun remarked on the " conspicuous progress in the art of portraying high ranking military officials and political committee members " in recent fiction, but so far we have not come across any noteworthy characterisation of this type.

An important point to remember in a consideration of old and new war fiction is the slow growth and formation of old war stories. The long period of time over which the stories were recited and the revisions given to them by various hands after they had been written down subjected them to a long process of romantic amplification. When they finally emerged in their finished forms, they had become war romances rather than war stories. Their reciters and authors, indeed, are at one with Communist writers in their attitude that war is unavoidable and that killing one's enemy, unless he surrenders, is a duty that requires no second thought, but here their resemblances end. Regarding war from a distance of time, when battles had cooled into historical events, authors of war romances usually took the stand of spectators, some of them pompously, as, we might say, philosophers of history, and drew the conclusion, as in the *Romance of the Three Kingdoms*, that history repeats itself and that a period of tumult is followed by a period of peace and order. Being spectators, they could also afford to moralise. They agreed that a war story should end on a note of restoration of peace. For this reason, even such a novel as the *Romance of the Generals of the Yang Family*,[24] which is a narrative of straight fighting from beginning to end, has for its last sentence: " From henceforth peace reigned in all four corners and thus this book also comes to an end." The change of the *Water Margin* from one hundred and twenty chapters to seventy chapters by Shih Nai-an and his concluding it with a dream of Lu Chün-i, in which he witnessed the beheading of all his sworn brothers and the flash of the words " Peace under Heaven " in blue, reflects the deep-rooted idea of ending a story of war and violence on a note of peace and serenity. The Communists, characteristically, often introduce, at the end of a story, slogans for fresh fighting or scenes of renewed enthusiasm for more fighting. Even a story as *Flames of Fire in the Front*, which draws its conclusion at the complete victory of the Communists over the Nationalists, flashes no cool blue words promising peace, but proclaims their victory in blazing flames. The story writers are participants in the struggle themselves and they know that their task is not yet completed.

[24] *Yang-chia-chiang Yen-i*, a story of the military careers of the Sung General Yang Yeh and his sons.

Residual Femininity:
Women in Chinese Communist Fiction

By C. T. HSIA

IN Chinese Communist literature, men and women are primarily seen in their likeness as workers rather than in their sexual and emotional unlikeness as human beings. Women, as much as men, are praised for their socialist zeal and heroic capacity for work and condemned for being socialist sluggards indifferent to production. But despite its repudiation of " human interest " as a symptom of capitalist or revisionist decadence,[1] even this supremely practical literature cannot begin to exist without some superficial attention to personal problems, and these problems, inevitably, attest to the persistence of biological instincts and immemorial habits of human civilisation. Until the techniques, Communist or otherwise, for dehumanisation are perfected, men and women will remain subject to irrational passions, and if circumstances permit, they will fall in love, get married, bring up children, and in other devious ways contrive for pleasure and happiness. In tracing the lot of Chinese women under Communism, I will therefore take for granted that the primary purpose of their earthly existence is to contribute to and assist in production and examine rather their residual personal problems in the context of the overriding importance of socialist construction. The results of my investigation, if my women characters,

[1] Orthodox Communist critics in China have of course no quarrel with " human interest " in its broader neutral meaning; in that sense, whatever a character does or fails to do is of human interest. Their quarrel with the revisionist critics is over the more dramatic kind of " human interest ": the problem whether under strong emotion or other unusual circumstance a person habitually seen in his " class " character may reveal his essential " human " character. The test case is whether a Communist hero may turn coward when facing death. The revisionists think he may; the orthodox Communists maintain, on the other hand, that to impute cowardice to a Communist hero is to distort and malign his Communist character. In his long address to the Third Congress of the All-China Federation of Literary and Art Circles on July 24, 1960, Mao Tun cites the following situations of " human interest " for special condemnation: " That a hero facing death must show a weak longing for life, that there must be mental conflict or hesitation when a man has to sacrifice his family for a just cause, or that a man may set free an enemy for the sake of ' humanity.' " Mao Tun continues: " The revisionists like this kind of ' human interest,' but we are against it. To us, this smacks of the bourgeoisie and petty-bourgeoisie, not the human interest of the proletariat. In particular, the signs of weakness in a hero going to his death are intolerable distortions of a hero's character and not a matter of human interest at all." The quotations are taken from the English text of Mao Tun's address as given in *Chinese Literature* (December 1960), p. 34. The issue of " human interest " is inseparable from the persistent debate between orthodox and revisionist Communists on " human nature," of which see *infra*, footnote 34.

drawn invariably from short stories, are at all typical, will show, not surprisingly, the pathetic adjustment of their feminine instincts and interests to the jealous demands of Party and state. The exceptions that I will take notice of—sympathetic victims and challengers of the impersonal Communist bureaucracy—are all heroines of revisionist fiction that has been subject to vehement attack by the press.

Space permitting, I would have liked to conduct my inquiry in a strictly historical fashion: a year-by-year survey of the changing condition of women under changing political and economic circumstances during the twelve years of Communist power. Though in its main emphases Chinese Communist literature has remained unchanged since the proclamation of the Mao Tse-tung line in 1942, writers, of necessity, have responded to particular drives and campaigns through the years, and in so doing, have reflected the changing complexion of the new society. Roughly, the change has been toward greater dehumanisation under the increasing necessity for collectivisation so that the literature of the Yenan period, with its permitted bucolic simplicity, is quite different from the literature of the post-1949 period, and the literature of the early and middle fifties is quite different from the literature of the Great Leap Forward and after, when the foundering of the commune system in a sea of apathy has meant for the people a regimen of impossible toil and actual starvation. Since the late Yenan period, production has always remained "the theme of all themes,"[2] but in reading the more recent literature, one recalls a time when labour was not seen as a night-and-day process, when the material rewards for labour were confidently and rightly expected.

These changes have been duly reflected in the behaviour of women characters in fiction. In 1943, in his celebrated story "The Marriage of Hsiao Erh-hei," Chao Shu-li could suggest the popularity of a village beauty in patently idyllic terms: "With or without excuse, the village lads would always want to exchange a few words with Hsiao Ch'in. When Hsiao Ch'in went laundering, the lads would immediately go laundering; when Hsiao Ch'in climbed trees to pick edible leaves, the lads would immediately do the same."[3] In spite of its great absurdity as a description of Chinese village life, the passage enjoys in retrospect a poignant pastoral charm because after 1949 any comparable description in a story of contemporary life would have been out of place. In a story about life in a commune, it would have been unthinkable. Granted that washing clothes and picking leaves are useful work, the youths in Chao Shu-li's story are nevertheless motivated by their desire to get

[2] Cyril Birch quotes this phrase in his valuable article "Fiction of the Yenan Period," *The China Quarterly*, No. 4, October–December 1960, p. 3.
[3] *Chao Shu-li Hsuan-chi* (Peking: 1951), p. 59.

closer to a village beauty rather than by their desire to build Socialism. Their behaviour is reprehensible, and the girl, in causing these regular commotions, is also censurable as a distracting and disruptive influence. Following this line of reasoning, one can understand why Fang Chi's story "Let Life Become More Beautiful" (*Jen-min Wen-hsueh* [*People's Literature*, or PL], March 1950), also about a village beauty, became one of the earliest stories to merit severe censure from the *People's Daily*.[4] Like Hsiao Ch'in, Hsiao Huan, though very faithful to her chosen lover, welcomes attention from all her admirers. The village militiamen would gather at her house every evening, giving her a bad reputation. But when the local cadres have failed to recruit able-bodied youth for the Liberation Army, it is she who incites eleven of her friends, including her lover, to volunteer for service. Throughout the story, the author is quite self-conscious about his heroine's objectionable popularity, and he apparently thought that her meritorious action as an inspirer of patriotic zeal would have vindicated her honour. But he didn't realise that if it is wrong to attract so many militiamen to her house, it is positively wicked of her to rally these men to a worthy cause when the cadres have failed. The Party brooks no rivals. A beautiful girl in Communist China has to suppress all vanity lest in her small circle she unwittingly supplants the Party as the primary object of adoration.

"The Heirloom" (1949), another story by Chao Shu-li, confidently asserts the kind of prosperity which is seen to have eluded the grasp of the Chinese in the years of their increasing collectivisation. The story depicts, quite ably, the comic contentions between a feudal-minded woman and her enlightened daughter-in-law Chin-kuei who, as a labour hero and chairman of the local women's association, is enjoying with her husband the blessings of the new Communist order. But the mother, bound to extreme frugality by her habitual poverty, disapproves of her spendthrift ways. Who has ever heard of a daughter-in-law who uses half a bucket of water to wash a head of cabbage, squanders one catty of oil each month for cooking, and has her uniforms fashionably made by a tailor? Good-humouredly, Chin-kuei eventually convinces the woman that under the new régime extreme measures of economy are impractical and uncalled for. Yet following the establishment of the commune system, the roles of the two women have been reversed: it is now the tradition-bound woman who would insist on token comfort and luxury, and it is her progressive husband or daughter-in-law who would force her to conserve all capital for Socialism. In "Corduroy,"

[4] In its May 1950 issue, PL publishes two letters from readers attacking the story, one reprinted from the *People's Daily* (*Jen-min Jih-pao*). Fang Chi's self-criticism is featured in the following issue.

a recent story by Hsi Jung (PL, July–August 1961), the backward wife of a commune director badly wants to buy a few yards of corduroy to make a suit of clothes for her prospective daughter-in-law, a labour hero. If in 1949 the chairman of a women's association is entitled to the luxury of custom-made uniforms, one would think that the wife of a commune director in 1961—after a dozen years of frenzied national reconstruction—would be within her rights to buy some cloth. But no, the poor woman doesn't have a penny to spend, since the dividend due to her family for their last year's labour, along with all the earnings of the member families in the commune, has been deposited in the commune trust as development capital. And her husband, a selfless worker, is firmly against her borrowing money to meet this unnecessary expense. Using her influence, however, she eventually gets the money from a sympathetic accountant (also censured for his wastefulness: because, while keeping accounts deep into the night, he keeps on using a smoky old lamp which consumes more kerosene than the glass-covered new lamp). But when the story becomes scandalous news, she has to return the money and the corduroy. Moreover, her husband instigates his future daughter-in-law to convene a mass meeting to criticise her: "Your big aunt is too backward in her ideas. If we don't criticise her now, I am afraid her backwardness will get worse." [5]

In 1949 the self-denying mother-in-law is backward; in 1961 the self-denying daughter-in-law is progressive. Conditions on the mainland may have deteriorated during the interim, but "progressive" and "backward" have remained a reliable pair of propaganda terms, supplying all the needed drama in stories about women (or about men and children). So far as women are concerned, the decisive event during this period has been the enactment of the Marriage Law in 1950, proclaiming the emancipation of all women from feudal bondage. During that and the following year, a great many stories appeared to welcome the new marital freedom of women. Nearly all these stories centre upon the conflict between the progressive and the backward—a theme hashed and rehashed since the May Fourth period—with the progressive children easily winning out against their backward parents, who are uniformly stupid in attempting to arrange undesirable matches for their offspring.[6]

[5] PL (July–August 1961), p. 61.

[6] These stories, of course, make no reference to the far grimmer reality. According to Chang-tu Hu *et al.*, *China: Its People, Its Society, Its Culture* (New Haven: 1960), p. 176, following the promulgation of the Marriage Law, "a rising number of suicides and murders, mostly of women, reached such an extent that in September 1951 the Government Administration Council . . . issued a directive to all local authorities calling for a general investigation in their respective areas." In February 1953 the National Committee for the Thorough Implementation of the Marriage Law disclosed that "between seventy and eighty thousand people were killed or committed suicide in a single year in China over marriage difficulties" (*ibid.* p. 177).

Between the marriage stories of the May Fourth period and the Communist period, however, there is a fundamental difference. The stories of the early period—and this is true even of Pa Chin's later massive assaults on the feudal marital custom, *Family* and *Spring*—are crude in the direction of sentimentality: a lachrymose exaltation of the emotion of love in the stifling environment of feudal oppression. The Communist stories, on the other hand, are crude in the direction of practicality: true love among the young is always cemented by their love for labour. The progressive daughters instinctively choose the labour heroes of their locality, while their mothers, guided by their feudal regard for property, would marry them into families that are comparatively well off. The contest between the progressive and the backward is, in the last analysis, a contest between two forms of prudence: the prudence of Communist youths who invest in labour and the discredited prudence of their elders who still bank on individual wealth. And in this contest the love factor necessarily receives only minimal and perfunctory attention.

By 1950, writers on the mainland did not have to be told that romantic love was disruptive of Party discipline and destructive of Party loyalty.[7] They knew that while the cheerful and hard-working lovers might brighten the socialist scene, any personal attachment that manifested a deeper emotion than a jaunty cheerfulness was potentially subversive. Once they have removed the feudal obstacles to their union, therefore, the Communist lovers remain positively cheerful. They do not pine for each other's company, and they are happily resigned to an infinite postponement of their marriage as long as more imperative duties claim their attention. On their wedding day they are more likely than not to perform some feats of unusual valour; during the wedding ceremony they invariably pledge themselves to work much harder in the years ahead. These brave deeds and promises are necessary to atone for what appears almost as the inherently criminal character of marriage as a private union between two individuals.

With his brief story "Marriage" (1950), Ma Feng set the trend for cheerfulness. In that story the heroine Hsiao-ch'ing, on one pretext or another, postpones her wedding. When her lover Ch'un-sheng wants to set the date again following her stint in the nearby city as a trainee in hygiene work for women and infants, she good-humouredly lectures him:

> "See how impatient you are! I've just returned from study and the village hygiene work for women and babies hasn't started yet and we

[7] Cyril Birch, *op. cit.*, p. 5, quotes an early critical pronouncement by Chou Yang, "Love has retired to a position in life of no importance; the new works have themes a thousand times more important, more significant than love." Chou Yang, of course, is merely echoing Mao Tse-tung's belittling view of love maintained in his *Talks at the Yenan Literary Conference*, 1942.

are discussing our personal problem. That would certainly set a bad example among the people! I think maybe after the Chinese New Year. . ." Not waiting for her to finish, Ch'un-sheng said with a smile, "I am too individualistic. I agree with you. . ." [8]

The date is finally set, after further postponements. As luck would have it, before they can register on that day, Ch'un-sheng has to help unload and load a truckful of cargo and then run five or six *li* after a secret agent and grapple with him in a river. One of his ears is bitten and torn, and his left foot suffers a bad cut. Begrimed, drenched and bloody, he has now shown sufficient socialist zeal to be granted the privilege of marriage, and his bride, who that same morning has delivered a baby and therefore made good use of her training in hygiene, can now eye him affectionately without fear of reproach. "Hsiao-ch'ing now could no longer suppress her passion and she dashed over to clasp Ch'un-sheng's hand. For a long while she was speechless, but it looked as if her pair of big eyes were saying, 'You are so lovable!'" [9]

In the second half of 1956, when writers were beginning to enjoy some illusion of freedom, one critic attacked the trend started by Ma Feng's story and wondered if only ascetics are fit for Socialism.[10] Another critic, Huang Ch'iu-yun, catalogued the formulas employed by writers to make love look trivial, silly, or mechanical, and rightly attributed this fault to their fear of the puritan critics who would denounce any elaborate love scene as a sign of "petty-bourgeois mentality" and "vulgar capitalist taste." [11] Granting the primacy of collective welfare, he then hurled the question that would be repeatedly asked by the rightist and revisionist critics during the "hundred flowers" period: "Then what is collective welfare? Isn't this a hope that every individual will live a little better? And to live better, won't that include love and family happiness?" [12]

Among the uncensured fiction, it is the rare story that conveys some feeling of love despite the prescribed formula of cheerful prudishness. Liu Chen's "Big Sister Ch'un" (PL, August 1954) is such a story. Big Sister Ch'un, a member of the Youth League, is constrained by her mother to marry a medium-income peasant, while her own choice is Ming-hua, a turned-over peasant now serving as Party secretary to a neighbouring village. The outcome of this conflict is of course foreseeable, but in the author's account of the lovers' courtship, there are some fine moments. After having fallen in love with Ming-hua, Ch'un gives him two pairs of shoes made by her own hand. "He was now twenty-

[8] Ma Feng *et al.*, *Chieh-hun* (*Marriage*) (Peking: 1953), p. 2. This slim anthology includes six stories on the marriage theme of the 1950–51 period.
[9] *Ibid.* p. 7.
[10] See Li Feng, "To Start with 'Marriage,'" PL (August 1956), pp. 111–112.
[11] Quoted phrases taken from Huang Ch'iu-yun, "On 'love,'" PL (July 1956), p. 61.
[12] *Ibid.* p. 60.

two years old and had always worn shoes made by his mother. This was the first time he was ever wearing shoes made by someone else. His heart felt an indescribable sensation." [13] Later, she goes to his village to attend the theatricals at a fair. "She stood near the top of a hilly slope, scanning the thousands of faces in the open theatre. Truly, she was searching for him as if he were a pearl in the ocean, but she finally located him. Her pleased face turned crimson. She thought that in this multitude of people every one had his own features but there was no one better-looking than he, or more pleasing to her eyes." [14] But, characteristically, despite the two brief scenes just cited, the author dare not explore love at a more intimate level. The lovers soon leave the theatrical performance for a secluded peach tree grove. After a brief avowal of their love for each other, the scene ends quite disappointingly:

> Ming-hua tightly clasped her two hands.
> They talked till dark and then each went his own way home.[15]

(Judging from my limited experience of Communist fiction, it seems that unmarried lovers express their deepest feelings only by holding hands. Only babies are kissed. Married couples may embrace when under the exhilarating influence of good news, such as the admission of the husband to the Communist Party or his promotion.) [16]

As a marriage story of 1954, "Big Sister Ch'un" would be quite dated if it did not concern itself with the then vital issue of the launching of the agricultural co-operatives. The progressive Ming-hua is a member of his village co-operative, while the man Ch'un's mother has chosen for her is an independent. After months of lonely estrangement from her married daughter, the mother is surprised on her first visit to her new home that the young couple live in a state of abundance even though Ming-hua has long been known for his poverty. The awakened mother will naturally work now for the collectivisation of her own village.

In the stories about agricultural co-operatives, mostly written during 1954 and 1955, the younger generation plays a decisive part in the

[13] PL (August 1954), p. 40. A girl making shoes for her lover, however, is a quite common situation in marriage stories. In Wang An-yu, "Li Erh-sao Getting Remarried," included in Ma Feng *et al.*, *Chieh-hun*, the widow Li also makes shoes for her lover.

[14] PL (August 1954), p. 41.

[15] *Ibid.* p. 42.

[16] In Ai Ming-chih's "The Wife," a story subsequently discussed in this paper, for example, Yueh-chen, while in bed with him, "tightly embraced her own husband," on receiving the news that he would soon become a Party member. See *Tuan-p'ien Hsiao-shuo Hsuan, 1949–59* (*Selected Short Stories, 1949–59*) (Shanghai: 1959), II, p. 466. This two-volume anthology is part of a uniform series entitled *Shanghai Shih-nien Wen-hsueh Hsuan-chi* (*Selected Shanghai Literature of the Last Decade*).

struggle between the progressive and the backward.[17] Theoretically, no one can force a well-to-do farmer, who has bettered himself after the land reform through sheer industry, to join the co-operative in his village, but he is always compelled to do so under the influence of his son or daughter who has fallen in love with someone already participating in the collective enterprise. As in the marriage stories, love here again serves a practical purpose: to make the recalcitrant parents fall in line and thereby increase farm production. In " Song of the Forward March " (PL, March 1954), a story in which the author has retained much of his pre-liberation skill for scenic and character description, Shih T'o [18] probes well the mind of the young under powerful pressure to join the majority. Ta-pao, twenty-three years old, is smitten with a progressive girl whose family has already become a part of the co-operative, but his father has remained a stubborn independent. Under the circumstances, he feels ashamed and humiliated, developing an acute case of inferiority complex toward his girl. To educate (or to spite) his father, he leaves home to join some technical expedition in the North-east, which causes his father infinite pain. His two crops already ruined by bad weather, he now applies for membership in the co-operative and undertakes a fruitless journey to seek his son. The following year, on his second visit to the village, the author's sympathy is impressively with the defeated old man: " His body was not sturdy to begin with, now he was bent with age to an extraordinary degree. His wrinkled and dry skin was almost in direct contact with his bones; the lines on his face had deepened; formerly he had only a few white whiskers; now they were over half white." [19]

In " Song of the Forward March," Shih T'o has written an exceptional story which abandons the prescribed cheerful note to probe a more complex and bitter reality. His observations on Ta-pao show especial psychological acumen: " I didn't then realise that the country youths, though their outward expression is stolid and imperturbable, approach the city schoolchildren in their inner simplicity." [20] Precisely: it is not so much that the young are progressive and enlightened as that, under Communist education, they are conditioned to join the crowd, to compete with their peers and emulate their betters. And love, inevitably, plays an important role in sharpening one's appetite for competition and emulation.

Ai Wu has written a number of stories on the theme of love-inspired emulation, of which " Return at Night " (PL, March 1954) is the best.

17 The most famous work depicting the co-operative movement under the guidance of progressive youth is perhaps Chao Shu-li's novel *San-li Wan*, discussed in my *History of Modern Chinese Fiction, 1917–57*, hereafter *History* (New Haven: Yale Un. Press, 1961), pp. 491–495.

18 For a critical study of his pre-1949 career, see the chapter on Shih T'o in *History*.

19 PL (March 1954), p. 51.

20 *Ibid*. p. 51.

An established pre-liberation author with many impressive titles to his credit, Ai Wu is perhaps the most accomplished short-story writer in China today. Though his themes are predictably trite, his techniques have remained thoroughly Western so that he avoids alike the heavy touch of propaganda and the traditional Chinese naiveté of telling the "whole story," cultivated by many Communist writers. "Return at Night," therefore, is delightfully superior to most Chinese Communist stories.

The hero of this story, K'ang Shao-ming, is a cheerful and talkative factory youth with few worries; the one thing that possibly bothers him is that his membership in the Youth League is still pending. One night, after a long meeting, he has missed his last train and has to walk a long distance in bitter cold to reach home. Luckily, a buggy passes by and he gets a ride with a girl driver, who is quite severe and is lashing her horse on to maintain a fast pace. K'ang Shao-ming enjoys nothing as much as talking and joking with girls, but after repeated promptings, the girl only tells him curtly that she is trying to make her night class at her village:

> Noticing that the girl driver had finally cast him a glance, K'ang Shao-ming explained to her airily, "Comrade, you don't know how hard we work." Then with a cheerful sigh: "Tonight, for instance, I even missed the train, really too damned busy."
>
> "We then are different. However busy, we have to make night school."
>
> The girl driver proudly gave this brief answer, then applied her whip to make the horse gallop ahead.[21]

Finally she has to water the horse. She halts the buggy and borrows a trough of water and a lantern from a village house. "K'ang Shao-ming . . . then hurriedly stepped down from the buggy and held up the lantern for her. The hair around the horse's mouth was encrusted with white frost, but as it dipped into the trough for water, the frost gradually melted. The girl driver's fresh and delicate cheeks, frozen to a thorough red like an apple, were radiant with beauty. A girl so pretty he had never before seen, he was in a daze." [22]

Meanwhile, the boy's begrimed face, exposed by the same lantern, has amused the girl, and she becomes more talkative. She particularly inquires about an old, special-class model worker in his factory. She also tells him that she works in a model co-operative. Before alighting, he asks for her name, which she gives. But he is hurt because she doesn't return the courtesy but drives on without looking back. Without his usual cheerfulness, he proceeds to walk home preoccupied by the thought, "This young thing, her eyes are set so high. She only sees

[21] *Ibid.* p. 40.
[22] *Ibid.* p. 41.

special-class model workers."[23] Later, while serving him supper, his mother finds him particularly pensive.

Ai Wu sketches the two characters sharply against a night journey, and in keeping with the scenic method of the modern short story, he doesn't tell us whether the boy will see the girl again, not to say whether their " romance " will ever prosper. It is a masterful study of a boy's awakening to love, but in a Communist story, this awakening is concomitant with an equal awakening to his sense of responsibility as a factory worker. His talkative jocularity will get him nowhere; to be at all deserving of the girl's attention, he has at least to work as hard as she, if not to strive for the distinction of a special-class model worker.

In a much less successful companion piece, " Rain " (PL, April 1957), Ai Wu reverses the situation to depict a girl's silent adoration for a studious factory youth. For over two years since the hospitalisation of her father, Hsu Kuei-ch'ing has been forced to discontinue school to serve as a train conductor on a commuting line. Quite envious of high school girls in her deprived state, she especially reserves her admiration for a factory youth who for over a year now had sat next to a window on his evening ride home and concentrated on reading or solving mathematical problems. Occasionally, when preoccupied with a tough problem, he would miss his regular stop and alight at the next station. He was so studious that never once would he glance at her or greet her while handing her the ticket. But the girl has of course fallen in love. Under his good influence, she would study every night, in spite of extreme fatigue. One evening she walks home through a heavy thunderstorm particularly depressed; her mother thinks she is sick, but actually she is worried about her hero, who has again missed his regular stop this evening and will have to walk home thoroughly drenched and exposed to the danger of lightning.

Among factory workers and their wives, the same condition of emulation obtains. One spouse, usually the husband, devotes his waking life to work, and the other has to catch up with him to reinvigorate a marriage gone stale with new socialist zeal. In " The New Home," another skilful story by Ai Wu (PL, October 1953), the heroine, a country wife just arriving in the city to join her husband, is quite miserable because, too busy in the factory, he has broken his promise to meet her at the railroad station. But in the company of his friends who greet her in her new home and tell her of his spirited dedication to work, her resentment gradually melts until, following their departure, she grows positively ecstatic in contemplation of her apartment: " The walls were snow-white, the window panes were shining. The new iron-frame bed was covered with a white sheet with a red floral design. The

[23] *Ibid.* p. 43.

oil-painted table and chairs were all gleaming. On the wall there was a new portrait of Chairman Mao, which made her especially happy."[24] When her husband comes home later in the evening, she is already imbued with a new spirit for "study."

In the above story, the emphasis is of course on study. The new furniture may dazzle for a while, but with the husband rarely at home, even the benign portrait of Chairman Mao will soon pall. Only through study and through full participation in the life around her can a factory wife live a tolerably happy life. But some wives, though efficient housekeepers entirely devoted to their family, adjust to their new life rather slowly. In Ai Ming-chih's story, "The Wife" (*Wen-yi Yueh-pao,* February, 1957), Yueh-chen is worried about her husband's growing indifference following his promotion to a position of greater responsibility and consequent total preoccupation with his work; she is even alarmed that he may abandon her for a younger woman. Trying the bourgeois trick of making herself more attractive, she goes to a beauty parlour to give her hair a permanent. But her somewhat shocked husband only comments teasingly, "Ha, how you've fixed your hair. It looks now like a duck's rear."[25] Heartbroken, Yueh-chen now steels herself to the challenge of attending study sessions in the afternoons. Not too long after, she surprises her husband one night with her new literacy and even helps him copying figures. From then on, she has regained his affections and becomes known in the neighbourhood as a model wife.

In "The Warmth of Spring" (PL, October 1959; translated in *Chinese Literature* [CL], July 1961), by the highly praised new short-story writer, Miss Ju Chih-chüan,[26] the heroine has to embrace a far more rigorous work schedule to earn her husband's renewed appreciation. Ching-lan goes regularly to the meetings of the neighbourhood women's committee, though without enthusiasm; for the past month, furthermore, in addition to taking care of her husband and two children, she has been putting in eight hours of voluntary work every day for the committee's Production and Welfare Co-operative. But her husband remains unimpressed, even with a special shrimp dinner she has prepared one Sunday to arouse memories of their shared poverty in the early days. Following this fiasco, she turns to her committee work with new zeal, determined to help fulfil the co-operative's challenging new assignment of turning out ten thousand transmitters within seven days. Now her husband begins to show new interest: he even calls for her at her workshop late one night and treats her to a bowl of noodles at a snackbar. In her

[24] PL (October 1953), p. 6.

[25] *Tuan-p'ien Hsiao-shuo Hsuan, 1949–59,* II, p. 462.

[26] Mao Tun was the first critic to praise her highly, in his article "On the Latest Short Stories," PL (June 1958). Wei Chin-chih parrots this praise in his Foreword to *Tuan-p'ien Hsiao-shuo Hsuan, 1949–59,* I.

complete dedication to socialist labour, Ching-lan feels that " that invisible, intangible 'barrier' had vanished completely." [27]

Along with her husband's appreciation, a woman so dedicated, of course, gets public praise: Ching-lan's name gets cited in the workshop bulletin for her contribution to " technical innovation." For factory wives in fear of losing their husbands as for children of backward peasants eager to join the co-operative, it is the terror of isolation that drives everyone to behave like a schoolboy, in quest of group conformity, praise, and appreciation. A bowl of noodles, a smile from one's husband or sweetheart, or even an official citation may not mean much, but these gestures of encouragement surely soothe the spirit when one is under the constant dread of being backward and not wanted. If the stories about factory wives reflect at all the actual conditions, then their socialist zeal is not so much an expression of disinterested love for country and Party as an inverted expression of bourgeois " togetherness "; in a Communist society a woman is closer to her husband when sharing his kind of drudgery than when merely content to perform her traditional wifely functions.

This Communist variety of domestic fiction can be seen to have much in common with the type of American middle-brow fiction intended for women readers. They pose the same problems though the solutions they offer are entirely different. When faced with the loss of her husband's affections, a typical heroine from a story in the *Ladies' Home Journal* will try to improve her physical appearance, social poise, or culinary skill; quite unlike her Chinese sister in a similar quandary, she will curtail her busy schedule of outside interests to cultivate an image of pliant femininity. In America as in China, a husband's preoccupation with his work or ambition is a source of domestic discord. But whereas, in a typical American middle-brow novel like *Man in the Grey Flannel Suit*, the husband gallantly relinquishes his ambition to become an executive and settles for a nine-to-five job so as to preserve domestic peace, the Chinese husband is denied this recourse to bourgeois chivalry, and it is entirely up to his wife to catch up with him in endurance and zeal to maintain a semblance of spiritual unity.

At the Third Congress of the All-China Democratic Women's Federation (September 1957), " to diligently and thriftily manage the home " was proclaimed to be as much a woman's duty as " to diligently and thriftily build the nation." [28] But if the short stories are any evidence, housework is only tolerated, if not actively despised: a woman's mere

[27] CL (July 1961), p. 80.
[28] See the woman leader Chang Yun's address to the Congress, included in *Chung-kuo Fu-nü Ti-san-tz'u Ch'üan-kuo Tai-piao Ta-hui Chung-yao Wen-hsien* (*The Third Congress of All-China Women's Delegates: Important Documents*) (Peking: 1958), pp. 12–46.

contentment with housework, as shown in "The Wife" and "The Warmth of Spring," indicates a want of socialist zeal. Not only progressive girls shudder at the idea of being tied down to domestic chores, but even old women get restless at home and want to serve in a public capacity. In "A Promise Is kept" (*Wen-yi Yueh-pao,* May 1959; reprinted in PL, August 1959), another story by Ju Chih-chüan, a grandmother is seen enjoying a new contentment and pride as a worker in a toy factory. Since both her son and daughter-in-law earn good wages in factories, she would be actually more useful at home doing the chores and taking care of the grand-daughter. But how empty she used to feel when on May Days she was left all alone while her son and his wife were marching in the parade! And how she hated cooking rice! "She took down the pot and sat musing in the kitchen. This was the responsibility she had—a task which could never amount to much but was a nuisance if she forgot about it."[29]

But with the nation-wide conversion of the co-operatives into large-scale people's communes in 1958 and 1959, millions of regimented women were of course relieved of the odious task of preparing meals for their families. They were not only liberated from the kitchen, but thanks to the military mode of their new existence and the provident service of the nurseries and kindergartens, they were to a great extent emancipated from their traditional servitude to husband and children as well. Story-writers reporting on the commune experiment now wrote with expected enthusiasm of their new freedom and much enhanced socialist utility. Quite unlike the stories about factory wives, these stories would assert the superior zeal and dedication of the new women often at the expense of their prejudiced or incredulous menfolk (for the cliché of progressive vs. backward must be maintained to provide dramatic interest), praising their infinite resourcefulness in a great variety of jobs now opening to them: as captain of a production brigade, mess hall superintendent, pig-raising expert, obstetrician, or meteorologist. A young writer, Li Chun, explored this vein with conspicuous success and emerged as the foremost eulogist of the new women under the commune system. In his most celebrated work, "The Story of Li Shuang-shuang" (PL, March 1960),[30] he traces the happy evolution of a

29 CL (December 1960), p. 54.

30 In addition, Li Chun has written two important stories on the new women: "Mother and Daughter" (PL, October 1959); "Sowing the Clouds" (PL, September 1960). The high value assigned to these stories by the Communist literary leadership can be gauged by the fact that English translations were made available to readers of *Chinese Literature* soon after their original publication: "Mother and Daughter" (December 1959), "The Story of Li Shuang-shuang" (June 1960), "Sowing the Clouds" (January 1961). These stories also immediately prompted highly favourable critiques: see, for example, Wei Ch'ün, "In Praise of New China's Women—Three Stories by Comrade Li Chun" (PL, June 1960) and Jen Wen, "The Achievement of 'Sowing the Clouds'" (PL, November 1960).

peasant woman from the drudgery of cooking at home to the challenging excitement of cooking for the masses in the mess hall; the title heroine has appropriately become a national symbol for emancipated women. In comparison with other propaganda tales of this type, this story is not without distinction: appropriating the style of Chao Shu-li for the occasion, the author has actually surpassed his master in his ability to sustain the mood of pastoral comedy in his more effective scenes. But these scenes are dominated not so much by the heroine as by her comic foil, the husband Hsi-wang, whose backward but endearing ways are done remarkably to life.

But precisely because of their new enlightenment, the exemplary heroines of the commune stories are so taken up with their public duties that they rarely have time to attend to personal business. In Li Chun's "Mother and Daughter," for example, the younger heroine, Chu-chu, finds time to lecture her prospective father-in-law over his objections to her volunteering for service as a midwife, but not once is she seen in her fiancé's company and even his name remains unrecorded in the story. One gets the impression that she is so happily busy with her manifold tasks that she scarcely needs the luxury of a romantic attachment. But if women in the communes have ceased to be distracted by feminine frivolities, they are, on the other hand, seen with rather odd frequency in the habit of bearing children. The disproportionate number of stories about childbirth serves no doubt to call attention to the improved obstetric and maternity service now provided by the communes. A typical story like Ju Chih-chüan's "Quietly in the Maternity Hospital" (PL, June 1960) harps on the gratitude a lying-in patient ought to feel when contrasting her good fortune with the primitive care her peasant mother received while giving birth to her a generation ago. But in celebrating the new era of socialist welfare, the story-writers also give occasional glimpses of the psychological condition of women while in a state of confinement and convalescence. In the two examples that follow we will see that, while one woman, understandably though atypically, still demands her husband's tender care, the other, far more noble-minded, actually refuses to attend to her condition because of her total preoccupation with her work.

In Ho Fei's "A Big Family" (PL, December 1961), a young wife has just given birth and is now resting at home. It is two days before the Chinese New Year, and a snowstorm is raging. When her husband, the captain of a production team, comes home that afternoon from work, she again reminds him of two pieces of long-neglected business: to repair the leaking roof and to pay a visit to her mother, who hasn't seen them for months. The first item of business is particularly urgent as the health of the convalescent mother and new baby might be endangered living in an unheated house with a leaking roof. Her husband agrees but immediately leaves home for more important business: to get provisions for the public dining hall at the commune headquarters some twenty *li* away. He pushes a cart through tortuous mountain paths in a worsening storm and returns the same night to his village, pushing a loaded cargo. But on reaching the dining hall, he proceeds to decorate the hall and prepare for a big New Year's Eve dinner so that for over forty-two hours he works incessantly with time out only for two meals. In the meantime, of course, he has completely forgotten his wife's request to fix the roof. When he finally returns home on the morning of the New Year's Day—with the snowstorm still raging—he is therefore agreeably surprised to find that in his absence the roof has been repaired by friendly neighbours and his family well attended to. Under the commune system a wife may not always count on her husband in times of need, but she is part of "a big family" and should be happily resigned to its efficient service. She should make even fewer demands than a factory wife on her husband's precious time.

Unlike the young wife in the preceding story, the heroine of Lin Chin-lan's "New Life" (PL, December 1960) scorns the traditional feminine weakness for attention; in fact, she feels so guilty about wasting time for childbirth that she would rather risk her life than stop working. She, a captain in charge of vegetable production, cultivates with her comrades a tract of land situated in a mountainous region completely detached from the other units of the commune and unreachable by normal means of transportation. Because of this geographical difficulty and because, with her pelvis so narrow, she is certainly going to have a hard time giving birth, the old doctor from the commune headquarters has urged her to come down a month earlier from her isolated spot to make ready for hospitalisation before the baby is due. But how could she neglect those eggplants growing so plump under her care? So she refuses to go; now in the third night of her confinement she is dying. But later that night a young woman doctor arrives in the nick of time, after an extremely arduous journey, to save the lives of mother and son.

The young doctor, who dominates the second half of the story, serves as an appropriate occasion to introduce a subject so far undiscussed in this article—the professional woman. Ever since Mao Tse-tung decreed the worker, peasant, soldier line for literature in 1942, intellectuals have played a relatively small role in fiction. But stories about women teachers and especially about women physicians and nurses, are not uncommon, since their socialist utility is quite self-evident.[31] In so far as these

[31] In the commune stories, to be sure, many heroines are seen actively engaged in a professional capacity. But these hardly literate nurses, obstetricians and meteorologists, usually teenagers and invariably drawn from the ranks of the peasants, have

stories evince a feminine interest, it always takes the form of the heroine's unreserved preference for the selfless nobility of her profession over any selfish hankering after personal happiness she may have retained. The young doctor in "New Life" is typical. On her return journey, elated by her amazing success as an obstetrician and the gratitude of the overjoyed villagers, she pauses in the hills to pour out her thoughts to a fellow doctor, her regular correspondent and possibly her lover. She writes of her new-found happiness, "I've been thinking and thinking that this is far sublimer and far greater than any kind of personal 'happiness.' Perhaps they are two entirely different things. . . ."[32]

The heroine of the significantly titled story, "Love" (PL, September 1956), a young physician named Yeh Pi-chen, comes to the same conclusion, but under far more trying personal circumstances. Writing at a time when adverse criticism of mechanical descriptions of love was being widely heard, the author, Li Wei-lun, had apparently attempted a full-blown romantic exercise, though the end product is unbelievably sentimental. But the story has nonetheless escaped censure because it positively and unambiguously affirms the incomparable nobility of socialist "love" over individualist romantic "love." Pi-chen is finally to part from her colleague, Chou Ting-shan, whom she has loved so hopelessly for so long. Dr. Chou also loves her passionately but a few years previously he had pledged his honour to marry and cherish a nurse, when under a temporary misapprehension that his love for Pi-chen was hopeless. On the eve of his departure, Pi-chen is quite miserable, but she is saved from spending the night in unendurable agony because she is soon called to attend a dying patient. She saves her life and thus forgets her own unhappiness in contemplation of the happiness she has brought to the patient's family. Early next morning she bids farewell to Dr. Chou with great calm:

> "Now go, Ting-shan! Don't worry about me; I'll be all right," she interrupted him. "The emotion that I ought to have conquered I have now conquered. For your happiness, for the happiness of you two, I am very glad. . ."
>
> Yes, she had conquered that almost unconquerable emotion. Why had she done this? It was because of love—a Youth League member's and a true doctor's deep and sincere love for the people, for her own profession. Could any other kind of love be more sublime, more beautiful?[33]

My examination of Chinese women under Communism begins with cheery peasant brides united with their labour-loving heroes for greater

merely undergone a crash training programme so that they are hardly professional in the accepted sense of the word. The young doctor in "New Life" is, of course, a professional.

[32] PL (December 1960), p. 41.

[33] PL (September 1956), p. 53.

productivity and ends with women doctors potentially or actually renouncing personal love for the greater love of mankind. Superficially, these stories seem to have little in common. Yet they, and all the other examples in between, stress the importance of self-adjustment to facilitate socialist construction. The greatest hero is he who exercises the greatest self-denial for the sake of Communism. Though complete self-denial is biologically impossible, one should progressively demand more of oneself and expect less of the others so that one may ultimately approach the ideal Communist person—a cheerful automaton whose one passion is love of labour. The cumulative effect of this propagandist emphasis may well have been to persuade readers on the mainland that socialist dedication is all that matters in life and to reconcile them to further calls for self-sacrifice: even to an experienced non-Communist reader, a few of the more felicitous tales in praise of Communist endeavour may not prove unappealing in so far as a self-denying hero or heroine attempting a difficult task normally excites admiration. But the seeming dignity of this heroism is ultimately pathetic because it draws no sustenance whatever from the deeper springs of the human being. To a model Communist all feelings are expendable except his passion for labour: he must above all simplify his emotional existence to promote greater zeal and efficiency.

In the last story discussed, "Love," it is not so much that spinsterhood is generally recommended for women doctors as that a happy, simple solution must be given for complicated emotional problems that threaten to reduce one's efficiency. As a literary product of the autumn of 1956, the story is, of course, quite uncharacteristic of Communist fiction in that is gives unduly prominent attention to personal problems and borders on tragedy, even if of the soap-opera variety. And the tragic attitude, inasmuch as it sanctions freedom of the will and sympathises with man in a state of psychological and moral bewilderment, is the very antithesis of the positive attitude of Communist zeal.

The women characters in the stories we have examined—whether dedicated workers, anxious emulators, or prudent conformists—are all efficiently untragic. Indeed, when compared with their benighted sisters in traditional Chinese fiction—such well-known heroines as P'an Chin-lien, Wang Hsi-feng, and Lin Tai-yü—these women appear to have disowned all too successfully their Chinese inheritance, with all its feudal squalor and animal savagery. Always public-minded, they are above the temptations of lust, greed, and self-destruction and superior to sadistic and masochistic schemes for unashamed and selfish happiness. Yet with all their abject enslavement to a cruel social code and blind refusal to rise above the evil passions, the earlier heroines are nevertheless as memorably human as the new Communist heroines are not: they have not abdicated their ultimate freedom—the tragic perversity of the will that makes for good and evil. The new heroines do not inhabit that metaphysical realm; their human worth is nearly always pitifully equated with their socialist utility.

Yet even in Communist China, the cause of human dignity has not been without its defenders—the pre-Communist modern tradition of humanitarian idealism has persisted in spite of repeated massive Communist attempts to stamp it out. The purged writers—prominently the Hu Feng group and the " rightists " and " revisionists " of 1956–57—were nearly all condemned for their stubborn belief in an unchanging human nature with its undeniable rights to love, freedom, and the pursuit of happiness, though their more immediate crime was their impudent attempt to liberalise the literary bureaucracy and demand freedom of expression.[34] The creative output of these writers was not large since their most convenient weapon was critical and polemic journalism. But, especially during 1956–57, a number of stories were produced which protest movingly against the universal imposition of dreary conformity and unendurable toil under the régime. And in these stories, it was not an accident that women characters played key roles as martyrs of and fighters against Communist oppression. In the main stream of modern Chinese fiction, women have always been seen as warmhearted idealists intolerant of sham and hypocrisy, though easily crushed in their struggle for a meaningful and abundant life. But even their defeat is a triumphant form of self-assertion: the defiant and self-indulgent nihilism so characteristic of the heroines of the early Mao Tun and Ting Ling is poles apart from the anxious conformity of labour-loving women as seen in today's fiction. Until she was censured in 1942, Ting Ling, while a prominent writer in Yenan, characteristically opposed her warmhearted heroines to the coldness of Communist bureaucracy, in such notable stories as " When I Was in Hsia Village " (1940) and " In the Hospital " (1941).[35]

[34] For a detailed account of the Communist persecution of the Hu Feng group and the rightist and revisionist authors, see the chapter on " Conformity, Defiance, and Achievement " in *History.* In his Talks at the Yenan literary forum, Mao Tse-tung scoffs at the idea of an abstract and unchanging " human nature." All the purged critics and theorists—principally Hu Feng, Feng Hsüeh-feng, Ch'in Chao-yang, Liu Shao-t'ang and Pa Jen—were accused of advocating the bourgeois or revisionist theory of human nature. In his address to the Third Congress of the All-China Federation of Literary and Art Circles on July 22, 1960, Chou Yang refers to the persistent attraction of this theory even after the great purge of 1957–58: " At present the revisionists are desperately advocating the bourgeois theory of human nature, the false humanism of the bourgeoisie, ' the love of mankind,' bourgeois pacifism and other fallacious notions of the sort, to reconcile class antagonisms, negate the class struggle and revolution, and spread illusions about imperialism, to attain their ulterior aim of preserving the old capitalist society and disrupting the new socialist society " (CL, October 1960, p. 47).

[35] I have briefly treated Ting Ling's Yenan career in *History*, pp. 275–279. During 1957–58, the two Yenan stories were cited by the orthodox critics as evidence of

The revisionist stories of 1956–57 nobly carry forward Ting Ling's interrupted protest. Within the framework of an unquestioned faith in Communism's ultimate benevolence and a cautious hope for immediate reforms, they express nevertheless the fatigue and despair of a crushed humanity as well as the defiant idealism of a few chosen spirits battling against an impersonal bureaucracy.

Feng Ts'un's story "Beautiful" (PL, July 1957) laments Chinese youth for all its unappreciated nobility and self-sacrifice. As the woman narrator confides to the first-person author: "Today's youths, they all have a beautiful heart, a heart like a precious stone, like a crystal in its prismatic transparency. . . . The young are all so lovable. But they also have their own sorrows and troubles; at times, one is really worried about them."[36] The person that worries her most is her niece Yü-chieh, who has served for many years in a government cultural organisation. For the first few years she was the personal secretary to an important official in that organisation, assisting him day and night and imperceptibly falling in love with him. But thoroughly conditioned to self-abnegation, she cannot admit the necessity of personal happiness and muster enough courage to fight for that happiness. Furthermore, she shrinks from the malicious criticism going the rounds in the organisation that her exceptional devotion to work is due to her ambition to climb ahead, and from the frightful jealousy of the functionary's tubercular wife. So when, following the wife's death, he does propose to her, she refuses. But, of course, the functionary doesn't press his suit very hard; he is soon transferred to Peking where he meets an actress and marries her.

In the meantime, Yü-chieh works so hard for that organisation that she has absolutely no time to attend to her personal problems. Her sympathetic assistant comments bitterly: "You know our kind of work; there are no Sundays and no holidays. Even if you have a friend, you see him maybe once in every two or three months. This really is a problem."[37] Yü-chieh does have an admirer, a young doctor; but they both are so busy and she especially has so many meetings to attend that she doesn't even have time to answer his telephone calls, let alone go out on dates with him. To make things easier for both, she breaks with him completely. And yet she is now thirty-one; however "beautiful" her heart, she has let her grinding routine take over her life completely. The final affirmative note in the story rests on the rhetorical question that a selfless and dedicated worker cannot be unhappy: "You

Ting Ling's anti-party, rightist character. Their striking resemblance in mood and tone to the author's early bourgeois stories was also emphasised to show her unchanged commitment to individualist nihilism through the years.

[36] PL (July 1957), p. 26.

[37] *Ibid.* p. 35.

just wait and see, Yü-chieh will be happy. How could she be miserable?"[38]

Upon its publication, "Beautiful," though a rather poor story in my opinion, immediately aroused the wrath of important critics, who all attested to its subversive character as a disconcertingly moving tale: the plight of Yü-chieh must have appealed tremendously for its acute truth. My next example of revisionist fiction, Liu Pin-yen's "Our Paper's Inside News" (PL, June 1956; October 1956), however, is an excellent story; judging from my limited reading, it must be ranked with Lu Ling's "The 'Battle' in the Ditch" (PL, March, 1954)[39] as one of the two outstanding successes among the more ambitious longer stories to have appeared in Communist China. Both stories and their authors were vehemently attacked, Lu Ling's story in 1954–55, and Liu Pin-yen's in 1957–58.

Prior to its denigration, however, "Our Paper's Inside News" had been a sensation; the editors of *People's Literature* greeted the first instalment with pride: "While we are becoming accustomed to writings that oppose rightist, conservative [*i.e.*, orthodox Communist] thought, this 'special report' again raises a new problem: the existence in our midst of other situations that shackle people's constructiveness and creativeness and zeal for labour and obstruct the development of society [literally, 'life']."[40] The person intent on removing these shackles and obstructions is the woman reporter, Huang Chia-ying. In Part I, her attempt to reform the paper, the *New Light Daily*, which has served as a mere echo of the Central Committee of the Party, into a real organ of the people ends in deep personal frustration. In Part II, however, it is seen that she has won substantial support from the newspaper staff. The climactic scene depicts a staff meeting convened to debate the issue whether Huang Chia-ying, with all her reformist zeal and intransigent individualism, should be admitted as a Party member. Sensing the general disaffection with the bureaucratic line, the editor-in-chief, Ch'en Li-tung, speaks surprisingly in favour of her admission. Under her influence, the other conscientious members of the staff have already shed their former despondent, fatigued, or cautious selves to stand by her.

Huang Chia-ying, while on a field trip to a mining area, has been peremptorily asked to return to her office. When the story begins, she

[38] *Ibid*. p. 36. Li Wei-lun's "Love" also ends with a rhetorical question. Dr. Chou's parting words to Pi-chen are: "Good-bye, Pi-chen. I wish you the greatest of happiness. Who could believe that a girl like you can be unhappy?"—PL (September 1956), p. 53.

[39] I reluctantly exclude this story as a subject for discussion from this paper because its heroine, a Korean girl in love with a Chinese volunteer, is not Chinese.

[40] PL (June 1956), p. 125. The magazine's associate editor, Ch'in Chao-yang, was later persecuted not only for his own revisionist articles and stories but for his warm commendation of "Our Paper's Inside News" and his supposed collusion with its author.

is seen as a passenger on a night train, pondering over her experiences with the miners, her difficulties at the newspaper office, and her chances of ever becoming a Communist Party member. She has just written a long report on the conditions at the mine, but from long and bitter experience, she knows that such outspoken articles will never be published and so she has torn it to pieces. She tries to relax with a popular novel, but each time she opens the book she has to put it down almost immediately, thinking to herself: "Why have so many novels treated life and people in such a commonplace, flat and simplified manner as if, once liberated, people have all lost their capacity for intense feelings of pleasure and anger, sorrow and joy, have all suddenly become on the surface good-mannered and good-tempered, punctually attending meetings and punctually arriving for and departing from work?"[41] A biting comment on the pseudo-cheerfulness of Communist fiction, this observation also reflects the actual life of the people. Huang Chia-ying is convinced that a mechanical observance of duty and form has resulted in a paralytic submissiveness, killing all initiative and strangling all honest attempts at reform. For several years now, the miners she has observed on her trip sleep only four hours every night. They get up every morning at 2 a.m. to walk to work; by the time they return home, it is usually after 9 p.m. The work hours are long, but even more fatiguing to body and spirit are those endless meetings. The workers' efficiency naturally falls off, and yet if they fail to fulfil the production goals, the inevitable remedy is to hold more and longer meetings to incite them to greater zeal for study and work. As she later tells her immediate superior at the office in great anger, "When the greatest desire of the workers is to lie down and sleep for days on end, how can they study?[42] Yet nobody at the mines had the initiative and courage to recommend fewer and shorter meetings. Huang Chia-ying wonders aloud if it is to the credit of the Party to perpetuate this cruel farce of fatigue.

The same lethargy prevails in the newspaper office. Governed by fear and cowardice, the paper will never dare publish editorials and feature stories on any subject unless it has received instructions from the Central Committee on how to attack that subject. And the heroine's personal drama—her prolonged failure to receive Party membership—is also enacted against the same background of fear-induced conformity. While never doubting her zeal and courage, even her close friend and admirer, Chang Yeh, advises her to resort to the expediency of confessing her faults so that her application may be approved. The first part of

[41] *Ibid*. p. 7.
[42] *Ibid*. p. 14.

the story ends with Huang Chia-ying profoundly shocked by this counsel:

> So, even he was of this opinion! To want to join the Party and yet not to uphold the interests of the Party! To want to join the Party and yet to hide one's opinions!
>
> Huang Chia-ying suddenly stood still. She wanted to say something, to rebuke Chang Yeh harshly. But finally she didn't say anything; she turned around and walked away. Hearing Chang Yeh calling after her, she walked on in even bigger strides. Never, never, so it would seem, had she been so insulted. . . .[43]

Throughout, Liu Pin-yen has presented his heroine as a loyal Communist fighting ultimately for the best interests of the Party. Workers should get proper rest and care; newspapers should of their own initiative correct social and bureaucratic abuses and reflect the actual sentiments of the people; applicants for Party membership shouldn't bow before group pressure to belie their honourable record. Yet, in its harsh repudiation of Huang Chia-ying as an unbridled and rebellious individualist, the Party has declared its unaltered policy to uphold total obedience by the people as the best means to ensure socialist advance: perhaps one major reason why socialist construction in recent years has been increasingly foiled by general apathy. Unquestioned supporters of the Communist cause, the women characters in the approved short stories have all endeavoured to earn praise, to avoid reproach, to wrest a bare minimum of personal satisfaction from an impossible regimen of hard toil and emotional starvation. They are resigned, but not completely, to the spiritual barrenness of a sub-human existence. As the most spirited of revisionist characters, Huang Chia-ying exemplifies in contrast the tradition of warm sympathy and defiant idealism, the struggle for personal honesty and integrity against general indifference and corruption, that has always distinguished the representative heroines of modern Chinese fiction.

[43] *Ibid.* p. 21.

The Image of Youth and Age in Chinese Communist Literature *

By HELLMUT WILHELM

I

SPEAKING in a very general way, youth and age have been taken in traditional Chinese literature as two stages in a continuous development of which the first represents the preparation and the last the goal. Respective values attached to these stages were derived from this concept. In a civilisation where literature, even polite literature, was to a large extent an amateurish pursuit of the scholar-official, this evaluation does not come as a surprise, particularly since it will not be easy to find another civilisation which was as strongly ideology-motivated as was the Chinese. Established attitudes concerning youth and age were thus, in general, accepted and taken for granted also by the poet.

These attitudes were fixed at a rather early period of Imperial China. Already the *Li-chi* contains, in a variety of chapters, detailed notations about position and behaviour patterns of the different age groups. This is apparent, for instance, in the name applied to the very young: *tao*, a word which Chu Hsi explains to mean pitiful. When they, just as the very old, receive special treatment this is justified by the fact that they are *not yet* at their goal and *still* incapable of rational thinking.[1]

As a rule to advance from one age group into the next was tied quite strictly to the years of life. If exceptions were made and the young ones were attributed a status beyond their years of life this was brought about by precocious proficiencies of an adult nature. The chapter *Shao-i*,[2] for instance, is willing to bestow a higher status on the children of the knight class as soon as they are able to drive a chariot, and to those of the

* Much more than the references indicate, this paper is indebted to the volumes of Jaroslav Prusek, *Die Literatur des befreiten China* (Prague: Artia, 1955); of Chow Tse-tsung, *The May Fourth Movement* (Cambridge: Harvard Un. Press, 1960); and particularly of C. T. Hsia, *A History of Modern Chinese Fiction* (New Haven: Yale Un. Press, 1961).

The paper is furthermore indebted, in substance as well as in analysis, to suggestions from my colleagues present at the Ditchley Manor Conference. Especially I want to express my gratitude to Miss Li Chi who submitted the paper to a thorough and extensive review.

1 Chapter "Ch'ü-li." James Legge, *The Li Ki*, Vol. I of *The Sacred Books of China: the Texts of Confucianism* (Oxford: Clarendon, 1885), Part III, pp. 65–66.

2 Legge, *loc. cit.*, Vol. II, p. 74.

peasant class as soon as they can carry firewood. Practical services approaching those performed by adults were the criteria here. This principle is found universally applied all through Chinese history in almost any existing biography. A man worthy of a biography almost had to be a precocious child, and this precocity was almost without exception expressed in achievements expected from a higher age group, mainly early advancement in learning and proficiency in the performance of the rituals of filial piety.

The prevalence of proficiency over age has then become a theoretical postulate which is stressed in a great number of anecdotes. When the legendary philosopher Yü-tzu, for instance, had his first audience with King Wen at the age of ninety, and when the King exclaimed: " My, are you old! " Yü-tzu replied: " If you want me to catch tigers and pursue deer then I am old. If you want to use me to plan the affairs of state, then I still have to be considered young." As Wang T'ung's (583–617) *Wen-chung-tzu* (chapter *Li-ming*) succintly puts it: When Chia Chiung was asked by Fan Shih-yüan about age, he replied: " It starts with the capping ceremony." And when Fan retorted, " Really, can you have understanding at such a young age? " Chia answered, " The Master was a teacher of men when he was fifteen. . . . I have heard it said: virtue does not depend on years, and the Way (*Tao*) does not depend on position."

Corresponding status is lavished on the aged in the *Li-chi* and other Classics. Even at a period of life when they are not any more able to perform useful services, the concept of " caring for the aged " (*yang-lao*) secured for them a life of comfort, ease and veneration. To serve the old was an injunction which held good within and outside the family, and thus the hierarchy of age was a firmly established and generally accepted notion.[3]

There is, however, evidence that this was not always so. Reading the fourth hexagram of the *Book of Changes, Meng,* Youthful Folly,[4] the youthful fool emerges as somebody who certainly is in need of discipline and guidance, but on the other hand also as somebody who is in the possession of qualities which older age cannot boast. " Youthful folly has success," one reads here, and: " Childlike folly brings good fortune." And this is explained by the immediacy of youth, its unreflected imbeddedness in time, which the wisdom of the aged cannot duplicate. In the words of the *Book of Changes,* a higher degree of personal happiness which this involves is not so much in focus as actual results which can

[3] See, for instance, Legge, *loc. cit.*, Vol. I, pp. 240–243. See also *K'ung-tzu Chia-yü,* Chap. 41. R. Wilhelm trans. (Dusseldorf: Diederichs, 1961), pp. 178–179.

[4] Wilhelm-Baynes, *The I Ching or Book of Changes* (New York: Pantheon, 1950), Vol. I, pp. 20–24; Vol. III, pp. 40–45.

be achieved only by youth. Thus, youth is here not only a preparatory stage for adulthood and old age but has a function of its own which is denied to other age groups. (On the specificity of youth one can compare Wordsworth's " Intimations of Immortality from Recollections of Early Childhood " particularly Ode VIII.)

To be sure, this notion was lost when the poet-philosopher Yang Hsiung (53 B.C.–A.D. 18) projected some of the concepts of the *Book of Changes* onto a much more rigidly institutionalised situation in his *T'ai-hsuan-ching*. The twelfth tetragram of this book, *T'ung*, The Child, conceives of youth only as an age which has to be disciplined and which has to be guided. If this guidance is not accepted this will lead with necessity to obscurity or worse, and even proper guidance does not always guarantee success.

The insight of the *Book of Changes* into the specificity of youth seems however to have been preserved, at least to a degree, in later polite literature. As an example the first stanza of Lu Chi's (261–303) *Pai-nien ko* might be adduced here. Speaking of youth, he says:

> Their faces are like hibiscus flowers, the brilliance of their eyes is radiant,
> Their bodies are like a whirlwind, they walk as if flying.
> How stirring is the sight of these kids chasing each other!
> When dawn breaks they go out to play, when dusk settles they return.
> All their six emotions are untrammelled and at ease, their mind has no inhibitions.
> What are, compared with these, the pleasures of wine and meal?
> What are, compared with these, the pleasures of wine and meal?

The focus is here on the pursuit of happiness, but the greater capacity for happiness of youth is derived not just from its vitality and exuberance but specifically from its immediacy, which is implicitly denied to old age.

This last aspect, the incapability of age of untrammelled expression, has been the topic of many later poems. It has led to a—half humorous—reassessment of the value of different age groups and their proficiencies. Po Chü-i's (772–846) poem " Watching Boys at Play " reads:

> Just about seven or eight years old,
> Prettily dressed, three or four lads.
> They wallow in the mud and then fight on the lawn,
> The whole day they shout with joy.
>
> In the hall an old fellow,
> His sideburns recently show some white hair,
> Seeing kids play with their hobby-horses
> He invariably reflects upon the time of youthful folly.

Youthful folly is full of play and joy,
Old age brings much grief and sorrow.
Quietly contemplating these two,
I would not know who really is the fool.

Half-humorous laments about the shortcomings of old age have then become a poetic genre of which again Po Chü-i's collection is particularly rich. It led even to the debasement of that very quality for which adulthood and age are generally famous: wisdom. Thus Su Shih (1036–1101), in a poem commemorating the ceremonial bathing of his son, has the following to say:

Everybody hopes a son will show some cleverness,
But, I, with all my cleverness, have made my life a mess.
All I want is that the boy be ignorant and dull,
And reach the rank of minister with neither strain nor stress.[5]

It is the same " Gay Genius " however who did not want to see the dignity of status impaired for the aged. His position has been recorded and contrasted to the one of the philosopher Shao Yung (1011–1077) in the following way:

Su: " When old people stick flowers in their hair, it is not so much a shame for the flowers, it is a shame for their old heads."
Shao: " If you see flowers stuck in the hair of old men, don't laugh. Old men have seen more beautiful flowers."

Huang-fu Yung (Ming) who records these sayings in his *Chin-feng wen-lüeh* adds: " Shao Yung's attitude was vigorous, Su Shih's timorous."

Experience and breadth of insight thus might lead to the serenity of old age and to the assumption of freedom, even freedom from the prerogatives of higher status. Old age in this way achieves an immediacy which might be as trenchant as the immediacy of youth. Chu Tun-ju (*ca.* 1080–*ca.* 1175) once expressed this in the following song:

Growing old is such a joy!
Across this journey of the human world
Comes an understanding beyond things,
Comes an insight into the emptiness of things,
Crushing all seas of sadness, all mountains of sorrow.
Not dazed by flowers,
Not ensnared by wine,
Forever, free, free.
When my belly is full I lie down to sleep.
Waking up, I play my part.

[5] Trans. Peter Elizabeth Quince, quoted without permission.

Talk not about the past, the present, the future;
In my mind are none of these.
No desire to become an immortal,
Neither the wish to flatter the Buddha
Nor to follow the ever-hurrying Confucius,
For I am too lazy to vie with the virtuous.
Laugh at me as you may,
What is thus is thus.
The play over
I shall cast off my costume
And leave it to the fools.

The " joy " of old age is, to be sure, more conscious than the joy of youth, it might however be heightened by just this consciousness. To this must be added, however, the realisation of its short duration which gives a specific edge to the beauty of old age. Tersely this is expressed in a poem by Li Shang-yin (813–858):

Ill at ease at the dusk,
I drive to Lo-yu highland.
Infinitely beautiful is the setting sun,
But alas! so close to the eve.[6]

II

When, in our century, the onslaught set in on the traditional hierarchy of status and on traditional values and attitudes, it was significant that this movement included among its targets the emancipation of youth. Much of what has been said and done during this period was said and done for the young and by the young. It is no accident that the most influential journal of this period was called *New Youth*. Ch'en Tu-hsiu, its editor, started this journal with an opening article " Call to Youth " in which he said among other things:

> Youth is like early spring, like the rising sun, like trees and grass in bud, like a newly sharpened blade. *It is the most valuable period of life*. The function of youth in society is the same as that of a fresh and vital cell in a human body . . . With tears [I] place my plea before the fresh and vital youth, in the hope that they will achieve self-awareness and begin to struggle . . . [emphasis mine].[7]

Lu Hsün's evaluation of youth is equally forceful:

> Youth will be the first to give China her voice again. Talking courageously, advancing boldly, disregarding advantage and disadvantage,

[6] I owe these two translations to my colleague Vincent Y. C. Shih.

[7] Chow Tse-tsung, *op. cit.*, pp. 42–48. See also Benjamin I. Schwartz, *Chinese Communism and the Rise of Mao* (Cambridge: Harvard Un. Press, 1951), pp. 8–9 and *passim*.

> pushing the old aside: this is the youth's way of proceeding. (*Chüan-chi*, 4, 27.)

Many other journals employed the term "youth" in their titles, such as: *Young China, The Young World, Youth and Society, The Progress of Youth* and *Chinese Youth,* and associations and parties of different political colouring were founded to serve the double aim of emancipating youth from what was considered to be an over-aged status hierarchy and of harnessing youth to the promotion of social functions in general.

The response of China's youth was immediate and vigorous. Only two eye-witnesses shall be quoted here. One is Bertrand Russell, who once wrote:

> Throughout the East, the university student can hope for more influence upon public opinion than he can have in the modern West, but he has much less opportunity than in the West of securing a substantial income. But, neither powerless nor comfortable, he becomes a reformer or a revolutionary, not a cynic. The happiness of the reformer or revolutionary depends upon the course of public affairs, but probably even while he is being executed he enjoys more real happiness than is possible for the comfortable cynic. I remember a young Chinese visitor to my school who was going home to found a similar school in a reactionary part of China. He expected the result to be that his head would be cut off. Nevertheless, he enjoyed a quiet happiness that I could only envy.[8]

John Dewey was no less impressed by the performance of Chinese youth. In his rather chatty letters, he said:

> To the outsider it looks as if babes and sucklings who have no experience and precedents would have to save China.[9]

And at another place:

> You heard nothing but gloom about political China at first . . . and then the students take things into their hands, and there is animation and a sudden buzz.[10]

Even though the fierce attacks on traditional Chinese values were formulated not by the very young but by a slightly older generation,[11] China's youth was swift and radical in taking up the opportunity. These were the times when I became the involuntary witness of a scene in one of the *hutungs* of Peking, during which a father lectured his teenage son on classical attitudes, whereupon the son spat in his father's face, turned around and went away without uttering a word.

There were wide differences of opinion concerning the distinct social and political aims of this revaluation of values. The radicalism of modes

[8] *The Conquest of Happiness* (New York: Signet, 1951), p. 88.
[9] John Dewey and Alice Chipman Dewey, *Letters from China and Japan* (New York: Dutton, 1920), 178.
[10] *Ibid.* p. 193.
[11] Actually not so very old either. Hu Shih was 26 in 1917, Ch'en Tu-hsiu, the oldest among them, 38.

of procedure also varied by degree. There was however near unanimity concerning the postulate that literature had to be put at the service of the movement, thus reasserting the old slogan that literature was there to sustain the doctrine. A literary revolution formed part of the fundamental change. The demands of the extremists who wanted to discard all traditional Chinese writing do not have to be repeated here. As however the literary revolution was accompanied by a thorough language reform the result was that the Chinese literary tradition lost much of its prestige. This almost complete break with the literary past was one of the most fateful by-products of these turbulent times. What arose in its stead did not lack vitality and promise. It was however not given enough time to develop a general maturity and a degree of acceptance which alone could have made for a sustained growth.

That does not mean that all polite literature of the twenties and thirties was political, social, or ideological propaganda literature, even though much of it was. It does however mean that, to begin with, the old genres of poetry, drama and fiction were shunned and entirely new modes of expression were experimented with, and it does furthermore mean that the topics and problems to which emphasis was given were brought in line with what was considered to be the spirit of the time.[12]

This last focus is of importance. Whatever sophistication and refinement Chinese literature lost through the break with the past was, at least in part, compensated by a greater directness and an untrammelled devotion to new and in themselves exciting topics. And as the concern with, and the fate of, youth was part of the contemporary movement, youth as a topic is found much more frequently dealt with than in traditional literature. The period did not lack sensitive writers, and even though, for lack of generally accepted standards, literary products were frequently loosely composed and clumsily executed, the concern was to get to grips with the problems as such and not just to write a piece of exhortatory prose.

Among those who wrote about the very young and about teenagers the women writers stand out. Much of Ping Hsin's early short stories are concerned with boys aged between seven and thirteen, the time when unconscious urges and emotions lead the child beyond the containment of the self. She does at times succeed in capturing the unconscious and ununderstood longings of the very young with a trenchancy which is reminiscent of Thomas Mann's *Unordnung und frühes Leid*. All along, children are taken here as beings in their own right and an attempt is

[12] I am not concerned here with those few poets who continued to produce in the traditional fashion. Even though the quality of their output was exceedingly high, they were not then considered the representative poets of the day.

made to seize an image of how they experience their own life and not of an experience and a life which adults have provided.

Possibly the most accomplished story about a very young girl is Ting Ling's novelette *New Year,* where a strangely happy-unhappy child is depicted against the background of a decaying gentry clan. Also the Little Bud of her novel *Mother* shows some of these qualities. Youth is seen here as a way of life with its specific observations and its specific trials which are not shared by other age groups; it leaves the reader full of tenderness and full of marvel. The same cannot be said about Ting Ling's attempts in writing about teenagers. Stereotyped problems and pat situations are not entirely avoided here, and much of her teenagers' immediacy is spoiled by a sweetish gravy of Wertherian self-pity which was the craze of the age. The problem of love and sex, which does not appear to have been difficult of solution in her real life, is at times given a somewhat tortured expression and she even delves into the artificial problem of love and revolution. It has to be said, though, that her solution of this problem in her novel *Wei-hu* is her own.

Ling Shu-hua, the wife of Ch'en Yüan, also wrote a lot about children. Her most interesting stories are possibly those which concern themselves with teenage girls brought up in the old tradition and their difficulties and anxieties when confronted with the untraditional manners of their age peers.

Male writers have much more frequently focussed on the problems of adolescence rather than childhood. Yü Ta-fu's story "Sinking" is a typical example of a story on the tortures of sex, frustration, and guilt. It shares with many other stories of the period a spirit of jadedness and despair which few sensitive writers escaped.

Others, such as Yeh Shao-chün, have however dealt with younger children, their day-dreaming, their ambitions and their blessed ignorance. The only really happy human beings which Lu Hsün ever created were the poor village children in the story "She-hsi."[13] My favourite is Shen Tsung-wen's story "The Tiger Cub," a wild little rascal who is an underage orderly in the following of an ill-disciplined band of soldiers. Technically, too, this little story is a masterpiece.

The preoccupation with the more advanced stages of youth in the literature of this period gives room particularly to one trait characteristic of the times: defiance. Youth, defying the traditional status hierarchy, also defies its own elders. In Pa Chin's novels, for instance, particularly in his trilogy *Chia, Ch'un* and *Ch'iu,* this note is struck hard, resulting in overtly cacophonous relationships between youth and age in which he,

[13] Jef Last, *Lu Hsün—Dichter und Idol* (Frankfurt a. M.: Metzner, 1959), p. 50, has drawn attention to this.

as did most other writers of the time, openly sides with youth. It took a rare poet like Shen Tsung-wen to show that not even then was life all revolution. The old man and the little girl in his novel *Pien-ch'eng* are not governed in their relationship by institutionalised value patterns, traditional or otherwise.

Age, on the other hand, has not been so frequently and so successfully dealt with. Stereotypes which equate age with the reactionary, the stubborn, the narrow-minded, and the superstitious mar many of the elderly figures in the writing of the time. This is even true in some of Lu Hsün's stories. There does appear, however, an occasional insight into the special problems of age. The loss of spiritual and material security which leaves the aged desolate and lonely is, for instance, the topic of Yeh Shao-chün's story " Solitude."

These few selected examples will have shown that the tradition had definitely lost its grip on literature. We do not find any more the devoted and pious young scholar, nor do we find the wise old philosopher. Life had been torn wide open, and the images the writers selected were those offered by humanity rent apart. Gropingly and at times clumsily these images were developed and at times endowed with an overdose of sentimentality. However they were, as a rule, not any more dominated by old, and, as a rule, not yet by new patterns. There are moments in the literature of this period in which the images offered by life—life conditioned by the specific circumstances of this period—have been transfigured into images of literary validity. And it is youth, particularly childhood, and at times even old age which occasionally emerge almost entirely free of the slags of rationalisation. An implicit but trenchant symbol of this image is given in the last exclamation of Lu Hsün's *Diary of a Madman*:

" Save the Children! "

III

To get literature, which was thus lifted out of the gravity of tradition, into Communist orbit, the Chinese borrowed methods and concepts from the " Big Brother." As Mr. Boorman's article deals with the ideological and organisational control of literature, the point does not have to be developed here. Attention has to be paid, however, to the fact that the phenomenon " literature " with which the Chinese dealt showed properties vastly different from those of its Russian counterpart.[14]

[14] On the following see: Victor Erlich, " The Literary Scene " in Abraham Brumberg ed., *Russia under Khrushchev* (New York: Praeger, 1962), pp. 343–359; Hugh McLean and Walter N. Vickery eds., *The Year of Protest* (New York: Vintage, 1961), introduction; Harold Swayze, *Political Control of Literature in the USSR: 1946–1959* (Cambridge: Harvard Un. Press, 1962).

At the time of the Russian revolution, the Russian writers had not recently discarded their tradition. This tradition afforded the Russian poets a status, and artistic creativity a prestige, which the early engineers of the revolution did not dare to attack lightheartedly, in spite of the rather grim views on literature of Marx and Engels, and of Lenin for that matter. Trotsky was aware that artistic creation was " a deflection, a transformation of reality, in accordance with the peculiar laws of art." " A work of art," he added, " should in the first place be judged by its own law, the law of art." [15] And even Lunatcharsky, whom Lenin had ordered to pull the *Proletkult* closer to the party, still proclaimed emotional intensity and spontaneity as ultimate tests of greatness in art.[16]

Only after about a decade the vice began to tighten. Then, organisational and ideological control devices, symbolised by the names of Zhdanov and later Malenkov, were put into practice—devices which pulled down the literature of the Russians, and, later, the literature of the Eastern European countries, to an unprecedented level of drabness. However, all the coercion and corruption of writers which Milosz describes so vividly in his *The Captive Mind* could not quite extinguish the spark of creativity. There were still people who wrote books like *Doctor Zhivago*; and when the short-lived thaw set in in 1956, a respectable amount of creativity came to the surface again. In Poland it even appears as if this reassertion of literary values had more permanent character. Even after the reversal of the thaw, a Russian poet could still write:

> Believe in me!
> I shall begin by morn.
> Then out of melody
> A song is born.[17]

No Chinese author would have dared to yearn for such a creative trust. Nor could any corresponding revival of literary activities be observed during the—still more short-lived—" hundred flowers " period in China.[18] It may be argued that among the reasons for this phenomenon the limited amount of time during which the new, tradition-free literature had flourished was one. There had not yet been occasion to set into motion again the " laws of art " of which Trotsky spoke. By knocking out tradition Chinese writers had not only knocked out for themselves position and prestige which generally accepted values tend to yield, they had ventured into a world without precedents and bounds in which the very co-ordinates of artistic existence still had to be established. They had

[15] Erlich, pp. 346–347. Trotsky was evidently influenced by Plekhanov in his views on art.
[16] Erlich, *op. cit.*
[17] Tyomin, 1959. See Swayze, p. 264. Translation slightly altered.
[18] Roderick MacFarquhar, *The Hundred Flowers* (New York: Praeger, 1960).

furthermore done this under conditions which afforded greater urgency to " the revolution " than to the cultivation of new literary values. Most, if not all of those who live on mainland China today had committed themselves and their embryonic craft to " the revolution " (even though not necessarily the Communist revolution), thus subsuming the world of literature to a non-literary world.

To Lu Hsün, who was foremost and most outspoken in this commitment, the ensuing dilemma appeared with brilliant clarity; with his usual candour he once said:

> That is why I know: All revolutionary poets with their ideals and illusions are in danger of being crushed by the reality of the very movement of which they hopefully sing praise; and a revolution which would not destroy the ideals and illusions of the poets would only be a paper revolution. (*Chüan-chi*, 4, 48.)

He was enough of a poet to realise the incompatibility of art and politics [19] and bold enough to forecast accurately the brutal fate which would descend upon his confrères.

IV

The control apparatus was put into operation in China at a much earlier stage in the development of the revolution than in the U.S.S.R. The propaganda needs of the politicians at this stage still stayed their heavy hand to an extent. The initial impetus of revolutionary literature was furthermore still strong enough to sustain an output which was at least co-determined by the poet's craft. But already at that period pieces were produced to which Lu Hsün refers disdainfully as the " New Three Character Classics " and the " New Songs about Model Boys." (*Chüan-Chi*, 4, 91.) Into this category would, for instance, belong the *Stories for Children* by Yen Wen-ching [20] which tell animal fables with a point. There is the story of the bee who is industrious and progressive and is rewarded with honey, and the earthworm who is conservative and lazy and has to eat earth. Eventually the earthworm undergoes ideological remoulding and also contributes useful services. Or there is the story of the three conceited little kittens, who are good at school and whom their mother wants to do productive work (catching fish). An old rat seduces them into laziness which they shake off only after their mother has pointed out to them that it would be a rat who gave such advice. Or there is the red-beaked crow who follows the lion and sings his praise in order to get the entrails of the lion's quarry.

19 Dramatically expressed in Herbert Read's now famous formulation: Art is revolution.
20 *Chinese Literature* (hereafter, CL), No. 1, 1956, pp. 147–164. Written before the " liberation."

Early submission to Party patterns is shown in the then preferred topics and plots. The political emphasis of the period ruled out the portrayal of childhood and old age except for very specific purposes. During the time of accusation literature, one of these was to make use of the emotional impact of the image of a suffering child, exemplified, for instance, by Ma Fan-to's "Nursery Rhyme" which contains the lines:

> There are so many little darlings
> Looking for grass to eat.[21]

Or by the ballad-like songs of Li Tuan-cheng, of which one describes an old man ploughing with the son pulling the plough. The son, tubercular,

> . . . stumbles
> Starts to spit blood and
> Sinks to the ground . . . [22]

Another one describes a mother letting her hungry children have the last bit of bran in the house, even though she knows

> Ai-ya, tomorrow,
> What hope is there? [23]

Occasionally the image of youth is used to counteract the despair which accusation literature is liable to evoke in older people. This is, for instance, the case in Feng Chih's poem about the woodcutter Han P'o [24] whose gloomy story is told by a mother to her son, who then dispells her gloom by stating that in today's circumstances men like Han P'o might still suffer, however

> Tomorrow we will fight the landlords.
> Then he can settle accounts with his landlord,
> Then he does not have to take humiliation any longer,
> Then he will emerge into the clear day.

Among the better established writers were however some whose residual adherence to literary imagery, even when they were devout Communists, was slow in breaking down. Ting Ling may serve as an example here. Her stories written during the war, entirely Communist in content, still take children as children and youth as youth,[25] and thus achieve an impact which others of the contemporary writers could not boast any more. It is only in her Stalin Prize winning novel *The Sun*

[21] Rewi Alley, *The People Speak Out* (Peking: The author, 1954), p. 36.
[22] "Blood," Rewi Alley, p. 40.
[23] "The Last Bit of Bran," *ibid*.
[24] *Shih-nien Shih Ch'ao* (Peking: Jen-min Ch'u-pan-she, 1959), pp. 6–9.
[25] See the title story in her volume *Our Children and Others* (Shanghai: Ying-wen Hsueh-hui, 1941), and her volume *When I was in Hsia-ts'un*, edited by Hu Feng. English trans. *When I was in Sha Chuan* (Poona: Kutub, 1945).

Shines Over the San-kan River [26] that the youthful hero emerges as so much of a Party robot that he refuses to see his best girl only because she is associated with a landlord family. But even here the youthful girl seems to survive the vicissitudes of her social surroundings and the fickleness of her lover with a degree of serenity and unconcern which made Communist reviewers cringe.[27]

When, after the take-over in 1949, the control machinery was applied in full force it did not take long for the great silence to set in.[28] No amount of propaganda could cover up the fact that most established writers just ceased to write. Some of them tried to evade the issue by writing for children and ended up by falling into the trap they wanted to avoid and writing "New Three Character Classics." Among them were writers of some renown such as Chang T'ien-i and Yeh Sheng-t'ao (the former Yeh Shao-chün).[29] As this kind of activity was publicly promoted by contests for children's literature sponsored by the Chinese People's National Committee in Defence of Children and by the creation of special periodicals for children and a Children's Publishing House, Chang and Yeh soon found emulators. Chang wrote stories like: "How Lo Wen-ying became a Young Pioneer"; Kuo Hsü wrote a prize-winning story about "Commander Yang's Young Pioneers" in which a group of orphans help guerrilla fighters, etc. The apogee among such stories was Emi Hsiao's *The Youth of Comrade Mao Tse-tung*,[30] in which a bowdlerised version of Mao's early years is presented for the edification of the young. Children's rhymes went a similar way. For the use of children, ditties were coined which reflected the changing slogans of Party drives. Liu Yü deserves special mention here.[31]

New writers and the second raters who kept the presses busy had of course still less of a commitment to literary issues. They were not even aware of literary problems other than those presented to them by the Party. To follow the Party line for them meant the acceptance of sorely needed guidance. Youth and age are reduced to types which have nothing to do with either living or literary images.[32] Youth is derobed of its self-confidence and pluck. "Naughty" children get lost and have to be found again with the help of young pioneers (unsuccessful) and the police (successful).[33] Daring children are punished,[34] whereas a good child

26 Written in 1948. English trans. (Peking: Foreign Languages Press), 1954.
27 Feng Hsueh-feng, *loc. cit.*, p. 338.
28 See Swayze, p. 247, for a similar phenomenon in the USSR.
29 CL, No. 2, 1952, pp. 214; No. 1, 1955, pp. 195–196; No. 6, 1959, pp. 137–139.
30 Prusek, *Die Literatur des befreiten China* (Prague: Artia, 1955), p. 341.
31 Prusek, pp. 127–128.
32 See Erlich, pp. 352–353, for the role of the "typical" as developed by Malenkov.
33 Kao Hsiang-chen, "Chubby and Little Pine," CL, No. 1, 1951, pp. 115–124.
34 Hsiao Ping, "At the Seaside," CL, No. 1, 1951, pp. 106–115.

would forsake his cricket fights in order to do good co-op work,[35] or has to give up happily long planned-for fun (teasing of a new bride) in order to fight rural capitalism.[36] Young girls live dangerously as members of a forest survey team,[37] or exchange further education for the care of the cooperative's sty of pigs which they teach to keep clean and even teach to go to the toilet, whereupon they are rewarded by being transferred to the state farm.[38] In one story the daughter " follows where the mother leads," whereas the mother " follows where the Party leads." [39]

Recently a full-fledged novel has been devoted to a young girl. It is entitled *The Song of Youth* and is the first novel of Yang Mao, a woman in her forties.[40] The book was praised as the most notable novel published in 1958 and a film was based on its plot. It is the story of a girl aged eighteen when the novel starts and takes place between the summer of 1931 (Mukden incident) and the winter of 1935 (students' demonstrations). The heroine Lin Tao-ching has against her every, literally every, conceivable strike which " feudal " society could muster. Unerringly however she " grows from a democrat into a Communist " and the book thus reveals " how the petty-bourgeois intellectuals . . . gradually turned toward the revolution." As is the case in the stories mentioned before, there is nothing youthful in her—she is stereotyped and trite.

Age does not fare any better. There is the veteran Party secretary who with Marxist wisdom and the recollection of past exploits sets right a chaotic co-operative,[41] or the greying chief engineer who is dared by his son into learning Russian,[42] or the old broad-minded and imaginative farmer who is encouraged by the *hsien* Party secretary to found an agricultural producers' co-operative.[43] " Long years of bitter struggle had given him a wide outlook " and he " always took the socialist road." Many of these stories are of interest inasmuch as they reflect quite clearly the shift of emphasis in the Party line, such as a greater stress on experience during the latest period. They do however not portray youth or age either in a realistic or in a literary sense.

If further proof was needed, all doubts would be dispelled by a perusal of the products of the great literary leap which followed the " hundred flowers " period.[44] Here one will find poems like these:

35 Jen Ta-lin, " Crickets," *ibid.*, pp. 97–106.
36 Lo Pin-chi, " New Year Holiday," CL, No. 3, 1955, pp. 73–85.
37 Lu Fei, " Forest Girls," CL, No. 3, 1957, pp. 158–162.
38 Ma Feng, " Han Mei-mei," CL, No. 3, 1955, pp. 60–72.
39 Li Chun, " Mother and Daughter," CL, No. 12, 1959, pp. 72–85.
40 Serialised in CL, Nos. 3–6, 1960.
41 Hsü Kuang-yao, " Lao Tao," CL, No. 4, 1955, pp. 114–120.
42 Hsia Yen, " The Test," CL, No. 4, 1955, pp. 1–69.
43 Li Chun, " When the Snow Melts," CL, No. 1, 1957, pp. 3–62.
44 See S. H. Chen, " Multiplicity in Uniformity: Poetry and the Great Leap Forward," *The China Quarterly*, No. 3, July–September, 1960.

A little girl with plaits so long
Gaily dressed from head to toe,
Each day she's up early to carry night soil.
Her singing wakes the sun from sleep.[45]

The rather quaint contrast between the neatly dressed long-plaited girl and two buckets of night-soil loses some of its impact if read in the context of innumerable manure poems (this was the time of the fertiliser drive); also the waking of the sun is a stereotype which occurs in countless other verses.

For an old age poem, the following may serve:

I am past sixty but I can still work,
And I find it as easy as when I was young.
It's not that I'm boasting about my strength,
But here in my heart I have Mao Tse-tung.[46]

The death of the image of youth in contemporary Chinese literature is possibly best exemplified by a dithyrambic effusion of one of the poets laureate of Communist China, Liu Pai-yu, entitled: *The Glow of Youth.* In it, Liu does not talk much about youth but about Mao Tse-tung, the civil war, Party parades and the like. But then he ends up with the sentence: "This glow of Youth will become the torch of imperishable Truth, etc." [47] In Communist Chinese literature, youth has been degraded from an image into a slogan.

[45] Kuo Mo-jo and Chou Yang, eds., *Songs of the Red Flag* (Peking: Foreign Languages Press, 1961), p. 121.
[46] *Ibid.* p. 10.
[47] CL, No. 11, 1959, pp. 50–57.

Co-operatives and Communes in Chinese Communist Fiction

By C. W. SHIH

IN less than a decade, collectivisation has come to more than five hundred million Chinese peasants and a large portion of the urban population; it has transformed the socio-economic structure of the nation, causing general repercussions around the world and unascertainable effects in the country.[1] The development of this massive and significant collectivisation movement is reflected, in large measure, in Chinese Communist literature. This article first presents, following a general chronological order, fictional materials reflecting the co-operative and commune movements,[2] and then discusses summarily the artistic and social values of this literature.

I

As early as 1952, co-operatives had already appeared in fiction. In September of that year there was published in *People's Literature* (PL)

[1] Early in 1943, Mao Tse-tung asserted that the peasant masses had slaved for thousands of years under the system of individual economy—the foundation of feudal rule and poverty—and that the only way to change this state of affairs was by gradual collectivisation. Not long after the inauguration of the new régime in 1949, the drive towards collectivisation was initiated. By December 1951, the Party's Central Committee had issued to local cadres the " Draft Decisions on Agricultural Mutual Aid and Co-operation." Not published till February 1953, this document called for a " three-stage " programme: seasonal mutual aid teams, year-round mutual aid teams, and agricultural producers' co-operatives. In a speech in July 1955 Mao Tse-tung, encouraged by the progress of the co-operative drive, dispensed with the " gradual approach " and gave the signal for rapid collectivisation. Immediately there was a nation-wide " socialist upsurge," which led to almost total collectivisation of the countryside by 1956. Concurrently with the Great Leap Forward, the régime launched in August 1958 a drive for the establishment of communes. When 1958 began, most of the five hundred million peasants were working in 740,000 co-operatives, but by the end of the year these peasants and many city dwellers had been organised into 26,000 communes. Since the winter of 1958, there have been measures of modification and retrenchment. For more information on the development of the co-operatives and communes, see *Communist China 1955–59: Policy Documents with Analysis*, with a Foreword by Robert Bowie and John Fairbank (Cambridge: Harvard Un. Press, 1962) (hereafter referred to as *Policy Documents*); Felix Greene, *China Awakened* (London: Cape, 1961); Richard Hughes, *The Chinese Communes* (London: The Bodley Head, 1960).

[2] In search of materials that reflect current developments, I examined mostly short stories in periodicals. The short stories quoted here are almost exclusively from *Jen-min Wen-hsueh* (*People's Literature*: PL), a monthly published in Peking. Because of the semi-official nature of this periodical and because of the eminence of its editors and contributors as Communist writers, materials from this journal should provide a proper perspective for this study.

"The New Path," an informative story about the "spontaneous evolution" of an agricultural co-operative out of the problem-ridden mutual aid team in a little village. The story centres around Old Liang, a poor peasant who had come into his own after the "liberation." Suspecting that his newly purchased horse is being overworked by a co-farmer, he withdraws from the mutual aid team. This incident touches off a heated discussion among the farmers about the difficult relations between those who own draft animals and those who do not. Under the leadership of the cadres, a solution is finally found in the common ownership idea: all the draft animals are to be pooled and kept in a common stall and the cost of the upkeep is to be shared by the members in proportion to the size of their farms. The team leader later reports about a common-land ownership scheme which has been newly adopted by another group. Under this system, all the land is pooled, all boundaries are eradicated for tilling purposes, and each peasant is paid according to the work he has performed and the land he has invested. This plan wins the team's immediate approval because of its many advantages, among which are better overall planning and greater incentives for labour. When the year ends, the team has reaped a bumper crop in spite of early frost and has enlarged its size from twelve to twenty-five households, many having been attracted by the new benefits. Soon news of this development reaches the administration, which orders that this new group, with its common ownership in land and in farming implements, be called an "Agricultural Producers' Co-operative" (*Nung-yeh Sheng-ch'an Ho-tso-she*).[3] In this story we see the birth of the co-operative in its lower form, where, though the land and the animals are pooled, the farmers retain their titles to these possessions and receive remunerations accordingly. (Later, when the agricultural producers' co-operatives developed into the higher form, the farmers lost their titles and received only wages based on work.)

The economic, social and psychological pressures on the farmers to join the co-operatives seem to have been strong from the outset. Shih T'ou in his "Song of the Forward March" (PL, March 1954) paints a convincing picture of an individualist farmer's futile fight against the tide of Socialism. Old Chu K'e-ch'in gives everybody the same impression: he is very sure of himself. "He lived quite comfortably, never squandered any money, never owed anybody anything, and never attempted anything beyond his ability."[4] But a problem arises when his only son falls in love. The love between Ta-pao and Erh-mei is known throughout the village. Both families had belonged to

[3] PL, September 1952, p. 41.
[4] PL, March 1954, p. 44.

the same mutual aid team. The year before, through the efforts of Erh-mei, her family joined the co-operative. The boy is in a dilemma: on the one hand, his father stubbornly refuses to join, and on the other hand, his girl refuses to marry him until his household joins. Why should she go back now to domestic chores only, the girl argues. "Yes, things progress every day. Why should I go backward? Ever since we joined the co-operative, I work more, but I am happy. Now like men, I can participate in production and in the sharing of grains, and I can have an opportunity to learn. I feel sure of myself, and I walk erect."[5] Changes come suddenly for Old Chu. Both his crops of corn and potatoes are ruined, first by drought, then by heavy rain. His son, in disappointment, leaves home. Furthermore, he discovers that an average co-operative member gets more grain than he does. After much consideration, "the old man made up his mind; he voluntarily applied to join the co-operative."[6] Action and good examples, not force, are used to prove to the peasants the positive virtues of the agricultural collectivisation movement. This is the popular theme in the early stories on the co-operative.

In 1955, responding to the Government's call for intensive agricultural collectivisation, several full-length novels appeared, the most popular of which was Chao Shu-li's *San-li-wan*. San-li-wan, in real life, is a mountainous village in one of the early liberated areas of North China. Chosen as a model village during the land reform and mutual aid period, it organised in 1951 one of the first agricultural producers' co-operatives. Based on the author's actual experiences while participating in collective farming,[7] *San-li-wan* tells about the growing pains and joys of a co-operative expanding in size, reflecting the hardships and excitements of a compact Chinese rural community at a time of intensive social change.

In its effort to increase productivity, the co-operative in *San li-wan* resolves to mobilise the whole village to build a canal for irrigation purposes. The movement takes on added significance when, over the question of land for the canal, a series of struggles start. Ma To-shou, a middle farmer, refuses to give up, for the building of the canal, his "handle-land," a piece of land so called because of its shape. Ma had joined the mutual aid team not out of enthusiasm for collective farming, but out of the ignoble intention of making use of the team's labour force on his land. He finds a kindred spirit in Fan Teng-kao, who is head of the village and a Party member. A hired-hand

5 *Ibid.* p. 50.
6 *Ibid.*
7 See Chao Shu-li, "*San-li-wan* Hsieh-tso Ch'ien-hou" (San-li-wan and Its Composition), *Wen-yi Pao,* No. 19, October 1955, pp. 23–26.

before the "liberation," Fan had received a piece of good land during the agrarian reform and had since increased his holdings considerably by farm work and small-scale trading. Both Ma and Fan are reluctant to join the co-operatives.

At Party branch meetings Fan is harshly criticised for his capitalist tendencies, his bourgeois ideas, his misdemeanour of trading privately, and his warped interpretation of the Party's "voluntary principle" to cover his reluctance to join the co-operative. Ma argues that private ownership is still legal and that he will willingly relinquish his possessions once Socialism comes into existence. "Even the masses accept the Party's leadership to work for Socialism," retorts the Party secretary, "they do not wait for others to build Socialism for them before giving up their private property. If all indulge in private business, who are to build Socialism?" [8]

In the meantime, tired of the backward atmosphere in the house and determined to fight for the "handle-land," the progressive third daughter-in-law in Ma's household insists on a division of family property. Old Ma and his wife, as a final step, produce the settlement papers showing the division of property among the four sons—a document drawn up ten years earlier as a device to avoid possible trouble during the land reform. According to the settlements, the "handle-land went not to the third daughter-in-law but to the second son, now working in another town. When informed of the village's need this youth willingly relinquishes the land for the benefit of the collective project.

Here we see a group of people opposed to collective farming: middle peasants and peasants who have "turned over" (*fan-shen*) since land reform and who are unwilling to give up their private possessions; peasants who believe in individual farming; and a backsliding Party member who engages in private trading. Under the competent leadership of Wang Chin-sheng, Party secretary and vice-chairman of the co-operative, the recalcitrant farmers are all finally persuaded by words, examples, and action to join the march towards Socialism.

The prosperity which collective work and Socialism can bring to the villagers is neatly foretold in three large paintings by a local painter. The first one, picturing the village as it is, is called "San-li-wan Today"; the second one, showing the proposed canal, gliding through luxurious crops brimming with water, flanked by dikes and dotted with water wheels, is called "San-li-wan of Next Year" and draws the most attention from the villagers. "With a watercourse like this, we never need fear drought again," says one. "Build a canal this year; next

[8] Chao Shu-li, *San-li-wan* (Peking: 1955), p. 121.

year it will be like that," says another. "We can double the harvest—no problem at that. . . ." Women, pointing to the stretch of the canal by the village, make their comments. "Here we can wash vegetables." "There we can do our laundering." "We need not carry water again to our house; it is right at our door. . . ." Children also make their plans: "We can come here for bathing, catching frogs, and fishing." [9] The third painting, entitled "San-li-wan Under Socialism," is the most alluring—it depicts the village on a summer evening, bubbling with automobiles, well-built highways, electric poles, trees, new houses, and streamlined farms, with combines and cultivators rolling in the fields.

Before the launching of the Great Leap Forward and before production was carried on at frantic pace, romance merited frequent mention in fiction. Love is not pictured as blind fury but mainly as mutual admiration for the boy's or girl's progressiveness, capacity for work, and similar qualities that make for good Communist citizenship. In *San-li-wan* the author sets six country girls and lads astir, choosing and switching mates. The reasoning of Fan Chih-ling, one of the few village girls "having culture," gives an insight into the psychology desired of the new generation. Comparing two potential husbands, Fan meditates: "Yü-sheng constantly thinks about constructing a Socialist world; Yu-i constantly thinks about obeying his feudalist mother." Besides, she thinks, Yü-sheng lives among models, tools, raw materials, and saws, and has as constant visitors Party members and cadres, whereas Yu-i lives among granaries, baskets, and utensils, and has as visitors uncles and aunts. "Enough, enough," [10] she says to herself and then makes her decision. When she gets up the next morning, it is not yet dawn. She quickly goes to see Yü-sheng, who, as expected, is still up working on his models. Very tactfully she proposes marriage. Interesting as these references to romance are, they occupy a secondary position in a novel about the serious struggle of the new and old forces in the Socialist revolution.

Another vivid account of the co-operative movement of this period is Chou Li-po's *Great Changes in a Mountain Village,* published in 1958. The story takes place in Ch'ing-ch'i (Clear Creek), a little town in Hunan in the winter of 1955. When Teng Hsiu-mei, a young woman cadre, is sent there to help organise agricultural producers' co-operatives, the town's people are not at all ready, as the great majority have not even been persuaded to join the provisional mutual aid teams. They listen to the new proposal with distrust and argue against it with their homespun sayings, such as "If a mother gives birth to nine sons, they

[9] *Ibid.* pp. 128–129.
[10] *Ibid.* pp. 140–141.

and the mother would have ten minds." Therefore how could scores of households be expected to work with one mind? Not discouraged, Teng and the local cadres talk incessantly to the peasants singly and in groups. After one month of intensive groundwork and after dissolving individual and mass resistance, they finally succeed in establishing five co-operatives, comprising more than two-thirds of the four hundred or so households in the area.

Just like these two works, the novels *Welcome-Spring Song* (1955), *Water Flows East* (1956) and *When the Snow Melts* (1956) [11] all have their plots focused on the struggle between the " progressive " and " backward " forces. Except for variations in emphasis and intensity, the short stories and novels about the co-operatives have fundamentally the same themes—class struggle and production—both essential to Socialist construction.

In the 1956–57 period, the " hundred flowers " policy and the relaxation of cultural control brought forth stories such as Liu Pin-yen's " On the Bridge Construction Site " (PL, April 1956) and " Our Paper's Inside News " (PL, June 1956; October 1956), voicing genuine criticism of the hardships and the suffocating conformity under the régime; but no stories openly voicing criticism of the co-operative movement appear to have been published.

In 1958, when the Second Five-Year Plan was launched with the dramatic slogans of the Great Leap Forward, a new mood of optimism and drive was immediately inculcated into literature.[12] The crusading spirit is well reflected in " Model Report," a short story first published in the *Yangtse Magazine* (April 1958), which was later reprinted in *People's Literature* (May 1958).

Inspired by the Great Leap Forward, a little mountain village where the inhabitants depended for their living solely on *t'ung* oil and other mountain crops pledged to enlarge the arable land from five *mou* (a *mou* is a sixth of an acre) to ten *mou*. When this pledge received an unfavourable reaction at a general meeting of representatives from several villages, the Party secretary, the next day, mobilised the whole group in his co-operative to look in the mountain for water. For several days and nights they searched high and low, but to no avail. On the seventh night, Old Wang chanced upon a damp patch. Overjoyed, the whole co-operative joined in the digging. When the last rock was removed, " Hua-la-la, a stream shoots out! . . . Wild with joy, the

11 Wang Hsi-chien, *Ying-ch'un Ch'ü* (*Welcome-Spring Song*); Li Man-tien, *Shui Hsiang Tung Liu* (*Water Flows East*); Li Chun, *Ping-hua Hsueh-hsiao* (*When The Snow Melts*).

12 For a description of poetry in this period, see S. H. Chen, " Multiplicity in Uniformity: Poetry and the Great Leap Forward," *The China Quarterly*, No. 3, July–September 1960, pp. 1–15.

people hugged each other, yelling, 'Long live Chairman Mao! Long live the Party!'"[13] In the same spirit, the villagers found nine springs in succession in these arid mountains. Without the help of any engineer, water was channelled all over the area: "Water listens to the masses and goes wherever they direct. Yes, the masses are the great, the most capable engineers!"[14] comments the author. As a result of the collective effort, fifteen thousand *mou* of farmland were cultivated.

In that same initial year of the Second Five-Year Plan, the régime started the commune movement. "In 1958 a new social organisation appeared, fresh as the morning sun, above the broad horizon of East Asia,"[15] announced poetically the Central Committee of the Chinese Communist Party after its December session. This new organisation represented a bold experiment in human living. Whereas the co-operative was organised for collective *work*, the communes, combining industry, agriculture, trade, education and military affairs, was organised for collective *life*. It represented a giant step towards the ultimate stage of Communism. In the initial period of this extreme social change, many writers took on the responsibility of interpreting to the people the workings and benefits of the new organisation.

It was with this mission in mind that Chou Li-po wrote his short tale, "Guest from Peking" (PL, June 1959). A few villagers gathered early one evening in Lao Kuan's room partly because it was raining and partly because they had a guest from Peking. The conversation soon turned to the mess hall. Because the free food they received was a thing too good to be true, many were worried about its continuation. "It will not be discontinued," says the city guest reassuringly, as if he knew more about the matter. After assuring the group of the rosy future of collective living, the guest re-emphasised: "Yes, in the future Communist society, because of great production, all kinds of things will be delivered to you without cost."[16] "Won't everybody live like an emperor then,"[17] marvelled a country woman at the end of the story.

In this little tale, the author attempts to drive home a basic Communist theory behind the communes—a theory emphatically stated in the now famous Wuhan Resolution of 1958: "Socialist society and Communist society are two stages marked by different degrees of economic development. The socialist principle is 'from each according to his ability and to each according to his work'; the communist

[13] PL, May 1958, p. 79.
[14] *Ibid.* p. 80.
[15] *Policy Documents*, p. 490.
[16] PL, June 1959, p. 12.
[17] *Ibid.* p. 13.

principle is 'from each according to his ability and to each according to his needs'."[18]

The mess hall, built on this Communist principle, is interpreted in the following story as a device arising out of the urgent needs of the people. "The Story of Li Shuang-shuang" (PL, March 1960) tells about a young woman, who in the midst of the Great Leap Forward, felt restless in attending only to domestic chores. "The Great Leap has lit the sky, how can I be tied down to my family like this?"[19] she questioned herself. The husband, who always spoke of her as "my cook," "my child's mother," and "the woman in my house," highly disapproved of her desire to join the others in the work on the village water projects. Fully aware of her duties to the family, Shuang-shuang tried hard to find a solution to the conflicts between domestic responsibilities and Socialist construction, and finally she hit upon the idea of a mess hall. In a clumsy, scrawling hand, she wrote a doggerel suggesting this idea and had her writing posted in the market place. After the doggerel had caught the country Party secretary's eye, the suggestion became a reality and Shuang-shuang became the staunch supporter of the mess hall.

This story illustrates not only how much a simple country housewife can help in the building of the new society, but also how she herself, in the tide of collective living, can be transformed into a progressive woman leader. Shuang-shuang was soon in charge of the new organisation. Her husband, once for two years in the pre-liberation days an apprentice in a restaurant, looked down upon the new mess hall and recalled with relish the "shredded chicken" and sea food delicacies. Upon hearing such nonsense, Shuang-shuang became very impatient: "I don't want to listen. . . . No matter how good the dishes were, they were for the evil landlords. What did we eat at home! . . . Now, though what is served in the mess hall is simple, it is cooked for us workers. . . ."[20] When Shuang-shuang pushed the food cart to the field and watched the farmers eat heartily, "she suddenly felt as if her sweat, from her work in the kitchen, had flowed, following the clear stream, into the lush field, turning into wheat and rice."[21]

The mess halls, nurseries, and similar organisations in the communes, releasing women from household duties, have helped to add an estimated 100 million women to the labour force. Formerly consumers, these women have now been turned into production labourers. In fiction,

[18] "Resolutions on Some Questions Concerning the People's Communes" (Wuhan Resolution), *Policy Documents*, p. 494.
[19] PL, March 1960, p. 15.
[20] *Ibid.* p. 19.
[21] *Ibid.* p. 27.

they are presented not only as competent workers, but often as production leaders in the workshops ("The Warmth of Spring," PL, October 1959), in the fields ("New Life," PL, December 1960), and on the construction sites ("Spot of Red in the Sky," *Chinese Literature*, May 1960). This last story, for example, tells how a spoiled, sickly girl, under the education of the Party, turned into a robust steel welder and the leader of the Youth League Shock Brigade. Her country mother, visiting her on the construction site in the city, was awed by the "mountainous blast furnaces and stoves being constructed." Although the daughter had written her that "We're building Socialism, the foundation of Communism,"[22] the mother could not help being amazed by what she saw. When she asked which of the steel plates on the furnace her daughter had welded, the girl replied: "Ma! How do I know? Many people are working on it together. We take a collective pride in the success of each of our projects. . . ."[23] The girl, like many heroines in other stories, was now not only an expert in what she did, but "red and expert."

The communes broke down not only the barriers between male and female labour, but also the barriers between mental and manual work, between the town and the country, and between civil and military life. Demarcations between work and study, peace and war were, to a great extent, eliminated. Production teams were led like military units. In Sha Ting's "The Contest" (PL, October 1960), for example, the leader of the First Production Brigade of the Shihmen People's Commune discussed with the cadres their plans for farm work in such military terms as "base" (*chü-tien*), "battle line" (*chan-hsien*), and "concentrate our fire" (*chi-chung huo-li*). "He had never seen fighting himself, but understood that they were now engaged in a battle with nature,"[24] comments the author.

Both the close co-ordination between the production forces in a commune and the expediency of labour mobilisation on a basis of a military discipline are illustrated in the following story about a production hero. ("Buddhist Immortal," *Hsin Kuan-ch'a*, March 1960). Chao Yung-fu, chief director of the electric station construction projects and also a Party secretary, was called by his fellow-villagers "Buddhist Immortal," because he was always there to extend a helping hand in emergencies. Now he was interested in the *ssu-hua*.[25] When drought

22 *Chinese Literature*, May 1960, p. 16.
23 *Ibid*. p. 21.
24 PL (October 1960), p. 10.
25 *Hsin Kuan-ch'a* (*New Observer*), March 1960, p. 11. "*Ssu-hua*," meaning "four transfigurations," is "organisation militarised, work materialised, life collectivised, management democratised." The translation of the slogan is by T. A. Hsia in his study of the language in the communes, entitled *Metaphor, Myth, and the People's Communes* (Berkeley: University of California Press, 1961), p. 1.

was threatening to burn the wheat in the fields, he hurried to the commune one morning and suggested the opening of an irrigation channel. " The suggestion was made in the forenoon, and by lunch time, four hundred people from eight villages had already started on the project.[26] The efficiency of labour mobilisation in a commune is even more strongly emphasised on another occasion. In the course of building the site for a third electric station in the area, the construction work ran into difficulty. After consultation with other leaders, the director decided on a shock operation that night. Immediately he assigned to each production brigade—The " Flying Tiger " Brigade, " Mu Kuei-Ying " [27] Brigade, the " Bayonet " Brigade—its special job. " In a flash, people, like soldiers, have drawn up in formation. . . . Just like an army organising for reinforcement after combat, they are quick in motion, high in spirit . . . and determined to win a great victory." [28] In spite of heavy snow and freezing weather, by dawn, the project was finished amidst joyous yells of " Victory ! "

The frenzy presented in fiction during the early period of the commune movement seems to have temporarily subsided. Short stories published in newspapers and periodicals recently indicate a certain relaxation of pace in the march towards Communism. In organisational matters in the communes, for instance, there have been signs of modification and retrenchment. Many stories reflect a partial reversion to small-scale planning by small production units and to family production in subsidiary occupations and on vegetable plots.

Both the tendencies to small-unit production planning and to family production are illustrated in a recent short story, " First Spring Day " which has its setting in a village on New Year's Eve. Although New Year was traditionally a time of rest and celebration for the Chinese peasants, we read in fiction that farmers during the early days of the Great Leap Forward volunteered not only to work on New Year's Eve and New Year's Day, but also to work for longer hours than usual. In this story we find, however, the repose customary to the occasion.

> Every family is busy with New Year's Eve dinner. The chimney smoke, floating over the roofs and vegetable plots, now rests on the little peach trees frozen purple in the wheatfield. . . . Snow flakes are coming down, in groups of three and five, dotting the air, slowly and leisurely. . . . The chimney smoke, the snow flakes, all these make

26 *New Observer*, March 1960, p. 11.

27 Mu Kuei-ying, a legendary woman warrior supposedly of the Sung Dynasty, is now singled out by the Chinese Communists to symbolise the fighting spirit of the female sex. The woman production leader in " The Contest " is also referred to as Mu Kuei-ying (PL, October 1960, p. 14).

28 *New Observer*, March 1960, pp. 12–13.

> the northern Heng-liang Mountain very misty-looking. Yu village is now wrapped in peaceful and joyful air.[29]

The old man Yu Feng-tai, a production brigade leader, is walking to the barn to relieve the stockman to go home for his New Year's family gathering. Feeling happy and at ease in the evening, he is making plans for the future:

> Now we have good green shoots, enough farm implements, enough manure—may be we should have more. A scholar never worries about having too many books, a farmer should never worry about having too much manure. The more the merrier! If every family raise two pigs, that would solve the problems of fertilizer for even next autumn.[30]

References to family planting of vegetables and fruit trees and raising of chickens and pigs are numerous in current newspapers and magazine stories. In many of these, the local production brigades and teams stand out as the foci of attention. This new interest in smaller production units in fiction is in keeping with information from other sources that the country, now suffering from economic setbacks caused partly by over-rapid expansion of large communal organisations, has reverted to smaller production units, which are given the right to make their own production plans, provided that they meet the quotas set by the higher levels. The present three-level structure, consisting of the commune, the brigade, and the team, allows the peasants in the smaller groups more initiative and incentive for work. The developments and shift of emphasis of the massive collectivising movement in its different stages have thus been reflected in Chinese Communist fiction.

II

This body of fiction on co-operatives and communes, considered from the aesthetic point of view, is highly formalised and limited, mainly because of its thematic preoccupation with the class struggle and with Socialist and Communist construction. Supposedly written for the workers, peasants and soldiers these stories though possibly instructive to the masses generally create a monotonous impression from the artistic point of view. Psychological treatment of character is generally lacking. Black and white characters created in the light of official ideology often result in stereotypes. Communist saintliness, best illustrated by the cadres and Party secretaries devoting every day and night to the cause of collectivisation, such as Wang Chin-sheng in *San-li-wan* and Teng

29 PL (April 1962), p. 9.
30 *Ibid.* p. 15.

Hsiu-mei in *Great Changes in a Mountain Village*, robs many a story of its human quality and interest.

This human quality and interest, though deficient, are not entirely absent. Traces of human conflicts, for instance, are clearly discernible, especially in the stories on the early phase of the collective drive. When the co-operatives were formed, there was a great degree of persistence of the old social habits, and the writers thrive on the conflicts between the old Chinese modes of thinking and behaviour and the new forces. This is exemplified by the conversion of the stubborn father in " Forward March " (PL, March 1954). He joined the co-operative chiefly as a measure to win back his only son, who had left home in protest against his old way of life. The Chinese attachment to family was thus used to bear on problems of transformation. The denunciation of the traditional way of life by this and many other peasants was not unaccompanied by tears. The cause of the heartbreaks sometimes came from their genuine affection, transcending material interest, for their land and animals. In " Advance Together " (PL, June 1953) Wang Lao-ch'ing fought desperately to keep one little plot of land while letting the rest of his holding go to the co-operative, because this little plot, as he told the co-operative chairman, was left to him by his uncle on his deathbed. Later, when his mule was to be absorbed into the co-operative, he stayed home all day to give the animal a thorough grooming, " more ceremonious than sending a daughter off on her wedding day." Looking at the mule for a long while, he felt, " suddenly, a flush of warmth in his heart." [31] Very poignantly told also are the inner conflicts of Ch'en Hsien-chin, an old man in *Great Changes in a Mountain Village.* After forty years of hard and honest work in the fields, he had given up hope of ever getting anywhere, and his only wish now was to keep intact the few pieces of land he and his late father had cultivated, so that they could be handed on to his sons. Sensing, however, that these had to go to the co-operative soon, he sadly confided to his wife, " No matter how you look at it, I cannot bear to give up the few pieces of hill land." In order to comfort him, she tried to point out the bright side of the picture:

> " Everyone is handing it over ; public horses are for the public to ride. We shall be spared a lot of worries ; in the future, we shall only have to work and eat."
>
> " That's true," said Ch'en Hsien-chin reluctantly and was then silent.

[31] PL (June 1953), p. 34.

Early next morning, when the sky was barely lightening, he went alone to the field and wept.[32]

In the description of these tortuous experiences and inner conflicts of the peasants, the writers lay bare the truths of the heart. As William Faulkner asserted in his Nobel Prize speech, " the problem of the human heart in conflict with itself . . . alone can make good writing, because only that is worth writing about." [33] In spite of his political beliefs and literary commitments, a conscientious writer, in his attempt to present life as he sees it, cannot but touch upon the truth, the " old verities " of the heart—love, pity, compassion, and sacrifice. Faulkner again said in his speech that " I believe man will not merely endure, he will prevail. He is immortal, not because he, alone among creatures, has an inexhaustible voice but because he has a soul, a spirit, capable of compassion and sacrifice and endurance." When a story-teller presents truthfully and skilfully these universal feelings of the heart, his presentations, regardless of the overall scheme of his work, become art, and such presentations are found, though in fragments, in the works of veteran Communist writers on collective farming, such as Chao Shu-li, Shih T'ou, Li Chun, and Chou Li-po.

The didactic quality of this literature as prescribed by the régime far outweighs the artistic. The Yenan line, except during the brief " hundred flowers " interval, has been enforced with increasing strictness since the Communists came to power. As an instrument in the class struggle, fiction has been amply used to show the masses the way to happiness through collectivisation. Socialist realism purports to represent things not as they are but as they are supposed to be. It is in this context that fiction on co-operatives and communes has presented for the general public a series of idealistic characters; the most prominent of these are the cadres, who, in their leadership of the collective movement, show infinite patience with the peasants, uncompromising courage in the fight against the feudalistic and the capitalistic, fanatic devotion to work, and, above all, unswerving loyalty to the Party. Also often idealised in fiction are the common peasants, who are grateful to collectivisation and to the Party for their new plenty, who are hardworking and full of initiative, ready to overcome any hardship or disaster, and who are cheerful and uncomplaining, willing to sacrifice personal and family concerns for the cause of the co-operatives and communes. Among these characters stand out the progressive youths, noticeably women, who often perform

[32] Chou Li-po, *Shan-hsiang Chü-pien* (*Great Changes in a Mountain Village*) (Peking: 1958), pp. 163–164.

[33] William Faulkner, " Nobel Prize Speech," *Les Prix Nobel en 1950* (Stockholm: 1951), p. 71.

amazing feats with inventiveness and ingenuity. All of these are concerned with the one great goal: Socialist and Communist construction. Many of the ideal traits presented in fiction, it seems, are meant as remedies for the particular ills of Chinese society: the static way of living of the tradition-following peasants, who, for thousands of years, have toiled in the fields painstakingly with the same tools and methods; the reserve and the retiring attitude of Chinese peasant women, who, always taking a subordinate position in life and in work, never ventured to explore their own talents. These characters are intended, no doubt, to serve as models for the people in their personal lives, work and ideology and in their loyalty to the Party.

Fiction is also employed to instil in the people confidence in the unprecedented collective way of life. In Socialist realism, the change from the old to the new is brought about not by the natural laws of development, but by concerted human effort. Stories about bumper crops every year, about gigantic projects accomplished with superhuman speed, about water courses and hills removed and transplanted at will are repeatedly presented to show the people the strength of collective work. Tales illustrating the new freedom of women from household chores, the healthy way of life for the young in the nurseries and schools, the security and peace of the old in the Homes of Happiness, and the high future standard of living replete with automobiles, electricity, and other luxuries for all are probably designed to enhance people's support of and hopes for collectivisation. To what extent this literature has succeeded in its persuasion, it is hard to assess. But with the increase in literacy and with the great accessibility of Communist literature to the masses, there can be little doubt that fiction must have helped to spur collectivisation.

Against this background of literary regimentation, the value of these stories about the co-operatives and the communes as social documents is to be appraised only with many reservations. Written with the Socialist-realist approach, short stories and novels depicting idealised characters and achievements reflect more often the régime's aspirations rather than the realities under the collectivisation movement. With the background of literary control, a study of the frequency of themes, types, and situations, is helpful, but not adequate as evidence for the norm of collective life in Chinese society. The absence of government officials and high Party authorities in fiction, for instance, does not exclude the important role they must assume in the collective movement. And the general air of jubilation present in Communist fiction does not necessarily mean that all is well. Thus an understanding of the extent and implementation of the Party's control over writers and their works is essential for any attempt to learn about life in the co-operatives and communes from Chinese fiction.

With an understanding of this tendentious quality of Communist fiction, one can derive from these stories helpful information about the lives of millions undergoing drastic changes in a Chinese society in rapid transformation. In the early and mid-fifties, for instance, Communist fiction was occupied thematically with the central problem of the struggle between the old and the new forces in the co-operative movement.[34] Although the emphasis was always on the conversion of the backward, the opposition—a feature of interest to the outside world—is inadvertently presented with much detail. The rich peasants and landlords had all been liquidated during land reform and thus posed no problem when the co-operative movement started. The middle peasants and peasants who had newly acquired the sweet sense of possession during the land reform however, often became the antagonists in the collective movement as is illustrated by the stories about the co-operatives. In this enormous agricultural country with its tradition of private ownership and family economy, the property idea constituted indeed a basic problem and a great obstacle in the transformation to collective farming.

Some references in Mao Tse-tung's speech " On the correct handling of contradictions among the people " indicated that the co-operative movement had not all been unchallenged. Some, he said, " have stirred up a miniature typhoon: they are grousing that co-operative farming won't do, that it has no superior qualities." [35] Fiction reports many a different approach used to overcome these miniature typhoons. Propaganda is employed on a large scale to convince the people of the superiority of collective life. In fiction, we read about the young and old, the men and women, the literate and the illiterate, all constantly going to meetings or classes to learn to understand and to accept the new way of life. In " The Contest " (PL, October 1960), the young Party secretary, as a successful leader of the First Production Brigade, tells the other cadres that " no matter how good the methods, the first thing is still political and ideological work." [36] Old wounds are often reopened to remind the peasants of their woes in the pre-liberation days and thus to enhance their sense of gratitude to and support of the new régime. The most effective weapon in the struggle for collectivisation in the earlier stories is not, however, ideological persuasion, but material gains. When farmers see that a co-operative, because

[34] See Albert Borowitz, *Fiction in Communist China 1949–53* (mimeo) (Cambridge: Massachusetts Institute of Technology, 1954).

[35] Dated February 27, 1957, in *Policy Documents*, p. 283.

[36] PL, October 1960, p. 12.

of more scientific methods and because of collective effort, can bring forth a better crop, they usually voluntarily apply for admission. Although the opposing forces are presented at length, the emphasis is on the struggle, and the author's sympathy is with the new, because, in the end, the recalcitrants are always persuaded to join the co-operative.

As the stories quoted in the early part of this paper indicate, the shift of emphasis of the régime's policies, and the progress and regress of the collectivisation movements are extensively reflected in fiction. In the Great Leap Forward period, for example, a definite acceleration in the pace of Socialist and Communist construction is seen everywhere in fiction. Communes with mess halls and factories involving a reorientation of lives for hundreds and thousands are organised in a matter of weeks. Water reservoirs and irrigation projects are completed in a matter of months, sometimes under colossal handicaps and in almost impossible situations. Thousands of *mou* of arable fields are cultivated in previously arid mountain land. Since the winter of 1958, however, newspaper and periodical stories show a certain relaxation of pace in the march towards Communism.

The preoccupation with certain themes makes Chinese Communist fiction appear monotonous, but this preoccupation could be interpreted as an indication of reality. In the stories about both co-operatives and communes, the people are always working and learning. Although this repeated theme of Socialist construction is tiring, other sources confirm the omnipresence of work in the lives of the Chinese in recent years. For example, in real life as in fiction, the Communist régime, since its assumption of power on the mainland, has been busy on water projects. Unpredictable rainfall and floods have for centuries been the scourge of the country. Building reservoirs and canals, dams and dikes has been the most prominent feature of collective work as well as one of the most frequent themes in Communist fiction.

Revealed also in the pages of these stories is the transformation of the traditional Chinese society with its values and taboos. One of the many structural changes brought about by collectivisation is the weakening of the solidarity of the family, which was, until the advent of collective living, the all-important stronghold of a Chinese citizen. The abolition of the family farm and family economy has reduced parental control over the young; with the loss of the financial control goes the unquestioned parental authority. The proverbial filial piety and children's obedience are no longer detectable in stories about life in the co-operatives and communes. Progressive sons and daughters are often seen lecturing their parents and guiding them to the new way of life. The equal opportunity to work and to earn wages has raised the economic and social status of the women and the young and has given them a new sense of importance and freedom unthinkable in the peasant class in the pre-Communist days. The system of arranged marriages, primarily contracted for economic reasons, has collapsed in the new society. The village boys and girls in *San-li wan*, for instance, choose their mates and contract their marriages freely without parental help and without reference to their families' economic situation. Families as units, as indicated by fiction, have been preserved in the co-operatives and communes; but with the passing of private ownership, the family economy, the hierarchy of age, parental authority, and arranged marriages, the families today are very different in appearance and substance from families in the old society.

No matter how fictionalised the characters and situations are in Communist stories, a study of average men and women against their background yields information essential to the understanding of their lives in the collectives; and no matter how orientated a writer is, his first-hand observations and his own experiences in a revolution cannot but supply some valuable knowledge otherwise unobtainable. Thus we may conclude that Chinese Communist fiction because of the literary regimentation under the régime is limited in value from the artistic point of view; it does however, provide glimpses, ironically as well as intentionally, of life in the collectivising movements in mainland China.

Industrial Workers in Chinese Communist Fiction

By RICHARD F. S. YANG

IN the opinion of the Communists, the significance of the Literary Renaissance in modern China beginning with the May Fourth movement of 1919, lies not in that it introduced the colloquial language as the new medium for literature, but in that it ushered into China a new literature which replaced the " old-fashioned, out-of-date literature of the bourgeois class." But the new literature which the Communists had hoped for did not fully develop until the political revolution led by the Communists succeeded, and a new régime was established in 1949. To implement the literary revolution and to introduce the people's new literature, the Communist régime called the first conference of the All-China Federation of Literary and Art Circles in July, 1949 at which the government spokesmen expounded the concepts and scope of this new literature and outlined a programme for " literary workers " to follow. Since these expositions were indeed the expressions of the policies of the new régime on literary reform and are therefore pertinent to the discussion in this paper, they must be cited here as a point of reference.

The definition of the new literature was outlined by Kuo Mo-jo, the leading cultural figure of the Communist régime. Using the words of Mao Tse-tung where he defines the character of the Chinese revolution in his *New Democracy*, Kuo answers the question "What is the new literature since the May Fourth Movement (of 1919)?" by saying that " the new literature is no longer the out-of-date, old-fashioned democratic literature, but the people's anti-imperialistic and anti-feudalistic new democratic literature created under the guidance of the proletariat." [1] Kuo then went on to review the development of this new literature since the May Fourth movement. He told the delegates that " the past three decades saw the literature of the landlord-class disarmed in theory and that of the Kuomintang Fascist capitalists denounced by the people and writers throughout the country. But apart from this, a controversy has also taken place between two schools of literary workers: one championed

[1] See the speech made by Kuo Mo-jo at the First All-China Federation of Literary and Art Circles held at Peking, in July 1949. His speech and those of other government spokesmen are included in a pamplet entitled *The People's New Literature* (Peking: Cultural Press, 1950), pp. 43–44.

'art for art's sake' for the benefit of the feeble, *laissez-faire* capitalists; the other advocated 'art for the people's sake' in the interests of the revolutionary masses. After thirty years of struggle, the theory of the former school has gone completely bankrupt with the result that the 'art-for-art's sake' writers have lost almost all their readers and have afterwards had to change their views about life and art and to adopt the literary principles of the working class." [2]

A further directive for the writing of the new literature was then made by Chou Yang in his speech. He said, "Now that the revolution is fundamentally victorious, China is entering a new historic period of vast economic, political and cultural reconstruction. Our writers must continue to unite with the masses, integrate with reality and actively participate in the people's struggle for liberation and in every sphere of the new democratic reconstruction. They should further and better reflect this struggle and reconstruction by means of various forms of art. This stage of national reconstruction is essentially one of converting an agricultural nation into an industrial nation. Formerly, because we were an agricultural nation, the great majority of our works of art reflected rural struggle and production. Writings depicting industrial production and the working-class were extremely few. . . . At present, the working-class, the peasants and the intellectuals are the leading forces of the people's Democratic Dictatorship. Our writings should describe these three forces. . . . Yet stress must unquestionably be placed on the workers, peasants and soldiers, because they are the soul of the war for liberation and national reconstruction." [3] He then further instructed the literary workers that in order for them to become revolutionary artists, they must study politics, namely Marxism, Leninism, the principles of Mao Tse-tung and the basic policies of the government,[4] and maintained that authors must "penetrate into life, into the masses and practically examine and personally experience the conditions" under which policies were effectuated.[5]

The significance of this conference is that it laid down both the guiding principles of the new literature and the directives for writers to follow in their creative activities, at a time when the triumph of the revolution seemed to make them, for the first time, completely fulfillable. Prior to 1949 Communist writers had for the most part been able to depict the lives of only the peasants and soldiers; now, with the conquest

[2] *Ibid.* p. 48.
[3] A speech made by Chou Yang, deputy head of the Communist Party's propaganda department, *ibid.* pp. 118–119.
[4] *Ibid.* p. 122.
[5] *Ibid.* p. 124.

of the urban areas completed, they could come to grips with the problems of the proletariat proper.

Yet there are disappointingly few novels on the subject of industrial workers, though there are many pamphlets containing biographical or autobiographical stories giving " factual " descriptions of workers, mainly the so-called " labour heroes " (whom the Communists call " model workers "). A typical one is *The Banners of Workers.*[6] Such " factual " accounts at least enable one to detect the qualities that characterise the " labour hero." There seem to be four: (1) he must be of proletarian origin oppressed in the old society; (2) he must take part in the Revolution, either in the struggle against the imperialists or in the struggle against the " feudalists " (Kuomintang, in this case); (3) he must be a member of the Communist Party; (4) he must perform some unusual deed or exploit, carry out a difficult task or assignment, or break a production record. These qualifications should be borne in mind when one examines labour heroes in Communist literature.

As mentioned already, novels about workers during the last decade have been extremely rare. For this paper, I shall examine three: *Our Day of Festivity,* written by a young, unknown writer named Lei Chia in 1952, *Spring Comes to the Yalu River,* written by the same author in 1954, and *Steeled and Tempered,* written by a veteran writer, Ai Wu, in 1961. I believe that these three works, covering not only a span of ten years but also different activities in industrial development, should give us some insight into the role of industrial workers in fiction.

In examining the first novel, one cannot but agree with the dictum that " Heroes are made, not born." If one is guided by an impression of large numbers of labour-heroes in the " pre-Liberation " days and expects to find the same in the new literature, one is bound to be disappointed. For the workers described in *Our Day of Festivity* are not model workers or labour-heroes, but a group of common labourers with problems and troubles that are familiar to us. The writer, adhering to the principle of realism, does not hide the problems and difficulties of industrial reconstruction. This particular novel deals primarily with developments in the paper industry in Communist China. Let us take a look at the following paragraphs in which certain problems are discussed at a conference:

> . . . The problem of the division of labour is an old one and has been discussed several times. The problem is: when labour is not divided, the entire job becomes nothing but a mess; but when labour is divided, complications also develop. This is because the working staff is of rather a low quality. But the cultivation of a high-quality staff takes time

[6] *Kung-jen-te Ch'i-chih* (*The Banners of Workers*) (Tientsin: 1949), pp. 1–14.

> and besides, there are few people of good enough potential to be trained. Therefore the problem of division of labour has resulted in a deadlock. . . .
>
> . . . The problem of housing was also discussed. Here it seemed to involve the serious problem of "average-ism." Once this problem came up, it was not easy to solve. Someone at the meeting mentioned that medicine and drugs should be carefully and watchfully guarded, for some people had found out that certain workers' families had asked for more drugs than they could actually use. So waste was the result. But how should restrictions be imposed? After much heated discussion, they agreed that a rise in price was perhaps the best solution. But the majority of the workers was opposed to an increase in price. . . .[7]

Thus the organisers of the industrial reconstruction of the new China were faced with such basic problems as the training of staff and skilled personnel as well as with related problems such as housing and medicine for the workers. In describing these kinds of problems the author seems to want to present an undistorted portrait of the workers to his readers.

But when we read further, we find more interesting passages in this novel. The following is the author's description of the conference scene:

> . . . Some of those present at the meeting put their heads sloppily on the back of a sofa, with their bodies slanted downward. It was hard to say whether they were sitting or lying. Some of them had fallen asleep, with one foot on a chair, holding the other foot with their hands and resting their chins on their knees. Cigarette butts were strewn all over the floor. The conference room was filled with smoke. None of them could remember their own production units. Nor could they hear the noise of the machine, the sound of the motor, the splattering of water, the shriek of the saw-machine, or the crackling of paper dried in the drying machine. Nor could they see their tired co-workers, with sleeves rolled up, dirty faces stained with oil and their bare feet. They were just lying here and there, and their minds had been numbed by the discussions. They were as tired as those working in the factory, with sleeves rolled up and faces covered with oil stains. . . .
>
> . . . The presiding chairman, Hu Chao-shan, also began to feel tired and bored. The meeting had gone on too long, and was completely out of control. When someone had a point to make, he was immediately interrupted by someone else, and the speaker had to find yet another person to express for him what he had wanted to say. Besides, the meeting had turned into small group discussions, with one group here and another group there, each discussing its own problems. Hu Chao-shan thought to himself: "Without meetings, problems cannot be solved. But when meetings are called, problems still can't be solved." [8]

This reflection of the presiding chairman is perhaps truthfully reflecting the situation confronting the workers during the early days of the

[7] Lei Chia, *Wo-men-te Chieh-jih* (*Our Day of Festivity*) (Peking: 1952), p. 14.
[8] *Ibid.* pp. 14–15.

Communist régime. It reflects perhaps the writer's perception of the inability of the workers to cope with the gigantic task of national reconstruction. But the problems did not end there. As one reads on in the novel, one finds that many other problems and troubles were facing the organisers of the programme of industrialisation. Take, for instance, the relationship between the old and skilled workers and the young and inexperienced workers. The revolution had destroyed the old system of apprenticeship under which the young workers showed absolute respect and obedience to their masters, but it had failed to establish a new system to replace the old one. The problem is clearly presented in this novel in a conversation between the factory manager and the chairman of the workers' union:

> "Tell me, why is it that the old workers refuse to teach the younger ones skills?" asked the manager.
>
> "The younger workers have been spoiled. They have shown off too much in various movements and drives, and they have developed a tremendous pride and arrogance," replied Sun Yu-ts'ai (the union chairman). "The skills taught by the older workers are usually looked down upon by the younger group. The younger ones always want to learn the big skills in a hurry, and want to learn the whole skill at once. In my opinion, some sort of master-apprentice contract must be signed." [9]

That a legal contract should be necessary to control this kind of relationship indicates the seriousness of the labour situation as seen by the novelist.

If the problems were confined to the workers, the chances of industrialising the country under the leadership of the Communist organisers were reasonable. But according to this book, there was trouble also at the higher levels in industry. It seems that there was friction between the management and the labour leaders, a phenomenon which commonly occurs in the "capitalist" West but should not be allowed in a revolutionary state. Of course, the writer does not directly reveal this kind of problem in his novel, but if he reads between the lines, the reader cannot help but feel that the relationship between the top leaders was anything but friendly and harmonious. The following extract from the diary of the director of the factory exposes this problem:

> September 20. On two of the problems, namely, the distribution of raw materials and the question of whether the auxiliary plant should be closed down, I hold different opinions from those of Hu Chao-shan [the union leader]. His attitude can be said to be more aggressive. To accomplish the task, he has focused his attention on one point—that is to get hold of the 88-inch machine with which to attack the problem and to achieve victory. . . . Many other people share this viewpoint.

[9] *Ibid.* p. 50.

> They all believe that the sure way to victory is to get hold of the 88-inch machine. Thus at first sight, I seem to be mistaken. Consequently, the 88-inch machine has become a focal point for the entire plant. . . . But they have forgotten that the 88-inch machine cannot represent the entire factory. To raise and consolidate the productivity of the 88-inch machine is not equal to the raising and consolidation of the productivity of the whole working body. . . . The union leaders must be aware of the following point: the production task of the entire plant cannot be fulfilled by a part of the workers, but must depend on all the workers. . . . Yet Hu Chao-shan does not trust me. . . . Since the focal point lies in the 88-inch machine, he wonders why I do not agree with him. He thought I was on the negative side regarding the fulfilment of the task. But who would believe that my desire to fulfil the task has become an inseparable part of my life? I am only afraid that I can't achieve it. I am also afraid that even if I achieve it, I might lose it . . .[10]

Here the author, through the meditations of the manager of a factory who is a top Communist cadre assigned the job of organising the workers in a paper mill, reveals the real problem facing the Communist planners in the early days of their régime, namely, the disunity and lack of trust between the Party members and the workers and their union leaders. To make the workers think like the Party leaders think requires an accelerated programme of education. So later in this novel, we find that the manager of the paper plant tackles two problems at the same time: the promotion of production in order to reach the quota, and the education of his workers through political indoctrination in order to build up morale. At the end of this story, as in other Chinese Communist stories, the problems are solved; the quota is finally met and morale is built up. But the day of festivity does not come until the days of troubles and problems are over. Who then, is the hero of this novel? The author does not indicate any particular person. However, after we have read the whole book, we come to the conclusion that the manager of the factory, a Party cadre, not a member of the working class, is the hero.

The second novel entitled *Spring Comes to the Yalu River* (*Ch'un-t'ien Lai-tao-le Ya-lu Chiang*) was written by the same author, Lei Chia, in 1954. But the story described here relates something which happened in remote Manchuria at the time of the conclusion of the Sino-Japanese war and this is therefore one of the few Communist novels dealing with industry run by the Party prior to 1949. The setting is similar to the first story in that it concerns a paper mill. And the characters involved in the story are also similar—the workers and the cadres of the Communist Party. Although the story is set before the establishment of the Communist régime, it depicts, nevertheless, the life and struggle of the working class under the

10 *Ibid.* p. 142.

leadership of the Communist Party in the early post-World War II days in the regions controlled by the Communist army. In this novel the narration is much clearer, the description more vivid, the language is smoother and the plot more convincing than in his first book.

The story begins with the appointment of a cadre, Ho Shih-chieh, by the newly organised local government, to the post of director of a paper factory, which had been left by the Japanese. He was chosen because he is a native of Manchuria, born and raised in Antung where the paper mill is located. So Ho Shih-chieh goes home, is reunited with his family, organises the workers of the factory and manages to get the mill back into production. The task of taking over a paper factory is not an easy one for Ho Shih-chieh, because he had had little experience in paper making. But being a seasoned Party member and a trained cadre, Ho not only organises the workers and wins their confidence, he also overcomes the obstacles (including a case of sabotage) and difficulties (such as shortages of materials), and brings the plant back to full production.

This novel is designed as a paean to the capability and ingenuity of a Party member. He is painted by the author as a man with a warm and attractive personality. For example, in the first meeting with the workers, he discusses with them the necessary steps to be taken for the resumption of production at the mill. In the course of discussion, some of the workers mention that the chief trouble is the lack of some basic materials, especially copper net and wool cloth. Being a total newcomer to the paper industry, Ho Shih-chieh does not know what these two things are. So at the meeting he asks the workers rather naïvely what copper net and wool cloth are. Such a display of ignorance on the part of a manager would normally make the workers disrespect him. But in the hands of the author, Ho's frank admission of lack of knowledge is the key for loosening up the relationship between him and the workers. The incident is described as follows:

> "This seems to be the main difficulty," Ho Shih-chieh thought to himself. "How can this difficulty be overcome? Furthermore, what is copper net and wool cloth?"
>
> "What is copper net and wool cloth?" asked Ho Shih-chieh. Suddenly all voices ceased. Nobody answered him. Startled and inquisitive eyes began to focus upon him. "Why, he does not even know copper net and wool cloth."
>
> Ho did not feel that his question was strange. He was waiting very innocently for someone to answer it. Chou Ta-chung who sat beside him turned towards him and began to explain.
>
> The atmosphere in the meeting was suddenly loosened. . . . But Ho Shih-chieh did not see anything. He was listening to Chou Ta-chung's explanation. Having told him what copper net and wool cloth were, Chou pointed out that these were the most important

materials in a paper mill and that there were difficulties in obtaining them.

It was like a small screw turning loose in a huge machine; the entire meeting was set on a different but unknown course. . . . Finally Ho realised that this loose screw was actually his ignorance. . . .

When the explanation was over, Ho nodded his head. In a loud voice, he said very sincerely: "Now I understand. I am afraid there are still many things that I don't understand. I hope that you'll teach me later. Since someone mentioned this is the main difficulty, let's see whether there is any way to solve it."

"Not to understand is not to understand." This candid attitude of Ho's had apparently produced a strong effect on the meeting. . . . The modesty and self-confidence of Ho Shih-chieh, in the opinion of Yueh Ch'uan-shan and others present, indicated that he was a quiet but firm person. . . . Yueh Ch'uan-shan was greatly moved by Ho's modesty. He believed that this man was the ideal manager he had expected him to be. . . . (p. 95.)

However, the depiction of the workers as heroes in this novel is not particularly successful, although the author deliberately brings the workers into the limelight. A few passages in the book attest this point. For instance, the workers are given the credit for taking over and guarding the plant after the Japanese surrender, and they are described by the author almost as heroes:

Yueh Ch'uan-shan and Liang Man-fu ran to the factory. The Japanese were burning their records in front of their shrine. The burnt papers were flying everywhere. The shrine was being torn down by the Japanese. In anger, Liang Man-fu kicked everything as he went along. In the past when workers came to work, they had to bow before the shrine. If it weren't torn down by the Japs, they would smash and flatten it anyway.

Such trivial things should be put aside. The first important thing to do was to hoist the national flag.

On the sandstone right in front of the shrine, the workers spread a piece of wrapping paper with a bottle of red ink by the side. They were trying to remember the picture of the national flag. Suddenly a breeze blew up and the paper rolled up. The whole bottle of red ink was spilled over it. A few rain drops from the willow branches also fell on it.

Yueh Ch'uan-shan jumped up and, looking at the excited faces of the people, he shouted, "All right, this is just fine. Let us hang it up like this."

So they hoisted the red flag on the main gate. The workers stood around it. Their eyes were filled with tears, and their throats were choked. Some of them wept silently.

For many years they had hoped to hoist the red flag and chase the Japanese out. The red flag represented their hope. From now on, they would follow the red flag and march towards their mother-land, towards the Soviet Union and towards the peaceful, new world . . .

The Chinese workers called a meeting and organised a Workers

> Self-Protection Team. They decided to build a "second front" around the factory.
>
> The "second front" went into action at night. At one time, they seized a hand cart which carried the most valuable tools and equipment stolen by the Japanese. At another time, Liang Man-fu came face to face with the devilish and evil Japanese foreman and beat him up; Liang found the blueprint of the factory under his belt. . . . Yueh Ch'uan-shan was named captain of the Self-Protection Team. At night, he led a group of workers on patrol. During the day, he bought one hundred ears of corn. Squatting in front of the factory gate, he set up a charcoal burner on which he toasted the corn and sold it. . . .
>
> It was not until the day when the Red Army of the Soviet Union marched into Antung that the Kwantung Army [of the Japanese] was finally disarmed. September was approaching. The cold breeze which blew in from the sea from time to time did not cool off the late autumn heat. . . . (pp. 59–61.)

There was hardly any "heroism" involved in the workers' voluntary protection of the factory, although their action can be described as brave and patriotic. Throughout the novel, the workers are depicted as second fiddlers in everything. However, the problems and the struggles of the workers (such as their accusation of a counter-revolutionary in a mass meeting, and the emancipation of women workers from the old "feudal" bondage of forced marriage) are described here and can be regarded as new features in modern fiction. But although credit should be given to the author for his sincere attempt to write a novel about the working-class, the book itself cannot be said to be an interesting and moving novel.

The first full-sized novel with industrial workers as the main characters and industry as the main theme is Ai Wu's book entitled *Steeled and Tempered* (*Pai-lien Ch'eng Kang*).[11] Ai Wu is a veteran writer who achieved fame before the Communist era. His familiarity with the Western writing and his attractive style won him acclaim as a good novelist and he was one of the most promising young writers of modern China. But to accept the challenge of the Party leaders to write realistically of the life and activities of the people was a new experience for most Chinese writers and Ai Wu was no exception. He went to the people and lived with them. This novel is the product of his experiences in a steel factory located in Liaoning province, right in the heart of the industrial centre.

In this novel, the main characters are the Party cadre, Liang Ching-chun, the manager of the factory, Chao Li-ming, and a number of steel workers, notably Chin Te-kuei, the labour hero.

[11] Ai Wu, *Steeled and Tempered* (*Pai-lien Ch'eng Kang*) (Peking: Foreign Languages Press, 1961).

The author is very anxious to spotlight his hero immediately for at the beginning of the story, we are led to the scene of an accident, witnessed by the newly appointed Party secretary who is on an inspection tour with the manager of the factory:

> . . . When the two comrades reached the No. 7 furnace, the man who had fainted had already been carried to the clinic. They hurried to the back of the furnace to take a look. Four or five workers were scraping the tap hole in a frenzy, perspiring with feverish excitement. With a rubber hose, they connected a finger-sized hollow iron tube to a big oxygen cylinder. Then they turned on the oxygen and ignited the end of the tube inserting it into the tap hole of the opening while the tube was burning. When they pulled out its burnt end, it was all black again. They quickly replaced it with another one.
>
> Seeing that the tap hole would not open, with knitted brows Chao Li-ming (the manager) asked in a stern voice: " Who closed the tap hole of the furnace?"
>
> Immediately two or three workers turned their deeply flushed and perspiring faces, snapping, " This was closed by the men of the B shift." Adding with anger, " You can see what a mean trick they pulled."
>
> Stepping around to the front of the furnace, Chao Li-ming went to look for the foreman on duty and the technician to discuss what method should be applied to release the finished molten steel as quickly as possible. . . . At this moment, a tall young man dashed towards the tap hole in great haste. He had goggles hanging under the peak of his cap. He was clad in a dirt-soaked canvas jacket and trousers, his feet covered with canvas stockings and he wore slippers and canvas gloves. He was perspiring and his face was flushed. On reaching the tap hole, he asked the other workers to step aside so that he could handle the iron tube by himself. Connecting it with another oxygen cylinder, be asked to have two tubes burning at the same time as one was not sufficient. With two tubes burning, the flames around the tap hole spread out while purple smoke immediately gushed forth in rolling waves. All the other workers who were seizing a short moment of rest began to shout with delight, " Good fellow, that is really a master stroke! " Liang Ching-chun [the Party secretary] noticed that this young man worked differently and more energetically in his efforts to break open the tap hole. Unlike the other workers who threw away the ends of the iron tubes while they were still quite long, he inserted them deeper inside the furnace and kept them burning there till he could hold them no longer. That two tubes were burning simultaneously also helped a great deal, because the opening was being melted continuously and did not congeal again during replacement. Watching all this, Liang could not help silently admiring the operation (pp. 8–9).

But heroism lies not in the fact that he posseses better skill and handles things differently from others. Heroism involves bravery. So the story goes on:

> " Look, your glove's on fire! " some workers shouted out. Liang Ching-chun saw at once that the glove on the right hand of the tall young man had caught fire, but he did not take it off. He pushed the

> two burning tubes farther inside while a rolling red cloud of smoke came out of the tap hole, followed by golden tongues of flame and a cascade of sparks. He stood up at once, and, raising his right hand with the burning glove, threw it off by flinging his arm downwards in one swift stroke. At this very moment the operator in charge of the control board pushed the button of the tipping gear and the furnace immediately began to slant backwards. The molten steel, luminous with radiant heat, began to pour into the big iron ladle hung under the one-hundred-ton crane. It glowed and bright sparks splashed around while it spread a fog of glittering gold. Intense purple rays shot up towards the high ceiling rising continuously. The strong white beams radiating from the molten steel forced Liang Ching-chun to raise his hands to shade his eyes. He dared not keep his eyes open to watch the liquid metal for a moment longer. Just at the moment someone touched his hand and thrust a piece of blue glass in a small wooden frame in front of him. Liang heard a gentle voice saying, " Secretary of the Party Committee, you'd better take this eye-piece and then it'll be all right to look." Liang raised his eyes and saw a man of medium height standing beside him. He was clad in a white canvas overall and wore the same kind of cap as any worker but without the goggles. . . . Holding the eye-piece but not looking through it at once, Liang Ching-chun pointed instead at the worker who had just broken open the tap hole, asking, " What's his name?"
>
> " Chin Te-kuei, the C shift furnace chief of the No. 9 furnace," replied Ho Tse-hsueh (secretary of the Party branch of the open-hearth workshop). " He certainly knows how to make steel. He was the one who turned out the heat of steel in seven hours and five minutes today."
>
> Liang Ching-chun took a good look at Chin Te-kuei, then asked Ho, " Is he a Party member?"
>
> " Yes, he is a Party member " (pp. 9–10).

Such is the portrait of the hero in this novel. A labour hero must be a member of the Communist Party. He must also possess the other qualities which were discussed at the beginning of this paper. The author gives a biography of this model worker and points out the fact that he is from the proletarian class. " During his childhood, Chin Te-kuei had known poverty. His grandfather and father earned their living by selling their labour, helping others plough the fields." As a hero, he must have personal experience in activities against the enemy, either the imperialists or the Kuomintang. Thus we read that " When he was sixteen, the Japs surrendered. A Communist-led, armed operational unit appeared in the village and Chin Te-kuei was happy to enlist. 'Little devil, we are going to fight the Kuomintang, the landlords and the rascals. Aren't you afraid?' Captain Liu Ke-yu, a young woman, asked joyfully. 'Comrade Captain, I want to fight the landlords and rascals,' he answered her bravely. 'When I was young, I had to fight wolves all alone. . . .' " Thus Chin Te-kuei took part in the " War of Liberation " (pp. 16–17). With this background, Chin Te-kuei threw himself into the gigantic programme of industrialisation after the war was over, quickly gained an excellent record in steel production and was soon promoted to be chief of a furnace unit.

Throughout the entire novel, the author tries conscientiously to point his pen to the steel workers, though he also portrays the leaders—the Party cadre and the factory manager. The main theme in this story is the drive to produce more steel in a shorter period of time. Therefore, we read about the record-breaking accomplishments of labour heroes. But praise to one man usually causes jealousy in others. So we read about jealousies and rivalries among the workers, especially between the labour hero, Chin Te-kuei and another young worker named Chang Fu-chuan. The competition between the two goes from bad to worse when they find out that they have both fallen in love with a girl worker named Sun Yu-fen. So we read about the entanglements of the three involved in a triangle love affair. Finally, disaster results when personal hatred develops into schemes on the part of one to hinder the production of the other. We also read about the different attitudes towards production between the factory manager and the Party cadre—a case of friction usually develops between the technical personnel and the Party theoreticians. In this novel we also learn about the participation of Soviet technical experts in the production programme in China. All these different events and characters are touched upon by the author in his book.

It seems that the author does not try to conceal the conflict and friction between the technical staff and the Party officials. In fact, he gives his full attention to this problem and reports it in detail in his book. There are a number of places where arguments and disagreements occur between the factory manager and the Party cadre. The following episode can be used as an example:

> . . . After Chang Chi-lin had gone, Liang Ching-chun came in. He moved a chair over to the manager's desk and sat down. Ignoring him, Chao-Li-ming [the manager] continued to look at some statistical charts. This was the first time the secretary of the Party Committee had met such a cold reception from the manager. Paying no attention to Chao's behaviour, Liang Ching-chun said quietly, "Again a heat of steel at high speed today, only . . ."
>
> "The workers are very energetic," without raising his head, Chao Li-ming cut short Liang's words.
>
> Sensing that Chao's remarks contained a double meaning, Liang Ching-chun did not touch on what he had been intending to say but took up Chao's line of thought, "I would say rich initiative has not been fully developed in the rank and file. They have a lot of latent strength."

"I say if we keep on like this their initiative will never be developed," Chao Li-ming raised his head showing his eyes glistening with rage in his dark square face.

"Why?" There was a faint shocked expression on Liang's round plump countenance as his calm eyes rested on the manager.

"Just because we responsible leaders are not energetic, because we're blind to the urgent tasks arising from this wave of national construction." Chao Li-ming turned his eyes from Liang and shook his head. [Liang said:] ". . . But if you take my absence from the office today as an indication that I am not energetic you are mistaken. I do not sit in the office doing only desk work. I haven't stayed in today, nor will I do so in the future."

"You don't get my point," Chao Li-ming then said. "I am not blaming you because you haven't been in the office. I mean that you haven't promptly done your job of calling a meeting of Party members and asking them to play a leading role in the contest."

"Today I visited some of the workers at the hostel and their homes, trying to get to the bottom of a few important problems." Irritated by the manager's impatience, Liang Ching-chun spoke with deliberate calmness, making every word carry weight. "I want to find out why the initiative of the workers is not as strong as it should be. Why hasn't it been fully developed? This is vital."

"Comrade, I agree with you. It is important. But that can be studied at any time, tomorrow or the day after. Don't forget that our most important problem today is to increase production. First of all, we must study how to push up our daily output, and how to launch the contest." Chao Li-ming tried his best to speak calmly at the beginning, but in the end he again grew a little impatient. "Comrade, let me tell you, anyone who is not wholeheartedly concerned with the problem of increased production is committing a mistake."

"It is precisely for that and to set off the contest that I went to the workers," Liang was also a little irritated now, but he contained himself. "I found out that some of the men are not satisfied with their furnace chiefs. That is why they are not doing all they can. You can't run a contest that way" (pp. 343–344).

So the argument went on. The manager's approach to this question of the contest was to set a model furnace and to rouse the Party members to take a lead. But the Party secretary's approach was to encourage initiative in every worker. Of course, the Party man eventually won, for under the Communist régime's leadership the policy of the Party must be carried out at any cost. But in this novel, the sharp conflict between the Communist Party and the technicians is clearly presented.

In this novel, we find that certain new features have been intentionally added and stressed, such as the very full description of the technical processes of steel-making. The technician's explanation of the condition of a furnace, for instance, is very interesting. This kind of information cannot be clearly given by an author unless he himself is familiar with steel-making. That Communist fiction contains such information is praiseworthy. For this and other reasons Ai Wu, the author of this novel, should be given credit for an earnest attempt to write a story about the working-class. However, after reading the book, we get the impression that the real hero is not the model worker but the Party cadre. It makes one feel that the author was assigned the job of writing a novel on the industrial workers, but that he did not write it with complete freedom.

Are we, then, in any position to comment on the new literature of Communist China, especially on the novels about the industrial workers? Frankly, no. That is, we cannot comment on it unless we fully understand the meanings and implications of the guiding policy, "art for the people's sake." For us, a piece of literature, like painting or music, whether for its reader's enjoyment or enlightenment, must arouse some sort of feeling or response from the reader. Literature, if regarded as man's spiritual food, must, like food, produce some kind of taste, be it sweet, bitter, salty or sour. If there is no taste, then it can be conveniently described by the Chinese phrase: "It tastes like chewing wax." Having read these three novels in Communist literature my own reaction is: "It tastes like chewing wax."

Twenty Years After the Yenan Forum

By T. A. HSIA

I

IN 1962, commemorative activities were held in Communist China to celebrate the twentieth anniversary of the publication of Mao's *Talks at the Yenan Forum on Literature and Art.*[1] In the same year, a group of scholars and writers working in America and Britain gathered near Oxford to ponder over Chinese Communist literature. Though the coincidence was not intentional, it did force on one's mind a disturbing sense of history. For no review of Chinese Communist literature, from our point of view or theirs, can escape the fact of control, and the control began with Mao's *Talks*. The success of the control, of course, is something to be celebrated in Communist China, but the defects in the Chinese Communist writing, noted at the conference in England, indicate the costs paid for that success. For these defects are made to order. It is beyond the power of any single writer in Communist China to correct them. He is bound to contribute to the collective errors if he wishes to avoid a political offence.

What is the political offence most commonly committed by writers in Communist China? The victims of the 1955 and 1957 purges, who were allegedly all punished for their various anti-Party activities, actually made one great mistake, according to Politburo alternate member Lu Ting-yi, Head of the Party's Propaganda Department (who recently became a member of the Party's Secretariat [2]):

> We regard revolutionary literature and art as an indispensable part of the whole revolutionary task. But they, from Wang Shih-wei to Hu Feng, and then to Feng Hsueh-feng, Ting Ling, Chiang Feng, etc., all maintained the supremacy of literature and art; [they maintained] that politics should be subservient to literature and art; that " artists should

[1] According to Liu Hsueh-wei (*Lunwen-hsueh-ti kung-nung-ping fang-hsiang* (*On the Worker-Peasant-Soldier Direction in Literature*) [Shanghai: 1949], p. 90, *cf.* note 5), the official publication date of Mao's *Talks* was October 1943. This is probably true, since so far as I can verify, Mao's *Talks* was not available in print in 1942. But in the Chinese Communist press, May 1942 is usually given as the official publication date, *cf. Peking Review* (June 1, 1962, p. 1): " Last week literary and art workers everywhere in the country started a round of commemorative activities, to celebrate the 20th anniversary of the *publication* (italics mine) of Chairman Mao's *Talks. . . .*"

[2] *People's Daily* (*Jen-min Jih-pao*), September 29, 1962.

> lead statesmen " or that literature and art should be made an independent kingdom.[3]

The difference between " we " and " they," therefore hinged on the question of the " supremacy " or " independence " of literature and art. It is never clear to me how artists, as artists, could have the ambition to " lead " the statesmen, though from the works of the former, the latter might derive displeasure as well as pleasure, incitement to anger as well as inspiration. A plea for the independence of literature and art is understandable because political power can do so much to direct, to molest and to persecute. But even such a plea had to be smothered for the sake of " revolution."

A leading article in *The Times Literary Supplement,* commenting on the Ditchley Manor conference, summarised well what one might think should have been the consensus of the conference:

> It would be difficult to dispute the conclusion of Mr. Howard Boorman's paper giving the political setting, that " the intermeshing of doctrine and discipline . . . is as dominant in the sphere of literature as elsewhere," or to doubt that the writers who rallied hopefully and confidently to the Communist cause make " a tale of ingenuous affection deceived."[4]

What I should like to point out here is that the binding nature of Communist doctrine on writers was never certain and the wayward fancy and independent mind of a Communist writer was seldom viewed with alarm as a breach of discipline by the Chinese Communist Party until the Yenan Forum of 1942. It was in that year too that the writers who had travelled " hopefully and confidently " to Yenan began to see what great demands the Party, in the person of its chairman Mao, made on them.

Liu Hsueh-wei, a leftist critic who was purged in 1955 as a member of the Hu Feng clique, published in 1949 a commentary on Mao's *Talks.* The book, entitled *On the Worker-Peasant-Soldier Direction in Literature,* tried to allay the fears in the minds of sceptics like Hu Feng as to the harm that Mao's *Talks* might do to the realistic tradition of the May Fourth movement. Liu's disregard of the fact of Party discipline made his book an inadequate study of the real power of Mao's doctrine. Naïvely, he welcomed the reassertion of the " worker-peasant-soldier direction " which, he believed, would lead out of the theoretical confusion experienced in the Creation Society period and the years of the Chinese League of Left-Wing Writers. His belief in the necessity for such a doctrine seems odd in the light of his later personal tragedy, but his review of the " theoretical confusion " in the leftist literary movement in China indicates that

[3] *People's Daily,* September 27, 1957.
[4] *The Times Literary Supplement,* August 24, 1962, p. 641.

a liberal tendency was observable even among the leftist writers before the watershed year 1942. Liu wrote:

> Without a refutation of the basic argument (that it is one's world-view that determines whether one is a proletarian or not, that the establishment of world-view depends on the attainment of materialist dialectics, and that to experience life is merely to acquaint oneself with the subject-matter of one's writings), the leftist literary movement developed a tendency for polarization. At first, what was deemed necessary was to write according to the "materialist-dialectical method," *i.e.*, according to the formula: the description of the birth of the new amidst the old, the tomorrow in today, the conquest of the old by the new, etc. As a result of this kind of formularist theory, formularist writings (in the foreign "eight-legged" style) were mass-produced. And because of this misconception, there was also a growth of the paranoia peculiar to petty-bourgeois intellectuals. A writer might consider himself unquestionably a "proletarian writer," if he were qualified to do so by that standard. But to write about real life with this "method" meant that nothing would look life-like; to write about workers and peasants by the use of this method meant that no worker or peasant would look like one.
>
> So the need was felt to liquidate the method. It so happened that at that time the theory of the "materialist-dialectical method of creation" was liquidated in Soviet Russia. The new slogan to take its place was "socialist realism." In order to hit the weaknesses of the immediate past, there was an emphasis on the "presentation of the true reality," "the necessity to write about what one is well acquainted with," the difference or even contradiction between "world-view" and the "method of creation," the difference between a Communist in politics and an actual writer for Communism, etc. These were, of course, not incorrect, but we treated them with a dogmatic attitude. Under the cover of such theories and slogans, we took the opportunity gradually, subtly, and naturally to conceive a breed of liberalism. On the strength of eulogising allusions to Tolstoy and Balzac, we began to develop a virtually uncritical worship of "classical works" and "classical writers." There began, even in the innermost heart of the leftist writers a reversion, an unconscious but no less true reversion to the path towards which the tendencies of the petty-bourgeois class are naturally directed. That is, we took ourselves as the first principle, while indulging in a free display of the true nature of the petty-bourgeois class. That was the process of moving from "formularism" to "liberalism," but by then we had already come to the last years of the left-wing Decade.[5]. . .
>
> When the theory of "world-view," which isolated theory from reality as well as from the writer, revealed its weaknesses, a remedial programme to replace it was sought for in the formula "to experience life." For a long period, we took this to be the only dependable solution of contradictions; we raised it from every side to a very high eminence. Then there was introduced into China *A Letter to Beginners in Writing*[6]

[5] Liu, *op. cit.* p. 17.

[6] The exact publication date is not available. But on a 1941 proscription list published by the KMT, there is the title *Kei ch'u-hsueh hsieh-tso-che-ti i Feng-hsin* (*A Letter*

from the Soviet Union Literary Advisory Committee, in which the first principles were "to lay your hands on life" and "to write about what you are familiar with." We did some earnest analysis of the merits of the theory, but aside from that, we did not study the differences in conditions between Soviet Russia and China, nor did we assimilate it with a critical attitude and point out its limitations when it was applied to us. As if it had spoken out what we had in our minds, we thought that this time all problems had been solved and all doubts dispelled. As a matter of fact, from 1933 to the Yenan Forum on Literature and Art, we took this as our guiding principle.[7]

How Socialist realism could lead to "liberalism" may sound paradoxical. But the realism of nineteenth-century Europe, in as diversified styles as there could be from Tolstoy to Balzac, provided a yardstick and a methodology not totally compatible with the requirements of propaganda. The hybrid known as Socialist realism, if not supported by political power, could easily shift its emphasis from Socialism to realism, especially when the writers who were supposed to practise it had already developed a disinterested love for the nineteenth-century masters who served as their models. Whatever the Russians said about Socialist realism, the Chinese interpretation of it is surely interesting. Perhaps the Chinese leftist writers of the 1930s did feel an embarrassing sense of freedom when advice from Soviet Russia, subsequent to the dissolution of the RAPP,[7a] began to sound self-contradictory and therefore less dogmatic. Another possibility was that they simply followed their own bent of mind, irrespective of the Russian theory. A crop of young writers, who were published in the pages of *Wen-hsueh* (*Literature*, 1933–37), adopted as a rule the realistic method. They were capable of independent observation and generally avoided paranoic gesturing. Fu Tung-hua, editor of *Wen-hsueh*, drew attention to this trend by citing a long list of its contributors which included Ai Wu, Ho Ku-t'ien (Chou Wen), Tsang Ke-chia, Wu Tsu-hsiang, Liu Pai-yü, Hsiao Chün, Tuan-mu Hung-liang, and Ch'iao Yin (Hsiao Hung).[8] Some of these are still well-known writers in Communist China; a study of their early writings will probably bear out the observations of Liu and Fu.[9]

Later developments also show how the de-emphasis of the socialist element in Socialist realism could act as a liberating force for Communist

to Beginners in Writing). The translator is Chang Chung-shih. See Chang Ching-lu, *Bibliographical and Historical Materials Concerning Contemporary Chinese Publications*, III (Shanghai: 1956), p. 221.

[7] Liu, *op. cit.* p. 60.

[7a] Russian Association of Proletarian Writers.

[8] Fu's article is found in Fan Chung-yun, ed., *China: The Last Ten Years* (Shanghai: 1937), p. 680.

[9] My brother gives high praise to Wu Tsu-hsiang and moderate praise to Tuan-mu Hung-liang. He is reserved about Ai Wu but censorious of Hsiao Chün. See C. T. Hsia, *A History of Modern Chinese Fiction* (Yale Un. Press, 1961), under the respective authors.

writers. Ch'in Chao-yang's critical essay " Realism—The Broad Path " (in contradistinction to the restrictive Socialist realism) voiced a strong protest during the " hundred flowers " movement.[10] He quoted K. M. Simonov who, like some others, had had the audacity to redefine Socialist realism in a parallel period of warm weather in Russia following Khrushchev's attack on Stalin. *People's Literature*, of which Ch'in was then an associate editor, announced the forthcoming publication, in Chinese, of Simonov's article, " Concerning Socialist Realism,"[11] which, however, never appeared, probably owing to a change of editorial policy as the " hundred flowers " movement changed into the Anti-Rightist movement. But Simonov's views are still available in Chinese. Another article of his, " Random Talks on Literature," was translated and published as a negative example since it contained the " representative incorrect point-of-view."[12] Some of Simonov's statements (*e.g.*, " We cannot say our literature in dealing with our post-war national life is all false; but a considerable part of our literature is half-true and half-false. And half-truth and half-falsehood is an enemy to art.")[13] must have found echoes, at least in 1957, in the hearts of Chinese writers.

Outside the left-wing groups, realism was also a method widely followed. The great changes in Chinese society dating from the late nineteenth century brought home a keen awareness of Chinese life. Not to mention the special effort made by the Chinese Writers' Union writers, the much underrated *Saturday* (*Li-pai-liu*) school of novelists, writing to entertain and little influenced by foreign models, could also turn out penetrating analyses of the manners and mores of the newly risen petty-bourgeois class and the decaying landlord class.[14]

Independent of the realistic method, but complementing it in many instances as the *yin* principle does the *yang*, was the theme of love, whether romantic or humanitarian, which was also adopted by a great variety of writers. A touch of tenderness, a susceptibility to emotions, and an indulgence in passion and melancholy are the traditional attributes of the Chinese writer (*ts'ai-tzu*, or the man of talent); after the May Fourth movement, the sentimental tradition was reinforced by the precepts and examples from Europe. Any unobservant or unthinking writer with a

[10] Ch'in's article is found in *Jen-min Wen-hsueh* (*People's Literature*, hereinafter PL), 1956, No. 9.

[11] See the editorial note in PL 1957, No. 7. Simonov's " Concerning Socialist Realism " originally appeared in *Novy Mir* (*The New World*), 1957, No. 3.

[12] Collected in *Pao-wei She-hui-chu-i Hsien-shih-chu-i* (*In Defence of Socialist Realism*), *ed. by Yi-wen-she* (Translation Society), I (Peking: 1958). Simonov's article originally appeared in *Novy Mir*, 1956, No. 12.

[13] *Ibid.* p. 429.

[14] The *Saturday* school carried on the sentimental tradition of the *Dream of the Red Chamber* and the satirical realistic tradition of *Ju-lin-wai-shih* (*The Scholars*). Its chief exponent Chang Hen-shui particularly deserves attention.

limited means of expression was likely to win praise for his competency to record his own moods or repeat some common sentiments. Novels written within a realistic framework, too, are also noted for their tender moments. This major trend does not come up in Liu Hsueh-wei's book on the "worker-peasant-soldier direction." With an effort of will, the leftist writers could indeed frown upon the showing of affection as a sign of petty-bourgeois weakness. But they, too, sometimes lapsed into sentimentality in their supposedly "progressive" works, probably because they had a need for it in spite of their revolutionary stance.

A minor trend before 1942 was the popularity of Lu Hsün's satirical style. I call it a minor trend, because the possibilities for developing it are limited. As exemplified by Lu Hsün's *tsa-wen,* satire requires a skill in irony, epigram, economy of expression, and subtle allusion, which is usually not within the grasp of younger writers. But Lu Hsün left a brood of imitators (after his death there even appeared a magazine called *Lu Hsün Feng*, or *In Imitation of Lu Hsün*).[15] The genre he made popular became a convenient vehicle to air a grievance or to register a protest at a time when occasions for grievance and protest were never lacking. One lesson that Lu Hsün taught the younger writers was how to hold emotions in check. It is clear from his writings that he seldom lost his temper or presence of mind. A skilled verbal fighter, Lu Hsün was not so particular about the code of chivalry as about the chance of victory. As a rule he avoided direct clash. He would sooner have recourse to sniping than come into the open "with no armour on his naked body." But he wrote very well. Within the short compass of the *tsa-wen*, the reader usually feels a pleasurable tension. He knows that from behind the apparently civilised manner, a dart will shoot forth, but he does not see at once how or when or where. Then, after a few minutes of reading, the trick is done and someone is hit. It is the neatness of the stroke and the unexpected angle from which the attack is launched that afford the peculiar intellectual pleasure. But wit, which gives the *tsa-wen* its sting, is after all not a powerful tool. It has little respect for fact or for logic. As it is too often caught in its own cleverness to convey much of a positive idea, the *tsa-wen* was a tolerable offence in the eyes of the Kuomintang censorship. So Lu Hsün's unique genius, unhampered by those who were supposedly his persecutors, raised the *tsa-wen* to a position which almost equalled the eminence of fiction and poetry.

At the Yenan Forum, Mao endeavoured to stem and deflect these three trends—realism (in fiction, and beginning with the thirties, in poetry

[15] According to Ts'ao Chü-jen, *Wen-t'an Wu-shih-nien: Hsu-pien* (*Literary Life during the Past Fifty Years: Vol. II*) (Hong Kong: 1955), p. 154 and Lan Hai, *Chung-kuo K'ang-chan Wen-yi Shih* (*History of Chinese Literature during the War of Resistance*) (Shanghai: 1947), p. 51, *Lu Hsün Feng*, a fortnightly, was published in Shanghai before the Japanese attack on Pearl Harbour.

as well), sentimentalism and satire—which hitherto marked the " directions " of modern Chinese literature. As a matter of fact, " petty-bourgeois " realism, sentimentalism and satire were all denounced as wrong. Henceforth, literature and art were to serve solely the Party under Mao, in the name of the workers, peasants and soldiers. Realism would be used for the praise of " progress "; love would bear the stamp of " class nature "; and satire would be directed only against the prescribed enemy. The change was great. As Chou Yang said in 1951,

> Comrade Mao Tse-tung's *Talks at the Yenan Forum on Literature and Art* pushed modern literature forward into a new epoch. If it is said that the May Fourth Movement was the first revolution in the history of modern Chinese literature, then the publication of the *Talks* and the consequent changes in literary undertakings can be said to be the second, and even more sweeping and profound, literary revolution.[16]

In 1957, Yang Shuo, a defender of the Party, took on two " rightists," Wu Tsu-kuang and Liu Shao-t'ang:

> Wu Tsu-kuang was indeed remarkable for his kindness to save people's face. He merely rejected the literary history of the past eight years [since 1949]. I think he would utter a sigh [about his conservatism] if he compared himself with Liu Shao-t'ang who had the impudence to reject all the Party's literary undertakings since the Yenan Forum on Literature and Art of 1942.[17]

To defenders and detractors alike, the Yenan Forum of 1942 was a major event in the determination of the nature of future Chinese Communist literature. For the first time in history, the Chinese Communist Party could boast of a " policy for literature and art." [18] All writers under the control of that policy were henceforth obliged to conform.

II

I have cited these three trends, not only because they were observable facts, but because Mao Tse-tung, as a speaker who concluded the discussion at the Forum, if not as a reader of modern Chinese literature, also noted the forces that he had to control before he could establish his authority. The striking fact about the Yenan Forum was, of course, the dominance of one man's voice. But another fact, often overlooked amidst the publicity that Mao's *Talks* receive today, was that the Forum was initiated as a meeting for the " exchange of views." [19] Of the over two

[16] Chou Yang, *Chien-chueh Kuan-ch'e Mao Tse-tung Wen-i Lu-hsien* (*Resolutely Implement the Mao Tse-tung Line in Literature*) (Peking: 1952), p. 72.
[17] Yang Shuo, " Rise! Defend Our Party!" PL, 1957, No. 8, p. 9.
[18] On May 19, 1942, a Yang Wei-che wrote in the *Liberation Daily*, Yenan (hereinafter LD) that the CCP did not yet have a policy for literature and art. Mao's important concluding lecture was to be given only four days later.
[19] Mao, *Talks. Selected Works* (in English), IV, (New York: 1956), p. 63. (This volume is hereinafter referred to as Mao.)

hundred people invited to the conference,[20] there were, according to Mao, scores who actively participated in the discussions.[21] Though a full record of the discussion is not available, the controversy was described by Mao as "great" and the debate as "heated."[22] Some of the more interesting opinions, summarily refuted by Mao, can be found today in Mao's *Selected Works*. They represented an assortment of the views of the "petty-bourgeois" writers in the May Fourth tradition: advocates of human nature and refined sentiments, romantics with their private dreams, satirists not too careful in the choice of their target, and cool, matter-of-fact realists who wanted to expose too much for the comfort of the powers that were. They had their say at the Forum, but after that they were not allowed to repeat their old "mistakes." Their thoughts and feelings had to be transformed and remoulded.

Mao's voice, which rose above and silenced the debate, had perhaps never carried so much authortiy as in 1942, the year of the first *Cheng Feng* (Rectification) Movement, a crucial year in his personal career, as well as in the history of his Party. Boyd Compton, in his introduction to a collection of documents pertaining to that movement, made the following observations about the increase in Mao's power during the *Cheng Feng* Movement:

> *Cheng Feng* represented a final stage in Mao's consolidation of leadership.[23]
>
> Since the 1942–44 *Cheng Feng* Movement, a Mao cult has grown in China with a strong family resemblance to both the emperor cult of Imperial China and the Stalin cult in Russia.[24]

The Yenan Forum on Literature and Art was convoked as an integral part of the *Cheng Feng* Movement, and Mao's *Talks*, which came out of the Forum, fitted well into the personality cult. A dictator already in many other fields, he was now strengthening his control over literature and art. He did not state his opinion as just another speaker at the Forum; nor did he withdraw to leave the individual artists to decide for themselves after they had listened to his contribution to the discussion. He was out to reform them.

In February of that year, Mao had talked about the reform of "literary style." The so-called "eight-legged style," which he attacked, the perfunctory, pedantic, repetitious, inexpressive and high-falutin' kind of prose favoured by certain Communist bureaucrats, has perhaps been

20 Ho Ch'en, "How Literature and Art in the Liberated Areas Marched Towards the People," *Ch'ün-chung Weekly* (*The Masses Weekly*) (Hong Kong), 1947, No. 15.
21 Mao, p. 69.
22 Mao, pp. 69, 92.
23 Boyd Compton, *Mao's China: Party Reform Documents, 1942–44* (Seattle: Un. of Washington Press, 1952), p. xxxviii.
24 *Ibid.* p. xlv.

the most durable style. In spite of the campaigns against it, it is still very much alive today. By including prose style as a target of his Reform Movement, Mao perhaps had in mind the " returned-students clique," composed of Moscow-trained Communists whose wide knowledge of Marxism-Leninism could be used to support their position. After their power and influence had been reduced, Mao did not really mind if his loyal followers (*e.g.*, Chou Yang) perpetuated the " eight-legged style " in their official and theoretical writings. Indeed, the interpretations of " Mao Tse-tung's thought " are crammed with so much borrowed thought in an utterly debased language that they belong nowhere if not to the " eight-legged " school.

Mao did not take up the topic of creative literature, *belles-lettres*, drama and fine arts until the Forum which was held in May. Here he began to attack the three trends that I have discussed. These trends, of course, produced both good literature and bad literature and representatives of the latter always outnumbered the former. But Mao's concern was not the merit of literature as literature. His " revolution " was to take " literary and art undertakings " (*wen-yi kung-tso*) out of the hands of individuals and small groups and give them to the Party. He perceived that so long as literature and art were left in the hands of individuals and small groups, however much their sympathies were professedly for the Communist cause, they had the power to cast doubts, to expose " contradictions," to raise questions about justice, to encourage independent thinking, to assert individual rights to happiness or, in a word, to undermine the power of the Party. In 1942, the danger became even more visible than before. There were clear signs of disaffection.

The writers and artists who had chosen Yenan when they were seeking a refuge from the Japanese invasion were making a happy decision. In fact, it was more than a refuge that they sought. They wanted to play their parts in the war against Japan, and the Communist leadership based in Yenan looked more likely to bring about victory. Many of them had accepted Communist leadership without question. For the hardships in the barren hills and on the loess plains in the north-west, they were psychologically, if not physically, prepared when they bade farewell to Shanghai or Peking, then Peiping. They would gladly lend a helping hand to the workers, peasants and soldiers; indeed, they would have no objection if wartime duties required them to live with them, befriend them and learn from them. Obviously, an illusion of personal heroism helped them to make up their minds to share their fate with the Communist Party. But there was also a common ground of faith between them and Mao. When Mao advanced his arguments at the Yenan Forum, he adroitly exploited their beliefs. " Do we need Communist leadership in order to win the war? Do we want to serve the workers, peasants and soldiers?" These were, in effect, the questions Mao put to the members of the Forum. His arguments sounded so powerful that I cannot imagine how those who were under the spell could stand up and answer "No!"

But the writers had to ask unpleasant questions when they came to Yenan. For instance, few of them had ever thought that some day they would have little to write about or that they would be even forced to cease to write. But such was their experience. Chou Yang raised a question in 1941:

> In Yenan, some friends interested in creative writing have felt that they cannot write anything anymore. But the life we have here is a new, meaningful life and creation here is free. Then why the cessation of creative activity, why is so little written?[25]

The question would have been puzzling indeed if life had been so meaningful or creation so free as Chou Yang claimed them to be. The puzzle was also noticed by Ou-yang Shan:

> To my question, "Have you written much recently?" a young acquaintance of mine who loves literature answers: "Recently my head has been so filled with revolutionary theory that not a single short poem could I produce."
>
> His immediate and unprepared answer reminded me of an article by Comrade Lei Chia in the *Wen-yi Yueh-pao* (*Literary Monthly*), No. 4. He reported that the Literature Branch of the Yenan Cultural Association had put the following question at its circuit forums:
>
> Why does literary production cease after a writer has made a study of Marxism-Leninism?[26]

Since the study of Marxism-Leninism had to be free from blame, Ou-yang Shan could only explain the otherwise unaccountable phenomenon by saying that the trouble with those barren writers was that they had accepted Marxism-Leninism in a dogmatic way. If they could only relate Marxism-Leninism to "life," then one would see.

The barrenness was not immediately relieved by Mao's *Talks*. One notable example was the poet Ho Ch'i-fang, who wrote in 1940 after his conversion to Communism:

> I also want to prove:
> I am a busy man,
> With several meetings a day,
> An enthusiastic administrator,
> But I am also a poet.[27]

[25] LD July 19, 1941, p. 2.
[26] LD May 19, 1941, p. 2.
[27] Ho, *Yeh-ko ho Pai-t'ien-ti Ko* (*Nocturnes and Songs of Daylight*) (Peking: 1952), p. 98.

But he could only disprove this proud statement when he explained his silence in 1944:

> Ever since the spring of 1942, I have ceased to write poetry. There are so many things more important than poetry for me to do. The most important of them is to study theory and to examine and reform myself through a number of concrete problems and concrete tasks.[28]

Ting Ling also said that she wrote nothing after "Eighteen," a short story about eighteen soldiers, a commemoration piece on the fifth anniversary of the Sino-Japanese War (July 1942). Said she:

> Then we did not have the opportunity (*chi-hui*) to write; all of us were swallowed up in the strong tides of reform and study. This lasted until the New Year of 1944 when the Party School mobilised us to write *yang-ko* plays. . .[29]

In the summer of 1944, a group of reporters from Chungking visited Yenan. Chao Ch'ao-kou, representing the independent *Hsin Min Pao*, commented on the literary scene:

> In fact, there are quite a number of famous writers residing in Yenan but their production does not seem to be plentiful. According to their own explanation, they are now engaged in "study." Therefore we cannot at this moment estimate the success of this literary policy. We should be fair and wait and see. We should not judge until we have seen the results of their "study."[30]

So the barrenness became all the more notable after the Yenan Forum. But why the two-year period of imposed silence from 1942 to 1944? Why did Mao subject the writers to the "strong tides of reform and study," instead of driving them to increase their productivity so as to resolve the doubts expressed by Chou Yang and Ou-yang Shan in 1941? A partial answer could be found in the general requirements of the *Cheng Feng* Movement: the Party needed better Communists more than it needed better or more productive writers. To Mao, an "incorrect" production was perhaps worse than no production. He was not so much concerned with the writers' lagging productivity as with their dubious mental health. Until they were cured of the traits of individualism in their attitudes, behaviour, and works, he found it necessary to keep them from publishing for the sake of public safety.

One of the "diseases" detected by Mao was the neglect of popularisation. His remedy was a return to "national forms" and "national styles" which he had already championed in 1938.[31] Why individual efforts to "popularise" other forms and styles should not be permitted

[28] *Ibid.* p. 238. However, this collection includes one poem for 1945, one for 1946 and another for 1949.
[29] Ting Ling, *Shan-pei Feng-kuang* (*Scenes of Northern Shensi*) (Peking: 1950), p. 92.
[30] Chao, *Yenan I-yueh* (*One Month in Yenan*) (Shanghai: 1946), p. 114.
[31] Mao, p. 62.

was never explained, except that to do so would have meant a betrayal of the interests of the workers, peasants, and soldiers. Instead of the divergent individual efforts, there would be a collective effort towards the creation of something that the people must love. Those who were to suffer from this policy were the novelists and the poets who knew their European models too well, the dramatists whose conception of their profession was limited to Western-style spoken drama, and the artists who practised oil painting. Their audience was perhaps never large enough in the eyes of Mao, but whatever audience they might once have had was now taken away from them. For the audience had no choice, any more than the author had. They could only accept what was offered them.

According to Lu Ting-yi, the immediate literary and artistic fruits of the Yenan Forum were, in the order of their appearance:

1. Folk dance and folk drama (*Brother and Sister Tilling Virgin Soil, The White-haired Girl.*)
2. Woodcuts in the " national " style.
3. Novels in the traditional style of story-telling (*Verses of Li Yu-ts'ai, The Heroes of the Lü-liang Mountain.*)
4. Poetry in imitation of the folk-song rhythm and idiom (*Wang Kuei and Li Hsiang-hsiang.*) [32]

This movement in Yenan, it seems to me, was a de-personalisation movement. The search for an identification with the " people " forced the artist to neglect his own inner needs, whether moral or aesthetic. Folk art, which might have had a broadening effect, led inspiration in Yenan into a narrow alley. But it is the virtual suppression, in the years following the Yenan Forum, of other forms and styles that would seem to be the most unfortunate consequence of the power of the Communist Party.

However, the alleged neglect of popularisation was a small matter in comparison with some definite signs of disaffection. From the available sources, it can be surmised that 1942 bore some similarities to 1957 as a year of crisis, a year of tolerance followed by persecution. Whereas in 1957, the Communist régime in China was alarmed by the rumblings from Europe, 1942 was also a year of great difficulty which perhaps required the stern measures of *Cheng Feng* to overcome. The seriousness of the situation, to my knowledge, has never been fully discussed, and I regret my inability to substantiate the facts quoted from *A Concise History of the Chinese Communist Party*, published in Shanghai in 1957. But these stark facts from official sources tell a great deal:

[32] Lu's Preface to *Wang Kuei and Li Hsiang-hsiang*. Reprinted in the *Ch'ün-chung Weekly*, 1947, No. 7.

> The Eighth Route Army dropped from a strength of 400,000 of 1940 to somewhat more than 300,000 of 1942. The population of the Liberated and Guerrilla Areas dropped from 100,000,000 to less than 50,000,000. Finance and economy in the Liberated Areas became also extremely difficult.[33]

The author of the *Concise History* then went on to quote a speech given by Mao in November 1942:

> For a while we were reduced almost to the state of having no clothes to wear, no oil to cook with, no paper, no vegetables, no footwear for the soldiers and, in winter, no bedding for the civilian personnel.[34]

The difficult living conditions, together with the controls, dampened the spirit of those who had dreamed about the " new, meaningful life " of their promised land. Complaints were heard from intellectuals, traditionally the articulate group, and writers were among them. Their unhappiness, expressed in whatever medium, " popularised " or otherwise, was readily communicated. Another irony was that they automatically abolished the " eight-legged " style when they came to speak out their genuine feelings. Mao Tse-tung saw the necessity to check their influence before demoralisation, of the sort that paralysed Chungking in the years to come, became widespread and uncontrollable. The possible trouble-makers were still a minority, but Mao did not like to see them increase in number. Faith in the future was somewhat shaken, but thanks to the organisational strength of the Party, discipline was maintained. The *Cheng Feng* Movement meant a redoubled effort at indoctrination—compulsory reading of documents and compulsory discussion, which had the effect of occupying the dissident's mind with the urgent business of revolution. And the method of " criticism and self-criticism," never so widely used before by the Chinese Communist Party, was an efficient device to sound out the hidden heresy in the depth of the soul of even an apparently docile comrade.

By " criticism," Mao meant free expression of discontent, but on the condition that it should be met by strong and organised rebuttal. Here the similarity between 1942 and 1957 requires some modification. In 1957, there was a period, lasting some months, for " blooming," followed by a period of withering counter-attack. In 1942, criticism was immediately countered by rebuttal. But even so, many unpleasant facts must have been exposed. Ai Ssu-ch'i, who had succeeded Ting Ling as editor of the Literary Page of the *Liberation Daily*, said on April 22, 1942:

> Yenan is now engaged in the " rectification of three styles " [the style of study, the style of Party work, and prose style]. One special

[33] Miao Ch'u-huang, *Chung-kuo Kung-ch'an-tang Chien-yao Li-shih* (Shanghai: 1957), p. 132.

[34] Mao, p. 106. If the reader checks the Chinese version, he will puzzle over the meaning of the phrase " for a while " found in the official English version.

> feature of the movement has been the enthusiasm to expose facts, which is entirely necessary. [Then followed a differentiation between two kinds of facts: " substance " and " superficial phenomena."] [35]

On June 5, the same paper carried an editorial on the topic " A Summary of the Study Movement during the Past Month." It noted that one of the lessons learned in the movement was:

> Maximum freedom should be granted for the expression of incorrect opinions; but there should be a readiness to organise rebuttal at any given moment.[36]

The effect of " criticism " was therefore much reduced in confrontation with an alert and organised opposition. At the same time, the dissident was required by " self-criticism " to expose his own weaknesses, *i.e.*, his " petty-bourgeois vices " according to Mao's definition, so as further to weaken the force of his " criticism."

When the Forum on Literature and Art was convoked on May 2, the *Cheng Feng* Movement had already thrown all government offices and schools in Yenan into a state of tension for at least a month. (Mao started the movement in February. On April 3, the Propaganda Bureau of the Central Committee issued an order to intensify it.) [37] How the " study groups " carried on their discussion gave some foretaste of what would happen at the Forum. The debate at the Forum was from the very beginning an unequal struggle. Prior to the *tso-t'an-hui* (" sit-and-talk meeting " is how the Forum is described in Chinese), Mao had prepared a number of people for what he asked of the meeting.[38] Then he delivered the keynote speech (the Introductory Lecture) to limit the discussion to five political and ideological topics (the artist's standpoint, attitude, audience, acquaintance with life, and studies in Marxism-Leninism) on which the dissidents would have had very little to say if they had wanted to avoid sounding like out-and-out reactionaries. The dissidents might have had some sort of organisation and preparation, too. But the odds against them must have been overwhelming.

We should not have learned so much about the dissidents of 1942, if the case of the so-called Ting-Ch'en clique of 1957 had not reopened so many old wounds. Jealousy among writers is an age-old habit and perhaps a forgivable sin, according to Emperor Wei Wen Ti of the third century A.D.[39] The quarrel between the two factions in Yenan, one headed by Chou Yang and the other by Ting Ling and Ch'en Ch'i-hsia,

[35] LD April 22, 1942, p. 4.
[36] LD June 5, 1942, p. 1.
[37] Compton, *op. cit.*, p. xxxiv and pp. 1–8.
[38] The fact is revealed in an editorial of *Wen-yi Pao* (*Journal of Literature and the Arts*), 1957, No. 7, p. 2. The title of the editorial: " Chi-nien, hui-ku ho chan-wang " (" Commemoration, Retrospect and Prospect ").
[39] Wei Wen Ti, *Tien-lun lun-wen*.

was not entirely concerned with principles. Jealousy and personal differences also played a part. The writers of the Ting-Ch'en clique did not begin as anti-Communists at all, but their fight for the independence of art compelled them to take a stand incompatible with that of the Communist Party.

Therefore, to treat the disaffection in 1942 as merely a manifestation of a " sectarian " fight among writers is to ignore the issues at stake. The voices that spoke for the supra-political value of literature are still preserved within quotation marks in Mao's *Talks*. The need for " humanity," " love " and " presenting the true reality " has recurred, over and again, all through these twenty years, to writers who were never connected with the Ting-Ch'en clique. Such a need was felt in 1942 after a shoeless and quiltless winter in the north-west had made the Communist system look all the more cold.

A great part of literature produced in Yenan before the Forum is lost. Magazines like *Wen-yi Yueh-pao* (mentioned above), *Ku-yü* (*Grain Rains*), *Ts'ao-yeh* (*Grass Leaves*) and *Shih-k'an* (*Poetry*) are hard to find. They had apparently all ceased publication by 1944, for Chao Ch'ao-kou noted that he found not a single literary magazine during his stay in Yenan. Handwritten journals posted on the wall, like the *Ch'ing-ch'i Tui* (*Light Brigade*), were of course even more perishable. From the files of the *Liberation Daily* and the collections of the works of that period, I can say that much that passed for literature was simply thinly-disguised anti-Japanese propaganda. (The same phenomenon was observable in Chungking.) If one is interested in individual expression rather than mass sentiment, though the latter was not manipulated so much before 1942 as after, one can recommend Ho Ch'i-fang and Ting Ling as two representatives of the May Fourth tradition. In Ho we find the suicidal progress of a sensitive soul, a Shelley in the Leninist era heaving his last sighs before he gives himself up to the historical movement. He wrote in 1940:

> And in May
> There is much too much good sunshine in daytime,
> There is much too much good moonlight at night. . . .
> I cannot get up from the bed, and walking into the woods,
> Say that each tree has a beautiful soul
> And weep with them.[40]

A mysterious urge was there, though he could not get up from the bed and cry, for whatever reason, in the woods. The tone had changed by 1942:

[40] Ho Ch'i-fang, *op. cit.*, pp. 20–21.

And then joyously to experience
My agonising rebirth.[41]

In her fiction, Ting Ling exhibited sympathy and tenderness against a background of harsh reality. Her best piece of this period may be the short story, " In the Hospital " (1941) which, however, has never been included in any of her collected works.[42] Perhaps she was forbidden to acknowledge it, because life in a Yenan hospital as Ting Ling understood it—the inhumanity in the system rather than the inadequacy of its material equipment—would be better kept out of the public eye from the Party's point of view. But " New Belief " (1939) is a powerful, though morbid, story.[43] A village grandmother is raped by the Japanese. She becomes abnormally talkative. Wherever she goes, she prattles about her experience as well as the sadistic scenes she has witnessed. Such exhibitionism is terrible enough, but then the Communist cadres hear of it and turn the pathetic old figure into a first-rate propagandist.

That a woman, with injured body and soul, should be exploited to advance a political cause may have had personal significance for Ting Ling. Another story, " When I Was in Hsia Village " (1940) is a variation on the same theme, but with greater tenderness.[44] A lonely woman cadre (the " I " in the story) is assigned to Hsia village. There she becomes acquainted with a lonely girl who is shunned by her fellow villagers as worse than a prostitute. She has contracted V.D. as a result of her relations with the Japanese. But she is still charged with a secret mission to go constantly behind the enemy lines, because she has Japanese friends and her youth and physical attractions can still enable her to get something out of them. She has a devoted lover in the shape of a young villager, but sick unto death, she has to rebuff his advances.

" Look, a Chinese woman was raped by the Japanese; so, down with Japanese imperialism!" was a theme repeated innumerable times by writers not only in Yenan but also in Chungking. Ting Ling's treatment of the theme was unique, which is a tribute to her genius. The story of the poor girl (or of the old woman) who was both a plaything for the Japanese and a tool of Communist cadres, though the latter used her only for patriotism's sake, poses a serious question about the inhumanity in human life, especially under the difficult conditions of war. Ting Ling's stories may have had some propaganda value at the time when they

41 *Ibid.* p. 182.

42 " In the Hospital " was originally published in the *Ku-yü*, No. 1, and was reprinted in *Wen-yi Chen-ti*, a Chungking journal. *Li Hsueh-wei* reviewed it in LD December 5, 1941, p. 4. A damning criticism is found in *Wen-yi Pao* 1957, No. 25, p. 11. Liu Pai-yü, also writing in 1957, said that the story was not available to him (*People's Daily*, August 28, 1957, p. 7).

43 This story is found in two collections: *Wo tsai Hsia-ts'un-ti shih-hou* (*When I Was in Hsia Village*) (Peking: 1950) or *Yenan Chi* (*A Yenan Anthology*) Peking: 1954).

44 This story is also found in the above-mentioned collections.

were published; but their meaning remains fresh today, long after the Japanese have been defeated. The realism in her fiction supplies an interpretation of life in its totality and ambivalence, in its terror and tenderness, over and above any philosophical theory. At least, there is no room for the Communist theory of the lovable masses in her picture of an apathetic, almost cruel, crowd of villagers, drawn from a sentimentalist's innermost knowledge. Obviously, the root of evil goes deeper than the accident of Japanese aggression.

The two stories may serve as an introduction to Ting Ling's "Thoughts on March 8"[45] which, in very articulate form, saw no hope for women in the so-called Liberated Areas unless men would agree to reform themselves. Poetry and fiction from Yenan with anti-Communist undertones seldom attracted so much attention as this essay did. For "Thoughts on March 8" is a clearly written essay about the deplorable condition of women in a place where they were supposed to enjoy equality, if not happiness. But it is not a satire, a genre Ting Ling is never good at. It is only a plea from the weak to the strong.

On October 23, 1941, Ting Ling had pronounced from the editorial chair of the Literary Page of the *Liberation Daily:*

> . . . It is said that this is not a suitable place for the writing of the *tsa-wen* and that what is needed here is only the reflection of democratic life and great construction.
>
> It may be in human nature to be intoxicated with small successes or to hate to be told that one is sick or that one needs to see a doctor about it. But that is also a sign of indolence and cowardice.
>
> Lu Hsün is dead. Customarily we say to ourselves that we should do this or that in order to live up to him. But we have not sufficiently acquired his courage in sparing no details. I think it will do us most good if we emulate his steadfastness in facing the truth, his courage to speak out for the sake of truth, and his fearlessness. This age of ours still needs the *tsa-wen*, a weapon that we should never lay down. Raise it, and the *tsa-wen* will not be dead.[46]

Here Ting Ling made a really brave gesture. She talked about "taking up the weapon"—but against whom? She went so far as to sneer at the "reflection of democratic life and great construction," which, as is well known, had been the main theme of Chinese Communist literature all through these years. She invoked the fearless spirit of Lu Hsün. We have seen indeed a number of avatars of that spirit, but none of them have been able to maintain a career of defiance for long.

[45] LD March 9, 1942, p. 4. It should be noted that on March 4, 1942, the Central Committee of the CCP gave instructions regarding the programme for the celebration of the International Women's Day. The propaganda was to emphasise these points: the establishment of the international women's anti-fascist united front, the promotion of unity in China, the active part that women should play in revolution, etc. Ting Ling's essay was an open defiance against such instructions.

[46] LD October 23, 1941, p. 4.

The first of the avatars was Wang Shih-wei. The day (March 13, 1942) after Lo Feng published " This is Still the Age for *Tsa-wen* " as a response to Ting Ling's appeal, there appeared in the *Liberation Daily* the best-known anti-Communist literature of the year: two essays by Wang Shih-wei under the title, *The Wild Lily*. Ten days later came two more essays under the same title. About that time, Wang also published, in the *Ku-yü*, " Statesmen vs. Artists," composed of thirteen pieces of causeries also in the *tsa-wen* style.[47] Judging from the performance of *The Wild Lily* alone, I do not think Wang was a particularly brilliant satirist. In spite of his occasional obscurity, Lu Hsün is remarkable for the cool decisiveness in his home thrust, his absolute irreconcilableness, and his utter contempt for whatever came under attack. These qualities, however, are not prominent in Wang. (Among the many disciples of Lu Hsün, Hsu Mou-yung, the one he disowned, seemed to have come the closest to the master's style in the essays he published, under various pseudonyms, in the 1956–57 period.) In his attacks on the hypocrisy and corruption of Communist bureaucracy, Wang seemed still to cling to some warm hope for amelioration. He did not put himself in an extremely hostile position as Lu Hsün might have done. The wild lily, the author explained, is the " most beautiful wild plant in Yenan "; only its bulb " tastes bitter." Hence some attractive but bitter advice he was trying to offer to the Communist Party, but the result was a long series of " struggle meetings " against the impertinent adviser until he was denounced as a Trotskyite. *The Wild Lily* had a very short life, but it anticipated the other breeds of doomed flowers by about fifteen years.

For the general literary situation at the time of the Forum, I shall cite two eye-witness accounts. These two pieces may give an exaggerated impression of the hostility and despondency prevailing in Yenan, since little is said about the staunch supporters of the régime. But what strikes us is the resemblance of 1942 to the 1956–1957 period. Here we get some foretaste of the works that embarrassed the Communist régime in the later period. Works like " On the Bridge Construction Site," " Our Paper's Inside News," " Beautiful," " Realism—the Broad Path," " The Development of Realism in the Socialist Age," etc., did not come from nowhere, though they were written by writers of a younger generation. They were rooted in 1942 or even earlier.

The first piece is from Ho Ch'i-fang:

> One of the principal representatives of the incorrect tendency was Hsiao Chün. He based his anti-people literary activities on the arguments found in a lecture given by Lu Hsün in 1927, " The Divergence

[47] This essay was published in the *Ku-yü*, Vol. 1, No. 4. Mentioned in LD May 26, 1942, p. 4.

> of Politics and Literature."[48] He exploited these statements of Lu Hsün's: "Literature and politics are in perpetual conflict." "Politics wants to preserve the status quo; thus it places itself in an opposite direction to literature as a symbol of discontent."
>
> It was not Hsiao Chün alone, or people of the same colour as Hsiao Chün, who were involved in the incorrect literary activities. But quite a number of writers participated. Even some writers who were Party members publicly supported him. Those who did not support him theoretically still showed their affinity with this tendency in their creative works. For instance, there were works of fiction which placed the cadres of the worker-peasant-soldier classes in a very bad light but poured out heartful sympathy to the petty-bourgeois intellectuals. Other works of fiction denounced the principle of revolutionary organisation that individuals should obey the collective; they demanded that the collective should obey individuals. The authors of such works were all members of the Communist Party. Of course, there were some Communist writers who contradicted this tendency: they opposed it with the slogan, "Praise the Bright Side!" But they were unable to combat it publicly on theoretical grounds so as to stop it completely. The "praise" found in their works still showed the more or less superficial petty-bourgeois sentiments.[49]

Here are the reminiscences of Miss Tseng K'e who joined the Yenan Branch of the Chinese Writers' Anti-aggression Association after her arrival in Yenan:

> The cell which I joined for my study programme was composed mostly of unreformed intellectuals who had not been in Yenan long. The great part of the more serious mistakes pointed out by Chairman Mao in his *Talks* was reflected in the Yenan branch of this Association.
>
> The most conspicuous were people like Hsiao Chün and Ting Ling. [On another occasion, she also mentioned Ch'en Ch'i-hsia and Lo Feng.[50]] They used every means within their power to "express themselves, spread their own opinions, and demand that people remould the Party and the world in their image."[51] . . .
>
> Even in everyday conversation, they talked about taking up the so-called weapon of *tsa-wen*. Clamorously they said that the youth and the writers should join hands in exposing the "darkness" in the revolutionary ranks and satirising the "weakness" of the people. They wanted politics to obey the demands of art. They exaggerated the aesthetic quality as if it were something mysterious.
>
> I remember one *tsa-wen*, "The Cock Crows," which was at once a satire on the writers who praised revolution and a diatribe of hatred

48 Lu Hsün's lecture was given at Chinan University in Shanghai on December 21, 1927. It was collected in his *Chi-wai-chi* (*Uncollected Works Collected*) with his approval. Lu Hsün, *Ch'üan-chi* (*Complete Works*), VII (Peking: 1958), p. 103.

49 Ho, "Improve Our Work with Mao's Literary Theory," *Wen-yi Pao*, 1952, No. 1, p. 125.

50 Miss Tseng mentioned these names at a forum sponsored by the provincial journal *Szechwan Wen-yi*, in celebration of the twentieth anniversary of Mao's *Talks*: *Szechwan Wen-yi*, Chengtu, 1962, No. 3, p. 87 *et seq*.

51 Mao, p. 91.

against the Border Region. It was a fable about a chanticleer who longed for daylight for which he would fain sing a paean. Then he saw a glimmering and he began to sing, for he wanted to announce the daybreak. But after his crowing, he discovered that all was pitch darkness about him. The time was midnight. He had been deceived by an illusion of dawn. He began to regret his impetuosity which had led him to get all excited before he sang that song.

In the wall-newspaper, *The Light Brigade*, there was a poem-in-prose, "Cupid Comes to Yenan." An extremely malicious calumny, it ridiculed the old cadres who were supposedly wanting both in culture and in an understanding of love.

There was a poet-cum-composer who deplored the inhumanity of the Communists who, according to him, understood his emotions less than a stone or a blade of grass did. The reason was simply that the nursery attached to his office did not afford an endless supply of milk and eggs for his children.

More typical was a short story, "Beyond the Realm of Consciousness." [52] It was about a girl student who loved art. When she came to Yenan, she thought that she might now develop her artistic talent in accordance with her wishes. Instead, she was assigned the job of a nurse in a hospital, since that was what the Organisational Department regarded as more important to the revolutionary task at that time. But she could never settle down for work. All the time she was crying that she wanted to go to study at the Lu Hsün Academy of Arts, the highest institution in this field. Since permission was not granted her, she became extremely distressed. She thought that the Party was strangling her talent. In her dazed state, her head was filled with poetry, music notes, the guitar, the crucifix, etc. Finally she became insane.[53]

It is interesting to note that Miss Tseng, the author of the reminiscences, was also once distressed over her failure to enter the Lu Hsün Academy. But then, she said, the Yenan Forum was convoked, and she was saved.

III

"In May, the weather in Yenan was neither cold nor hot. The River Yen had thawed; its muddy yellow waters rushed down the shallow bed, over sand and soil. The willow had turned green. The fragrance of the thorny-plum-blossoms (*tz'u-mei-hua*) filled the gullies and floated into the air. It was spring in Yenan." [54]

Against such a background of vernal smells and sights, which punctuated the monotony of the yellow plateau, the Forum on Literature and Art was in session. From May 2 to May 23, three sessions were held in the Auditorium, one of the few modern buildings in the ancient city where most people lived in caves. On the last day, the discussion stopped

[52] This story by Fang Chi was published in *Wen-yi Yueh-pao*, No. 14. A review is available in LD June 25, 1942, p. 4.
[53] *Szechwan Wen-yi*, 1962, No. 4, p. 65 *et seq.*
[54] "Commemoration, Retrospect and Prospect," *Wen-yi Pao*, 1957, No. 7, p. 2.

before dinner. The rays of the setting sun were still bright enough for a group photograph. Mao naturally took the middle seat in the front row. Before the focus was set, however, he stood up, went to Ting Ling, and gave his seat to her. Smilingly he said, "Let our woman cadre take the middle seat. We don't like to be rebuked again on March 8." Everybody laughed, to Ting Ling's embarrassment. Mao's good humour somewhat relaxed the tension of the discussion. But who would speak, on the next International Women's Day, about the status of women in Yenan?[55]

When the dinner was over, it was already eight o'clock. More people than the auditorium could accommodate had come for the anticipated concluding lecture by Mao. So the meeting was moved to the open air. In the courtyard, under the petroleum-gas lamps, Mao pointed out the direction for literature and art.

Like Khrushchev, Mao has his folksy ways of speech. According to a 1949 version, he used the word "buttocks" on two occasions where we now find a less offensive word in the standard version.[56] But neither version perhaps contains everything he said.[57] His casualness and conversational tone, his deep intentions notwithstanding, is lost on those who ponder every word of his as if it were divinely inspired truth.

As I have pointed out, one does not have to quarrel so much with Mao's theory as with the fact of control. Obviously Mao could not claim any originality for his theory. Though the Russian terms were not mentioned, what he required of literature and art was the fulfilment of the familiar Russian concepts: *ideynost* (ideological expression), *partiinost* (party spirit) and *narodnost* (national character). His dialectics, based on the law of excluded middle (either for the revolution or against it), permitted no ground for writers like Ho Ch'i-fang, who had had his private tears to shed, or Ting Ling, who had insisted on telling the truth about the revolution. The set of taboos he proposed placed a restriction even on those who favoured his kind of revolution.

Concerned with the political function of art, he did not at all touch the problems of imagination, aesthetic experience, or the workings of a creative mind. He omitted these and other problems unrelated to revolution but which creative artists have to struggle with. This obvious deficiency of the *Talks* gave something of an opportunity for writers to assert their independence. Ch'in Chao-yang said at a forum in 1956 discussing the "hundred flowers" movement:

[55] The anecdote is cited by Ho Ch'en. See footnote 20.

[56] *Cheng-feng Wen-hsien* (*Party Reform Documents*) (Hong Kong: 1949), pp. 276–277. For "p'i-ku," we find "li-tsu-tien" ("standpoint") in the standard version. Mao, *Hsuan-chi* (*Selected Works*), III, p. 859.

[57] In LD November 15, 1942, p. 4, Chiang Pu quoted Mao as having complained at the Forum about the writers "having neither life, nor Marxism-Leninism." This phrase is not found in the published texts.

> The method of creation is to be evolved by the writers themselves; it is a subject on which no man should be allowed to place any rigid restrictions.[58]

The veteran writer Mao Tun, in an article celebrating the Fifteenth Anniversary of Mao Tse-tung's *Talks*, said in 1957:

> Marxism is not to replace the method of creation. That no method of creation is included in the *Talks* is only natural. The problems proposed and studied today in literary and art circles are primarily and essentially the problems of creation which arise from the act of creation and which are to be answered only through this act.[59]

From this foothold of independence, Ch'in Chao-yang later went on to question the " dogmatism in literature " when he published his " Realism —the Broad Path." But Mao Tun tried to protect himself by bringing in the " political " factor in the method of creation:

> The world-view is not equal to the method of creation. But, all the problems pertaining to the method of creation are related, in a myriad of subtle and devious ways, to the world-view.[60]

Along the same line, Lu Ting-yi said that Mao Tse-tung's *Talks* were the " foundation of the method of creation." [61] Here is what might be the main topic of Communist aesthetics: how a method of creation could be built upon the ideological foundation; but this is a topic Mao Tse-tung did not go into. " The myriad of subtle and devious ways " in which the world-view affects the method of creation requires some fine analysis to develop into a literary theory. We do not get this from Mao; nor do we find it in the writings of his obedient mouthpieces whose " eight-legged " style proves nothing but their political " correctness." Indeed, Mao Tse-tung tried to maintain a double standard—the political and the artistic—in his Yenan *Talks*. But he never explained how an imaginative work that served the workers, peasants and soldiers could also pass the secondary—or artistic—standard. He recommended the reading of classics, both Western and Chinese—not very practicable advice, since it was to be taken together with the warning against their ideological impurities. Whatever benefit, in the way of methodology, a writer might derive from the study of the classics, he must beware of their ideological content. We have already seen the danger of following too closely the examples of Tolstoy and Balzac.

We have seen, too, Liu Hsueh-wei's discussion of the conflict between the world-view and the method of creation and how it led to the failure of the leftist literature of the 1920s and 1930s. The intrusion of an

[58] *Wen-yi Pao*, 1956, No. 14, p. 20.
[59] PL, 1957, Nos. 5–6 (a combined issue), p. 2.
[60] *Ibid.* p. 3.
[61] *People's Daily*, September 27, 1957, p. 2.

extraneous world-view has remained the most disturbing factor in Communist literature since 1942. The logical solution seems to be either a breed of liberalism which permits the writer to develop, within the limit of his talent, a method of creation which shows no respect to whatever political canon, or to write according to a formula, resulting in the complete triumph of the Communist world-view. But Mao's double standard has only added to the confusion and agony of the writers. There are no doubt a myriad of ways in the relationship between the artist's world-view and his method of creation. But the political situation being as it is in Communist China, the myriad can be reduced to a single factor of fear. The writer in Communist China, constantly and fearfully aware of his obligation to the Communist Party, may still engage himself, as all of us do, in a private struggle with ideas, emotions, images and words. But there is no guarantee that whatever comes out of an individual act of creation shall always support the Communist world-view. How to make room—and a large enough room—for the world-view that the Party hands him is a distressing problem to the creative writer in Communist China today.

The double standard is hard to pass. Therefore, we cannot say that the Communist Party is always satisfied with the merits of the literary products under its sponsorship. In 1952, to celebrate the Tenth Anniversary of Mao's *Talks*, the *People's Daily* editorially lamented the " ideological confusion " found in literary circles. The deplorable situation was said to be manifested in two aspects. The first was the " corrosion of revolutionary literature by bourgeois ideology." The meaning of this statement is clear, since we have seen the same corrosion in Yenan ten years earlier. The second aspect is more interesting, because it shows how the imposition of a political standard on literature and art began to reap its harvest. The " formularisation " and " conceptualisation " discussed in the following quotation bear some resemblance to the early proletarian literature of the 1920s, with the difference that the factor of fear was absent in the latter which was probably animated by " a petty-bourgeois enthusiasm for revolution." But a quotation at some length is needed to explain why the Communist Party was dissatisfied with the literature and art which might have been taken to be politically correct:

> Secondly, there is a tendency which seems to be in opposition to the above-mentioned [bourgeois] tendency but which actually represents also a loss of contact with the masses and with life. It is the tendency towards formularisation and conceptualisation in literary and art creation. This tendency comes from a Philistine (*yung-su-ti*) understanding of the political mission of literature and art. The works with this tendency have an empty content except for a medley of slogans and concepts. There is no life in them: the characters in them have neither flesh and blood nor any distinction. What is accomplished is

> merely a crude mixture of some superficial political concepts with a story according to a formula. Since such works are not profound reflections of real life, they do not perform the genuine educational function on the masses as they ought to. To produce such works, soon forgotten by the readers, does not require much effort. Comrade Mao Tse-tung says: "All revolutionary artists and writers of China, all artists and writers of high promise, must, for long periods of time, unreservedly and whole-heartedly go into the midst of the masses, the masses of workers, peasants and soldiers; they must go into fiery struggles, go to the only, the broadest, the richest source to observe, learn, study and analyse all men, all classes, all kinds of people, all the vivid patterns of life and struggle and all raw material or art and literature, before they can proceed to creation." [62] But our writers of the formularisation and conceptualisation school are the hopeless cases. They have altogether omitted the process of going into the masses to observe, to learn, to study, to analyse and then to organise, to concentrate, and to typify. They have never seriously engaged themselves either in the study of real life or in artistic creation. They treat only violently both reality and art with their eyes shut. They are the sloths among the literary and art workers; and of the sloths no genuine service to the people or to politics can be expected. Therefore, they are practically liquidating the genuine service that literature and art ought to do to politics.[63]

The prescription found in Mao's *Talks*, beginning with "going into the masses," etc., is not a sure remedy for formularisation and conceptualisation. Unlike the proletarian writers of the 1920s, who had probably more daydreams than experience, Chinese writers by 1952 had all studied some aspects of life. Among those who showed marks of "bourgeois corrosion," there were Ting Ling and others who had actually lived among the masses for quite a number of years. Their trouble was perhaps that they had too much experience to discover what the Communists call "the typical" and the "pattern of life." To present life as the writer understands it is hard enough; but to present life as the Communist Party orders it to be is not so easy as the editorialist of the *People's Daily* thought, unless the writer can harden himself, to "treat life violently and to keep his eyes shut." In 1953, Ch'in Chao-yang published an interesting book, *On Formularisation and Conceptualisation*. He was then not yet openly rebellious, but as an editorial assistant of *People's Literature* he was sorely disappointed at the manuscripts which it was his painful duty to read. His analysis of the basic weakness of Communist literature led, in 1956, to his conviction about the one criterion of literature, *i.e.*, reality instead of dogma. But his early opinion is also worth reading:

62 Mao, p. 77.
63 *People's Daily*, May 23, 1952. Reprinted in *Hsin-hua Yueh-pao* (*New China Monthly*), 1952, No. 6, p. 178.

> I have heard that among the literary and art workers in some place there is a current jargon, namely, "to put on ideological varnish." It means that the framework of a story is like a piece of furniture and that in order to give it a better look and a better market value, some varnish is needed. . . . It is most clearly shown in the "positive speeches" that the characters in fiction have to make. . . . Sometimes, the characters have to be beaten by landlords and enemy agents; and their wives and daughters raped. . . . To strengthen the "ideological quality," it is also possible to raise the standard of the characters, even by so little, and to improve the reality, even by so little. . . .[64]

Liu Hsueh-wei has described the formula for proletarian literature: the birth of the new amidst the old, the tomorrow in today, the conquest of the old by the new, etc. When Ting Ling sneered at "the reflection of democratic life and great construction" in Yenan she was also talking about a formula. Now Ch'in Chao-yang noted the possibility of "raising the standard of characters, even by so little, and improving the reality, even by so little." This possibility is actually a necessity for writers who are charged with the duty "to praise the bright side." To make room for the Communist world-view in a literary work is to adopt Communist formulas and concepts. The difference between the required mastery of the world-view and the defective presentation of formulas and concepts in a literary work is so small that I think that I am not far from the truth if I say that in Communist literature there is only a difference in degree of formularisation and conceptualisation. At least there has not yet appeared from Communist China a critical work that explains satisfactorily the use and abuse of Communist formulas and concepts in literature.

In 1942 Mao was quite confident of the future, though he also admitted the difficulty involved in thought reform:

> These comrades still stand on the side of the petty-bourgeois intellectuals, or, to put it more elegantly, their innermost soul is still a kingdom of the petty-bourgeois intelligentsia. Thus they have not yet solved or unequivocally solved the problem, "For whom are art and literature intended?" And this refers not only to the newcomers to Yenan; even among those who have been to the front and worked for a few years in our base areas and in the Eighth and New Fourth Armies, many have not solved the problems thoroughly. To solve this problem thoroughly, a long time is required, say, eight or ten years. But no matter how long it takes, we must solve it, and solve it unequivocally and thoroughly.[65]

Ten years after Mao made the vow, he saw the appearance of formularisation and conceptualisation. While admittedly the kingdom of petty-bourgeois intelligentsia remained in 1952, he had to divert his attention

[64] Ch'in, *Lun Kung-shih-hua Kai-nien-hua* (Peking: 1953), p. 60.
[65] Mao, p. 73.

to the "republic of sloths." Now another ten years has elapsed, and Mao's problems are not yet solved; instead they have increased. To his right, in addition to the perennial bourgeoisie and the petty-bourgeois intelligentsia, there has loomed the spectre of modern revisionism which, clothed as it is in Marxism or even Marxism-Leninism, gives nevertheless aid and comfort to the bourgeoisie. In 1962, commemorating the twentieth anniversary of Mao's *Talks, Wen-yi Pao* commented editorially:

> Our literature and art must carry on an irreconcilable fight with imperialist literature and art, revisionist literature and art, and all kinds of reactionary ideology that serves imperialism and the old order. . . .[66]

According to Chou Yang in 1960, the typical revisionist among Chinese writers was Hu Feng, who echoed the views of Georg Lukacs.[67] This may be true, but after the defeat of the Hu Feng "clique," I must profess my ignorance as to the identity of revisionists in Communist China. If revisionism is found in Soviet Russia, as other Communist Chinese documents suggest, then Soviet literature needs a complete reappraisal, a task which seems beyond the capability of Communist Chinese critics. How the fight against revisionism will be carried out in the "literary and art circles" in Communist China will be worth watching.[68]

Then, to Mao's left, there are the so-called dogmatists who, in spite of their loyalty to the workers, peasants and soldiers, are also said to be harmful to the Party's literary undertakings. Said Ho Ch'i-fang:

> Our struggle against dogmatism and the various tendencies towards crudity and violence that stem from a "Left" point of view is a struggle to oppose and correct the distortion of the Party's and Comrade Mao's direction for literature and art. Since this struggle belongs to the category of "contradictions among the people" . . . it has never approached the intensity of our fight against bourgeois ideology and revisionism. But the struggle has been renewed several times since the founding of the People's Republic. Those who represent this tendency also mouth their allegiance to the road of proletarian literature and art, but actually they want to take it to a dead end. They mouth support for Marxism and Mao Tse-tung's thought, but actually they are greatly distorting it, simplifying it and vulgarising it. Their subjective desire is for the promotion of literature and art; but the result of their effort is a retardation. With their withering touch, they destroy the products of literature and art; they separate literature and art from the people. Therefore though they are opposed to it, they are actually performing the function of supporting bourgeois ideology and revisionism. When their dogmatism, their crudity and violence becomes disgusting,

[66] *Wen-yi Pao*, 1962, Nos. 5–6 (a combined issue), p. 4.
[67] Chou Yang, "Wo-kuo she-hui-chu-i wen-hsueh-i-shu-ti tao-lu" ("The Road of Socialist Literature and Art in our Country"), *People's Daily*, September 4, 1960, pp. 6, 7.
[68] A recent instance of the fight is an article in *Red Flag* (*Hung Ch'i*) No. 21, 1962, p. 21, entitled "How Modern Revisionists Follow the Decadent Bourgeois Class in Literature and Art," by Li Shu-chih.

> impracticable, or conducive to bad results, they provide the opportunity and condition for the growth and spread of bourgeois ideology and revisionism. Our recurrent fight in this respect is therefore unavoidable and completely necessary. Without these struggles, the Party's and Comrade Mao's direction for literature and art can never be carried out and we can never hope to achieve everything in literature and art.[69]

This quotation from *Literary Criticism* (*Wen-hsueh P'ing-lun*) says something important about the failure of Chinese Communist literature. It stands out among all the " eight-legged " essays on Mao's thought and reminiscences of Yenan that came out last year during the twentieth anniversary celebrations. Since Ho Ch'i-fang refuses to mention names (" There has not yet appeared a typical ' Left ' dogmatist since 1949," said Ho), it would be rash for us to nail the accusation down to any single person, though, in my opinion, Chou Yang, Lu Ting-yi and others, including Ho himself (who has changed a great deal since his " rebirth " in 1942), may well qualify for the appellation of a " Left dogmatist." It should be noted, however, that the Left dogmatists of 1962 are different from the exponents of formularisation and conceptualisation of 1952. The latter are the " sloths " who are simply bad writers or driven by fear or a market sense to produce what was supposed to be correct; but the former are activists in a leading position. When Ho mentions " our struggle," I do not know if he is speaking on behalf of the Party. If he is, I must apologise again for my ignorance of " the recurrent struggles against ' Left ' dogmatists since 1949." True, complaints against them were plenty in the 1956–57 period (including a satire with a significant title: " Rather Left than Right " [70]), but in no instance, to my knowledge, did the Party ever support those who criticised the Left dogmatists. The leftists may still belong to the " people," but the rightists, if not " reformed," never. The most significant passage in Ho's article is his explanation of the miraculous survival of bourgeois ideology and the emergence of revisionism, which should not mean after all only a new label for an old crime. When the " Left " dogmatists lead literature and art to a dead end, says Ho, the rightists will then find reasons for self-justification. To discover such a gem of thought in what looks like a mire of " eight-legged " style is a great surprise. The conference sponsored by *The China Quarterly* turned out to be very critical of Chinese Communist literature. With a heavy heart, one agrees that the " crudity and violence " of Chinese Communist literary policy has provided outsiders with ample reason for adverse criticism. But if we agree with Ho here, a question will probably occur to many who have read his article:

[69] Ho, " Chan-tou-ti sheng-li-ti erh-shih-nien " (" Twenty Years of Battles and Victory "), *Literary Criticism*, 1962, No. 3, p. 5.
[70] An essay by Li Feng, *Wen-yi Pao*, 1957, No. 9, p. 11.

Is there a more powerful Left dogmatist in Communist China than Mao? Are there literary documents more " conducive to bad results " than his addresses to the Yenan Forum?

But here is a point where logic must stop for the sake of Ho Ch'i-fang and our fellow-writers in Communist China. To push the question further would be very embarrassing, indeed.

List of Contributors

Cyril Birch, formerly Lecturer in Chinese at the London School of Oriental and African Studies, is now Associate Professor of Chinese at the University of California, Berkeley. His publications include *Stories from a Ming Collection* and *Chinese Myths and Fantasies*. He has written articles on Ming fiction and on twentieth-century fiction and poetry.

Howard L. Boorman is Director of Columbia University's research project on Men and Politics in Modern China. He edited the special China issue (January 1959) of *The Annals of the American Academy of Political and Social Science* and is co-author of *Moscow-Peking Axis*. Mr. Boorman was formerly an American Foreign Service officer and was stationed in Peking (1947–50) and Hong Kong (1950–54). His articles " China and the Global Revolution " and " Liu Shao-ch'i: a Political Profile " appeared in *The China Quarterly*.

S. H. Chen is Professor of Chinese Language and Literature at the University of California, Berkeley, and is Chairman of both the Current Chinese Language Project and the Project on Studies of Chinese Middle Dynastic Histories at that university. His books and monographs include *Modern Chinese Poetry* (with Harold Acton), *Literature as Light Against Darkness, Biography of Ku Kai-chih* and *Lu Chi's Essay on Literature*. His article " Multiplicity in Uniformity: Poetry and the Great Leap Forward " appeared in *The China Quarterly*.

C. T. Hsia, formerly Associate Professor of Chinese at the University of Pittsburgh, is now Associate Professor at Columbia University. He is the author of *A History of Modern Chinese Fiction 1917–1957*.

T. A. Hsia, formerly a member of the staff of the Far Eastern and Russian Institute, University of Washington, is currently Associate Research Linguist at the Center for Chinese Studies, University of California, Berkeley. He was editor of the literary magazine in Formosa *Wen-hsueh Tsa-chih* and is at present engaged in writing a book on the leftist literary movement in China in the 1920s and 1930s.

Li Chi was a Boxer scholar at Oxford University in 1936 and taught English in China. She is currently Visiting Lecturer in Chinese at the University of Michigan, Ann Arbor. Her publications include *Studies in Chinese Communist Terminology nos. 1–6, Yin-yü and Tai-yü in Chinese Poetry, Wordsworth and His Prelude* (in Chinese) and *A Sketch of the History of English Literature* (in Chinese).

Yong-sang Ng, a veteran translator and editor, is now a member of the staff of the research project on Men and Politics in Modern China at Columbia University.

C. W. Shih has taught comparative literature and English Literature in China and the United States. She is currently Visiting Assistant Professor of Chinese at Stanford University.

Vincent Y. C. Shih is Professor of Chinese Literature and Philosophy at the University of Washington, Seattle. His article " A Talk with Hu Shih " was published in *The China Quarterly*.

Hellmut Wilhelm taught at Peking University from 1933–48 and is currently Professor at the University of Washington, Seattle. He has published in the field of Chinese intellectual and literary history.

Richard F. S. Yang, who taught Chinese at the University of Washington, Seattle, while studying for his Ph.D., is currently teaching at the University of Southern California, Los Angeles. He has published articles on Chinese literature and drama and is now compiling an anthology on Yuan drama. He also translated the first tales ever written in the colloquial language of thirteenth-century China.

Due